The Dream Directory

The Comprehensive Guide to Analysis and Interpretation, with Explanations for More than 350 Symbols and Theories

By David C. Lohff

AN IMPRINT OF RUNNING PRESS
PHILADELPHIA • LONDON

9   8   7   6   5
Digit on the right indicates the number of this printing

Library of Congress Cataloging-in-Publication Number 97-77965

ISBN 0-7624-0301-2

Cover design by Toni Renée Leslie
Cover and interior photographs by Jenny Lynn
Interior design by Maria Taffera Lewis
Edited by Greg Jones
Set in Baskerville Book

Published by Courage Books, an imprint of
Running Press Book Publishers
125 South Twenty-second Street
Philadelphia, Pennsylvania 19103-4399

*"There seems to be something in dream images
that reminds us of language. . . .
We have the feeling they might mean something."*

Samuel Taylor Coleridge
English poet

Dedication

For Kathy, who had courage enough to marry a seeker
and loved him enough to let him follow his dreams.

preface

◆

To dream is to experience something other-worldly, yet very personal and very much a part of our world. While everyone has experienced realistic dreams, most people would not say that their dreams actually happened. For example, you may recall waiting in the auto repair shop yesterday for three hours and then receiving a bill for five-hundred dollars—and you can remember the anxiety that situation caused you. On the other hand, you may recall the dream you had last night in which you were being chased by a pack of wild dogs, and you can remember the fear that rushed through your body. However, since you know it was a dream, you understand that it didn't actually happen.

Yet, to say "It's only a dream" devalues what many people hold to be one of the highest and purest forms of truth. Numerous testimonies exist of those who have acted or not acted because of a dream. People forego routines, change travel arrangements, sense potential disasters or tragedy, and feel premonitions—all based on dreams. Still others find themselves thinking that all the activities from a particular dream have happened sometime before. There seems to be knowledge revealed in the twilight between conscious reality and a dream world that is much less definable, but at times more "real" than the experiences of day-to-day life.

Dreams can hold great meaning and mystery at the same time. Whether one approaches dreams as the subconscious attempting to process the unresolved experiences of life or as a metaphysical phenomenon, it is useful to identify archetypes, images, and symbols to help us understand the dream experience. Interpreting dreams requires taking information and applying it to our individual circumstances to search for insight and meaning.

However, the knowledge contained in dreams can be elusive. What we recall from dreaming is often fragments or images that seem disjointed, but at the same time potentially meaningful. The interpretation lies hidden in visual images, emotions, or other thoughts and experiences that appear to coexist in the dream, but do not seem logical to our conscious minds. Like chasing vapors across our subconscious mind, we seek to capture the dream mystery.

Other times, our dreams seem forthright and clear in their messages. Some are even accurate premonitions. For example, one woman dreamed of triplets over and over while preparing for childbirth (this incident occurred before doctors routinely pre-determined the results of a pregnancy). When the pregnancy came to fruition and it was triplets, she was almost as surprised by the dream coming into waking life as she was by the triplets themselves. Moreover, she dreamt of two boys and a girl, which was consistent with her childbearing experience.

Since Aristotle, the interpretation of dreams has been a central issue in the debate of truth and meaning among human beings. That dreaming is a common human experience is the end of agreement in the battleground of dream studies. Theories on interpretation range from dreams as a random series of meaningless images to dreams as bearers of meaningful revelation. In between, one finds specific theories that cater to issues like psychological trauma, prehistoric evolutionary vision, personal discovery (sexual, physical, emotional, intellectual, and spiritual), wish-fulfillment, and a host of other possibilities. Trying to define the dream world is like trying to define images in the clouds.

While clouds are universal, the visual reminders they create are subject to personal interpretation. So too with dreams.

Dream content is similar to a mosaic, which includes numerous tiles of a variety of colors. Many times the tiles that are most intense in color or seem slightly out of alignment draw our attention away from the whole. However, the individual tiles (or parts of a dream) are not suggestive of the whole dream, which exists in multiple layers and in multiple meanings. Some dream images originate from global or cultural stereotypes, while others are defined by the inner workings of the dreamer.

While the psychological content of dreams defies scientific classification, the physiology of dreams has been thoroughly researched. Numerous scientifically observable cues allow the trained observer to see that the subject is dreaming. This research proves that dreaming is, in itself, a true and universal event.

Inside *The Dream Directory,* you will not find prescriptive answers to dreams and their meanings. Every dreamer must be willing to look three places simultaneously: in, around, and beyond. Dreams are mosaics. Within them you may find the world as you experience it, the world as it leaves its imprint upon you, and the world as you ultimately expect its outcome to affect your life.

Sweet dreams. . . .

introduction

◆

How To Use the Dream Directory

The "science" of dream interpretation is more like art than science. The relationship of dreamed events, persons, and objects to the dreamer's waking life often seems to be convoluted and illogical. However, searching for meaning in dreams will often reveal insights into life that are at times elegantly simple, profoundly meaningful, and personally challenging.

The Dream Directory works from the general towards the specific. While the information is useful and has meaning in itself, the interpretive meaning is brought to life by the reader—your engagement will open the door to your dream interpretation. After all, the dreams you want to interpret are yours, and nobody else's. Only you can decipher meaning within the myriad of images and emotions that come to you in your sleep. This directory is simply a tool that will help you acquire insight on your own.

Dream interpretation can be an asset to you, as searching rewards the seeker. It may lead to the knowledge and insight required to conquer irrational fears. You may gain new insight into relationships and the self-destructive patterns you may be projecting upon them. You may discover the goals you would like to achieve in your work, leisure time, and other endeavors. Ultimately, you may gain a window into your soul. The struggle is finding the courage to look, and having the patience to stick with it.

In the beginning, it is useful to understand the stuff that dreams are made of. What are those pictures fluttering about under closed eyes? Where did they come from? Why do certain dreams recur?

Book 1 is devoted to general discoveries and physiological knowledge about brain activity during sleep—especially during dream stages. It is useful to look in this section for entries concerning intriguing sleep/dream events such as recurring dreams, déjà vu, and nightmares. Knowing how your brain constructs a dream will go a long way in helping you understand what is in it.

Book 2 contains the symbols and icons of dreams, and comprises the bulk of the directory. Every attempt has been made to include the major symbols and experiences that most people encounter. To access the meaning in your dream symbols, start in general terms and work towards specific ones. For example, if you dreamed about a '65 Mustang, look under the entry "cars." Again, consider your dream as a mosaic. To look too closely at a particular tile in a mosaic deprives you of the whole image. The interpretation of a dream symbol lives within the context of the dream mosaic. Rather than pay inordinate amounts of attention to the facets of a dream that hold the most interest, it is important to step back far enough to view all the dream's tiles together, as a whole.

Finally, Book 3 offers different interpretive frameworks for experimentation—it discusses dream theories and theorists. There are many different approaches to dream interpretation. For genuine insight to occur, your dream interpretations and insights should be consistent with your waking worldview. Consequently, cursory treatment has been given to several major contributors to dream interpretation. Dream interpretation often includes a sense of spiritual, as well as psychological, insight. Therefore, several spiritual approaches to understanding dreams are also discussed.

As you use this directory to interpret your dreams, you may find the simple cross-referencing device employed here very useful. Many entries in *The Dream Directory* are related to other entries. Therefore, whenever a word appears that has its own entry, you will find that it is set in SMALL CAPITAL LETTERS. An index of all the entries that appear in all three books is in the back of the directory. This way, you can easily flip to other entries that are pertinent to your present study without wasting time or losing your train of thought.

book 1

◆

What Dreams Are Made of . . .

The study of dreams is not new. Throughout human history, people have been trying to understand what happens when we close our eyes to sleep. Ancient Egyptians spoke of dreams. So did the Greeks and Romans. And throughout time, RELIGIONS of the world have had their hand in the interpretation of dreams.

Medicine entered the scene around 1900, when Sigmund Freud invented psychotherapy. Physical medicine has been applied to dreams only in the last forty years or so. With advances in measuring the activity and structure of the brain, new theories about the dream event have entered the marketplace of ideas. Book 1 explores what we do understand about sleep and the dream event as a physical reality. And understanding how we come to dream may prove invaluable in our search for their meaning.

ACETYLCHOLINE

This is the brain chemical that is central to dream creation. Enhancing its presence increases dream activity significantly. What is unknown is whether this chemical is a "solvent" to clean the brain or a "stimulant" to enhance the overall function of the electrical environment. It has been synthetically produced at the Harvard School of Medicine and administered in sleep study experiments.

ALPHA WAVES

A particular state of operation of the brain that could be described as "focused relaxation." Alpha BRAIN ACTIVITY can be learned through meditation and occurs naturally during the transition from waking to sleeping. As a learned skill, alpha meditation allows the body to enter a twilight state between waking and sleeping while the mind continues a fairly disciplined, but relaxed, presence. During the transition from BETA to alpha brain activity, people often have a falling sensation.

The alpha wave is second in order of electrical intensity, falling below beta but higher than the other sleep pattern waves. The peak and valley amplitude is similar to that of beta, but the frequency is elongated as the subject ceases to respond to all outside stimuli and becomes more aware of internal stimuli through the induced sleep state.

ANXIETY

Although there is no proven correlation between the anxiety of a high-stress lifestyle and sleep disruption through stressful dreams, there is no doubt that the anxiety people face in their waking lives finds its way into their dreams. Indeed much of your dream content includes images and emotions that, when studied and interpreted by you, will point to possible solutions for your wakeful anxieties.

However, it is difficult to predict the kind of person that may have excessive dream anxiety. While you would probably expect an obviously anxious person to have more NIGHTMARES, this has not been proven and is likely not the case. In fact, those more likely to experience stressful dreams are the ones who hide their inward anxieties in waking life—they often have personalities that are susceptible to feelings of violation or threat. They are considered to have relatively weak PERSONALITY boundaries. Often these are the most outwardly placid people you will meet, but the most fretful dreamers.

Personality boundaries are popularly discussed nowadays with little understanding of what really forms them. (Is it nature or nurture?) However, people who have weak boundaries do seem to experience more frequent nightmares.

APNEA
This is a physical condition during sleep in which the tongue falls back into the throat and blocks the airway. At times, sleepers may go through extended periods (2–3 minutes) of not breathing due to the apnea condition. Some scientists have theorized that this causes the sensation of a NEAR-DEATH EXPERIENCE. However, there is no proven relationship between apnea and having bad dreams.

BETA WAVES
This is the typical brain pattern of a waking person. Not surprisingly, it represents a high level of electrical energy activity and response. On a graph, the image is one of compact peaks and valleys with relatively large changes in amplitude from peak to valley (low amplitude). Most of the environmental stimuli around you are being recorded in the brain at some level, either aware or sub-aware.

BIZARRE REALITY

The most common aspect of dreams is the bizarre sense of reality they present. Within a single, seemingly cohesive dream, your brain may construct a situation in which two of your acquaintances, who are strangers to each other, become a married couple operating a gondola in Venice, Italy. There may be a reason for all these connections, but it is obviously not obvious.

Because a dream is like a mosaic, you must look at the bigger picture: why do things that seem to be completely unrelated appear in the same dream? Perhaps their coexistence in the dream is not so bizarre after all.

See BRAIN ACTIVITY, MEMORY

BODY RESPONSE

In addition to the emotional reality of dreams, there can be a sense of physical realness that causes physical reactions by your body as it lay there ASLEEP. For example, it is common to be dreaming of something coming toward you and actually flinching your arm as you lie in bed. Although highly unusual, some people report sensing taste and smell in dreams. Others report having pain sensations as part of their dreams. These things usually occur in the early stages of the dream state.

Usually, the physical sensations one has while dreaming do not carry over into waking life. For example, if you dream that you fall out of a tree and break your leg, you may experience a sense of pain within the dream. However, after you awake, there is little chance that you will feel a lingering sense of pain in your leg.

BRAIN ACTIVITY

Asleep. Dreams have significant footprints that we can examine medically, as well as psychologically, to see what happens when we dream. Many of the observations that have been made regarding dreams are surprising. Perhaps most importantly, these observations provide understanding for the often unpredictable landscape of our dream environment.

Physically, dreams are easily identifiable. Electrical activity in the brain during a dream is widespread and apparent. The transmission of energy and images in the brain is handled by a network of neurons. These building blocks of the brain form an electrical network of capacitors (electric storage) and transistors (electrical channels).

What is interesting is the contrast between behavior of the body and the brain in sleep. The body is much less active in sleep. Respiration reduces by almost one-half the waking rate. Heartbeats reduce by 40% to 70% of waking, active rates. Metabolism and blood pressure also drop by significant amounts. However, according to scientists at Harvard Medical School, electrical neuron brain activity, even in deep sleep, decreases by only 5% to 10%!

While total brain activity even in deep sleep is only 5% to 10% lower, particular areas of the brain are more affected, relatively. The more affected areas are those responsible for concentration, learning, information organization, and MEMORY. During the sleep period, these areas are 50% less active most of the time and completely shut off during the REM stage.

See ASLEEP in Book 2

Awake. Deep in the cerebral cortex, the centers of learning, memory, and attention are hard at work. Information received by the brain is filed away as important or irrelevant and assigned to memory resources accordingly. The brain uses BETA WAVES as the standard electrical operating environment for waking activities.

The volume of information that enters the brain exceeds our CONSCIOUS ability to specifically handle each individual piece. Consequently, the memory resources are allocated according to the urgency of given moments. In any given moment, the brain has the ability to access related memories to assign meaning to the present circumstances.

Brain waves

There are four different types of waves that control brain function. These can be measured by an electroencephalograph (EEG), both while awake and asleep. They are measured in terms of frequency (cycles per second) and amplitude (voltage).

The four classes of brain waves are:

Beta Waves–these have high frequency and low amplitude. These are the waves that control the brain while wide awake, and are characterized by alert wakefulness.

Alpha Waves–these have lower frequency than beta, but higher amplitude. These waves are characterized by relaxed wakefulness.

Theta Waves–these have lower frequency than alpha, but higher amplitude still. They are characterized by very deep relaxation.

Delta Waves–these have the lowest frequency and the highest amplitude of all the brain waves. They are found at the deepest stage of sleep.

Conscious/consciousness

This refers to one's personal relation to time, place, identity, emotions, thoughts, and physical stimuli. Besides being aware of individual items from the above groups at any given time, there is a vast number of additional items that one may not be directly aware of, but that one may recall at will—this is called the SUBCONSCIOUS. Furthermore, there is another level of consciousness which contains an even vaster number of things that cannot be recalled at will under normal circumstances—this is called the UNCONSCIOUS.

CULTURE

Cultural issues and dream images are more complex than TRIGGER EVENTS, since they involve a system of personalities. In a given culture, members are taught to value, disparage, and treat as TABOO particular attitudes and actions. While the brain is indiscriminate in the data it absorbs, the PERSONALITY is very discriminating—based on culture— concerning its attitude toward those data. This can create conflicting impulses in the brain. The brain looks around to notice attractive members of the species for potential mating. It is a primordial urge to reproduce the human race. However, some attractive impulses may be identified with inappropriate persons: bosses, teachers, cousins, siblings, etc. The trigger event may be the attractive person or the inappropriate feeling. In either case, a primordial desire is linked to an intrinsic wrong. The mind has to sort the images and file them somehow. Often a dream with troubling or explicit content will follow as the brain tries to work through the conundrum.

There is another conclusion to be drawn from the trigger event phenomenon: the content of dreams may be culturally driven. In the late twentieth century, phones, computers, and televisions may be central features of many dreams. Celebrities may appear in our dreams. We may become a character in a particularly troubling news story we have seen on television, a star player for a team in the World Series, or a co-star to a heartthrob movie star. All of these dreams reflect different scenarios of the experience. It is important to realize that localized events have a way of working into our minds and becoming fodder for the dream mill.

Dreams with strong cultural content may tell us a lot about how we see ourselves in the world. Each of our lives includes certain amounts of hope and ambition, as well as fear and uncertainty. Culturally driven dreams represent to us who we have potential to be, given our aspirations and limitations.

Déjà vu

Déjà vu is an interesting psychological phenomenon that may leave goosebumps in its wake. Simply defined, it is the feeling a person gets when they sense that the events currently unfolding before them have been acted out previously. Generally speaking, two versions of the phenomenon exist.

One approach to déjà vu is clinical. It is believed that somehow the short-term MEMORY centers of the brain become primary, even if just for a moment. This in turn changes the perception of events from the general attention mind into the recalled mind for interpretation. Consequently, there is a flickering impulse that perhaps all this has been done before. In fact, it has not, but the perceptive centers of the brain have juxtaposed long enough to create a false perception of circumstances.

The second, more common event of déjà vu that most directly informs dream interpretation is the identifiable prior experience. It is not uncommon for people to dream of events that create an identified prior experience. This experience, or moments of it, is then acted out in waking life. This form of déjà vu leaves the scientist empty-handed. The past experience is concrete in the person's memory with no prior stimulus, but seems to spontaneously invade the waking life.

Is your life starting to remind you of the Bill Murray film *Groundhog Day*? Perhaps your dream is a revelation of a pattern with which you've grown too comfortable.

DELTA BRAIN WAVES

These are the BRAIN WAVES of the deep sleep pattern. These brain waves have the highest amplitude of the four types of brain waves, and the lowest frequency. It is the brain wave that occurs in Stage 4 deep sleep.

DREAM PHENOMENON

The dream is not only a universal event of humanity, but seems to include the entire mammal kingdom. BRAIN ACTIVITY similar to the type recorded during human dreams has been recorded in many higher order creatures. Of course, the ability to wake the ANIMALS and ask about their dream activity during the REM-like event does not exist. Yet the effect of REM deprivation in other animals seems to parallel the human findings.

Among other animals, all manner of experimentation has been done to observe brain events during sleep and dreams as well as deprive them of those experiences. While the ethics of such experiments may be questionable, the findings are universal not only in the phenomenon of dreaming, but also the necessity of it.

There is a direct relationship between brain complexity and the amount of REM sleep needed to sustain life. DOGS, CATS, RATS, and horses have been extensively studied in general SLEEP DEPRIVATION experiments, as well as particular deprivation of REM-type brain activity. The ability to socialize was compromised and many such subjects eventually died.

Amphibians and lower-order animals have also been examined to the greatest extent possible. It seems that the lower a creature's mind function, the less sleep is necessary in general and any kind of REM activity becomes nonexistent.

EEG (ELECTROENCEPHALOGRAM)

This instrument is used to measure BRAIN WAVES and electrical activity. In sleep laboratories, a collection of electrodes and probes is affixed to the head prior to sleep to record the subject's cerebral activity. The results are charted on a graph with brain waves illustrated linearly– this is called an electroencephalograph (also known as EEG). The EEG is the most important tool in the study of the physical qualities of dreams.

EGO

In Freudian psychology, ego is the central, waking dimension of who we are. First theorized by Freud, it has become widely accepted as a part of our PERSONALITY structure. Basically, the ego is responsible for mediating between the conflicting demands of the ID, SUPEREGO, and the outside world.

FOUR STAGES OF SLEEP

The use of the electroencephalograph (EEG) has provided science with direct results concerning the physical activity of the brain during sleep. Four distinct stages of sleep have been measured:

In Stage 1, the subject grows more relaxed as ALPHA WAVES begin to decrease; the eyes begin to show slow, rolling movements. This is the stage of sleep where the person is passing through the gates of CONSCIOUS toward the UNCONSCIOUS. The sleeper's muscles begin to relax and the heart rate slows. The sleeper in Stage 1 may experience a dream-like sensation, but may also be awakened easily and insist that he was not sleeping. After being at this stage for a short period of time without disturbance, the sleeper will descend to the second stage.

In Stage 2, the sleeper's BRAIN WAVES change noticeably on the EEG, experiencing rapid bursts. The eyes still roll slowly side to side, but anything that the person may be imagining at this point will likely be forgotten. After 10–20 minutes, the sleeper will likely descend further to the next level.

In Stage 3, the sleeper's brain waves slow down considerably in relation to waking, alpha wave activity. It is more difficult to wake the sleeper from this stage, as the muscles become more relaxed, the heart rate decreases, the body temperature declines, and the blood pressure drops.

In Stage 4, the EEG is characterized by very large and slow brain waves called DELTA WAVES. It occurs usually after about 30 minutes of sleep, and is known as the deepest level of sleep—it is basically like dreamless oblivion. After about 20 minutes in this stage, the sleeper begins to drift back up out of dreamless oblivion toward the surface. At this point, the sleeper's waves are similar to the Stage 1 of sleep, but the sleeper is very difficult to wake up. The sleeper has returned to Stage 1, but it is an unusual type of Stage 1 known as REM (rapid eye movement). It is at this point that the sleeper will likely have the most vivid dreams. After about 10–20 minutes in REM, the sleeper will begin to drift back down through the descending stages of sleep.

This cycle can repeat itself several times throughout one's sleep.

HYPNAGOGIA

This is the experience of drifting from waking to sleep. It is caused by the EGO's refusal to let go of the mind's thought processes. It is a characterization of Stage 1 sleep.

ID

In Freudian psychology, the id is the part of the PERSONALITY that generates base appetites. Unchecked, pure id cares only for the needs and desires of the self. In dream theory, it is perhaps the id dimension that presses many images into particular files of the brain—it chooses which aspects of the image are the most important to the person. Many theorists believe that the id reveals itself in dreams more than any other aspect of the personality, perhaps because the UNCONSCIOUS mind knows that the dreamer will not be responsible for actions taken within a dream.

IMAGERY (IN DREAMS)

Out of the potpourri of one's MEMORY images, the dream language is constructed. It can be frustrating because of the uncertainty of apparently unrelated images brought together in the dream state. However, the mind sorts these images as it has experienced them from earliest childhood. Thus, an image from childhood may be placed with an image from adulthood. When a trigger from waking life creates a dream experience, childhood and adulthood images, both seen as they were originally experienced, are knit together in the dream.

This is why we must step back and take in the entire mosaic of a dream before analyzing its individual parts. No one image of the dream may seem to match any other image precisely. However, by separating ourselves from the individual images we can look for dominant

thoughts and feelings. One gets the impression that the reality of the dream is not quite as bizarre or improbable as it looks on the surface.

In dreaming, the mind accesses all data in a similar experience. Thus an image from childhood may be intertwined with a more complex relationship from adulthood to create a dream environment. The dream is difficult to grasp because of the disparity between a childhood vision and an adult problem to solve. However, in waking, the dreamer senses the two are related, if only she could grasp the language of the dream.

In dream interpretation there are numerous variables to consider. Yet, properly seen in their context, the dream itself is an elegantly simple statement of life as you are experiencing it and the potential within it.

INSOMNIA

This is the inability to achieve adequate amounts of sleep. There are many potential causes for insomnia, including life-related stress, chemical imbalances, or physical conditions such as APNEA. Prolonged insomnia can be very dangerous to one's health, but often it can be treated by physicians.

INTUITION

Traditionally, this is humanity's sixth sense—to feel what cannot be seen. Intuition reminds us that there is often more to life than what is seen. Dreams often seem to confirm or stir intuitive understandings of ourselves and our relationships. This may be part of the reason why dreams seem so real to us. Intuition operates to inform or to promote self-awareness, but seems to operate outside of our direct CONSCIOUS experience of the world.

Lucid dreams

This is a dream where the dreamer realizes, "Hey, I'm dreaming!" It is a skill that can be learned through meditation and is useful in resolving RECURRING or particularly troubling dreams. It is not unusual to have an unsolvable problem in a dream that seems apparently simple in waking life. Yet the dream is troubling due to your lack of competence and lack of initiative while in the dream.

By developing lucid dreaming skills, the dreamer can exert a version of self-awareness onto the mosaic of dream images. The goal is to resolve the scene according to the power of the self in awareness. In certain circumstances, this cannot be done because the dream involves DEAD PEOPLE AS LIVE CHARACTERS in the dream or other dilemma. However, the dreamer can still use lucid dreaming to identify sources of emotional PAIN that may be resolved through the waking life.

Medical studies

Medicine has entered the scene only in the last 40 years or so. With advances in measuring the activity and structure of the brain, new theories about the dream event have flooded the marketplace of ideas. The work of both RELIGION and FREUD have been brought under critical examination. If dreaming is so important, why do we remember or understand it so rarely?

These studies seem to be gravitating toward the brain as an electrical environment. The two significant roles of dreaming are recharge and discharge. The recharge aspect has to do with allowing the attention, MEMORY, and learning centers to become prepared for the next day's activity. The discharge aspect reflects the need to clear isolated static-electric impulses so the brain can start with a clean slate the next day.

See BRAIN ACTIVITY

MEMORY

Understanding the work of the mind and SUBCONSCIOUS can provide an excellent framework for decoding dream language. Think about the brain as a sponge. Throughout life, countless images and stimuli are taken in by the brain without any discretion whatsoever (in addition to the ones that are taken in with discretion). These are filed by the brain according to appropriateness, topic, PAIN, pleasure, and TABOO. They are then accessed according to the needs of a person as that person continues on the path of life.

Visual images begin to be absorbed by the brain long before the ability to apply thought to those images develops. It is ultimately the ability to process verbal thought that creates self-awareness. However, verbal skills are among the last to develop, leaving huge amounts of data to file prior to reasoning skills being developed.

As you may recall, the brain receives all stimulation from the outside world without much discretion. It is then filed in the brain according to subject matter and made available for recall at a later date. Well, suppose a two-year-old boy throws a fit of ANGER out of desire for a piece of candy. Then, forty-three years later, he sees a beautiful woman outside his office. That night, he dreams:

> "I entered a store. I had lots of money and a list with me. As I got into the check-out lane, I virtually emptied the candy display, abandoning my cart and the list. The cashier (who I seemed to know) smiled at me and said, 'You seem to know what you want.' When I got home, my wife looked at the candy and walked out for good. I didn't care."

A 45-year-old man sabotaging his family for a grocery cart of candy is bizarre to the point of being ridiculous. However, there is nothing

surprising about a two-year-old throwing a temper tantrum. Moreover, during the tantrum, no one expects the two-year-old to understand the consequences of his actions. But the brain had filed both the candy and the beauty under "desire," so these seemingly unrelated experiences were matched in a dream image that night.

This is why we must step back and take in the entire mosaic of a dream before analyzing its individual parts. No one image of the dream may seem to match any other image precisely. However, by separating ourselves from the individual images we can look for dominant thoughts and feelings. (The contents of your memory, whether you are aware of them or not, may reappear to you at any time.) One gets the impression that the reality of the dream is not quite as bizarre or improbable as it looks on the surface.

MYOCLONIC JERK

This is the involuntary jerk that the body may experience at the early stage of sleep. It may cause some sleepers to wake for a moment, but it is nothing to be concerned about—it is very common. The myoclonic jerk indicates that neural changes are taking place, and after it passes, the sleeper continues the descent into unconsciousness.

NEAR-DEATH EXPERIENCE

Dreamers may awake, startled, having felt as though they somehow nearly died. However, this feeling is not related to physical events during sleep, such as APNEA. Certain metaphysical schools hold that this near-death sensation is precipitated by the inability of a soul to immediately reenter the physical body upon completion of the dream. However, it is impossible to comment with any authority on this unobservable claim.

Another possible explanation for this phenomenon is the simple understanding of death that each of us has. Though no person can know what death will bring, we all know that it will come to us one day. Because of this, death is something that is always on everyone's mind—even if it usually resides in the very back of the mind. It just may be the case that to dream of a near-death experience is a simple reminder of one's mortality.

See SLEEP PARALYSIS

NIGHTMARE

The name assigned to particularly frightening dreams; they usually cause the sleeper to wake, disoriented. Nightmares seem to decrease with age. Women tend to be more susceptible than men to nightmares. CHILDREN may be prone to a particularly intense version, the night terror. In this type of dream, the eyes may actually open, although there is no comprehension of the surroundings, just an immediate continuation of the dream state.

Nightmares have always fascinated, and sometimes terrified, people. Some CULTURES have believed (and some still do) that a nightmare was caused by an evil spirit oppressing the soul during sleep.

The word is also used to describe situations in waking life that have become grotesquely out of balance.

OUT-OF-BODY EXPERIENCE

This is defined as a feeling of being outside one's self, as a soul or spirit-being in travel. It occurs most commonly in dreams of intense derealization. These are dreams where the PERSONALITY, as defense against the trauma of the dream, develops a self-awareness that is not dependent on body awareness or limitations.

As with the NEAR-DEATH-EXPERIENCE dream, there are schools of metaphysics that revere the out-of-body experience as an ontic excursion into other potential realities. Within certain revisions of Hinduism, these excursions have implications for the eschaton, or ultimate resolution of being.

In most dreams, the dreamer experiences people, things, and situations from the vantage point of their own body. Some dreams, however, are so deeply rooted that the dreamer projects himself into a situation and then can see himself interacting with other people or things or situations.

See OUT-OF-BODY EXPERIENCE in Book 2

PERSONALITY

Among other functions that dreaming fulfills, the dream as a WINDOW into personality structure seems like an important aspect. Dreams are unique in that they seem to offer clues that can be characterized as "pre-reaction" as well as environmental. Certainly, there are other windows to the personality—behavior in relationship to others being the most directly observable.

However, regardless of which theorist you ascribe to, there seems to be a level of mind or personality that exists apart from, but is directly influential upon, the most observable personality traits. The construction of this sub-aware, yet highly influential level of personality may be most clearly accessed through dreams.

JUNG and FREUD look most directly to this SUBCONSCIOUS layer of personality. Freud calls it ID. Jung prefers to speak of a more universal self that is the common ground of all self-awareness within the human race. However, as theories of mind, language, and holistic self-awareness come into play, we see that personality boundaries may be less prescriptive than originally theorized.

The advent of gender-specific awareness seems to be the largest influence on this more comprehensive theory of self and awareness. Dream work has become a statement not only about the self, but the self in a particular body with particularized potential in the world. Jane Goodison, in her work *The Dreams of Women*, finds that her clients' dream work articulates their potential in terms of archetypal psychology and also within their awareness of being women.

What is important to see in dreams and personality is the relationship of your most basic self to the environment and relationships of this world. Many times, what we expect to become a dream does not, and the content of our dreams is something that we hold as the deepest and possibly truest source of our selves.

PHYSICAL RESPONSES

In addition to eye and BRAIN ACTIVITY, heart activity may increase due to the stress of the dream event. Sexual responses may be present as well. This may include orgasm, especially among teenage boys. Depending on the intensity of the dream, sweat and increased respiration may also occur during the dream event.

Also, people often report flinging their arms into the air as they lie in bed, a direct reaction to something about which they were just dreaming. This type of physical reaction usually happens in Stage 1 of sleep.

PREMONITION

This is a dream with particularly strong insight into future events. These may include dreams about impending disasters, DEATH of loved ones, or visits from friends or FAMILY. In these cases the dreamer may awake with a strong sense of needing to do something, either by way of completion of the dream or warning others about the dream. While the content of such dreams is subjective and therefore beyond investigation, there is much anecdotal evidence regarding such claims.

Because TRIGGER EVENTS arise out of our daily transactions, it is not too surprising that some dreams create feelings of premonition in the waking life. This is especially true of situations where dreams have content that reflects ongoing, drawn-out life circumstances. You may dream about a particular situation and resolution of it, then find yourself in a meeting the next day where circumstances unfold in very similar fashion to the dream you had last night.

See DÉJÀ VU

PROPHETIC DREAMS

The fare of religious interpretations, the prophetic dream often places the dreamer in a position of reckoning with ultimate reality. The dreamer will often awake feeling a heightened sense of awareness in relationship to God, the Goddess, or to whichever ultimate reality one prescribes.

In the Hebrew scripture, dreams (which happened while ASLEEP) and visions (which occurred while awake) are considered as sacred revelations inasmuch as they foretell what actions God may pursue. It is interesting to note that these sleeping and waking dreams are not differentiated, as the Hebrew word *chalam* is used for both events. In Sha'i Islam, the dream often has prophetic content and is considered the best pathway for receiving communication from Allah. For Hindus, a co-creation with the god Rudra for the purposes of karmic revelation can be received in a prophetic dream.

PSYCHOLOGY OF DREAM EVENTS

The study of dreams is not new. People have been trying to understand what happens when we close our eyes as long as there has been human history. Numerous minds, some of the greatest minds the world has ever known, have celebrated or been confounded by the sleep experience.

Because dreaming is a universal activity, it is one of the most accessible forms of psychological study. Not everybody has pathological fears or compulsive disorders that interfere with daily living, but everybody dreams.

REALISM IN DREAMS

It seems that in life, the moments that we recall for years to come are the ones that provoked strong emotional reactions. Many people have dreams that contain much of that strong emotional energy. This is why Robert Louis Stevenson wrote, "The past is all one texture." He saw that the power of his dream content is as much a part of his PERSONALITY and self-perception as the dealings of his waking life. MEDARD BOSS, an existentialist counselor and author, takes this work to its next logical progression. He contends that since we perceive ourselves as awake while dreaming, dreams are the being's continuation of waking activity.

Indeed, among dreams, there are especially LUCID occurrences. Both pleasant and foreboding, these shape much of our attitude toward dreams and dreaming. This is oftentimes troubling. We awake from sleep knowing that the images dancing about the mind were not actual occurrences in three-dimensional space and time, but we still feel the impact of their content in unusual ways.

It is as if our minds are being invaded by the writers of *The Twilight Zone* every time we close our eyes. In the classic TV series of the 1960s, Rod Serling led viewers through a surreal journey of deep-seated fears brought into everyday life. The reason it was so troubling was that no one really wanted to think of a world where such deeply disturbing thoughts—usually only experienced in a dream state—could become actual experiences in our mundane lives. But that was exactly what happened. The images didn't fit. Horrifying possibilities were knit together with ordinary lives.

This is what happens to us in dreaming, except that the images are not exclusively horrifying. In a dream, the improbable, or even impossible, is uniquely woven together with the mundane reality of our lives to reveal the most unbelievable scenarios and fantasies. The result is the twisted and bizarre—wonderful or troubling—reality of the dream.

Dream content seems unusually real for several reasons. The first is our adaptation to the visual mode of data entry. Eyes are the primary source of data entry as we form attitudes and discern our world. Thus the visual stimuli in the dream creates a powerful imprint on us. Secondly, dreams have a strong emotional content. Oftentimes, especially in very stark visualizations, we feel emotional content appropriate to the dream. This emotion is what brings the dream into reality for us. Sometimes, we will wake having felt an inappropriate emotion. This also brings a reality component to the dream as we think to ourselves, "Where in the world did that come from?"

Whether the emotions are appropriate or not, they are the content that brings the dream into our personal reality. Compare a dream to going to the MOVIES. There are some movies that divert the intellect and entertain without much engagement. Then other movies engage the emotional self. Years later we remember the scene when Bogie kissed Bergman in *Casablanca*.

So too with dreams. Because they originate in the dark theater of the mind, playing for an audience of one, we feel particular kinship to them. Since it is we who dream, the events are, for us, intensely personal emotional experiences. They are made real by our feelings toward them and in our reflections upon them.

RECURRING DREAMS

This is an often disturbing pattern within the dream life. People with emotional trauma and/or post-traumatic stress disorder seem to have recurring images in dreams most often. CHILDREN also are more susceptible to experience recurring dreams or dream images than most adults, although it is not uncommon for all persons to experience them at one time or another. The frequency is irrelevant. A dream that occurs three times a month or three times a decade may be considered "recurring." Interpreting recurring dreams can be useful in finding lifestyle patterns or relationship tendencies.

Often a recurring dream is either a reflection of life or a PROPHETIC dream about what lies ahead in life.

RELIGION AND DREAMS

Almost every major religion of the world accepts the possibility that dreams may contain divine communication. There are even accounts of persons becoming religious through dreams, as well as persons converting from one religion to another as a result of their dream content.

The dream experience includes reflections of the self in relationship to the world, in relationship to ultimate values, and in relationship to ultimate realities. As such, it seems fitting that some dreams have the power to prick the spiritual CONSCIOUSNESS.

For most of human history, the dream has been regarded within the realm of the supernatural or divine. The content of dreams was considered a divine revelation. Dream events were given spiritual or supernatural interpretations and the nature of dreams was considered eerie and somewhat feared. A priest, shaman, seer, or other "professional dream interpreter" would be called on to unlock the messages and intentions of the dream from a supernatural point of view. Now, while it is still viable to call on such people for advice, you can work to interpret your own dreams.

REM

Rapid Eye Movement, or REM sleep, is the phase of sleep identified with dream events—it is a special type of Stage 1 sleep. REM was discovered more or less by accident at the University of Chicago. Back in the 1950s, sleep researcher Eugene Aserinsky was observing sleeping infants during his residency. He observed vigorous eye movement occurring with predictable regularity. After witnessing the event among infants, he observed the same event in patients of all ages.

The REM state occurs naturally about every ninety minutes throughout the night. During the REM state, the larger muscle groups are somewhat paralyzed while BRAIN ACTIVITY increases. Presumably, this is to prevent bodily action or injury in response to visual stimuli. The eyes do in fact move vigorously and the minor extremities often become active as well. Talking in one's sleep may occur in the REM state. SLEEP-WALKING, on the other hand, is generally associated with deep sleep.

The REM stage repeats itself about four to five times per night. Each cycle lasts about ten to twenty minutes with the later ones becoming slightly longer than the prior ones. The most vivid and easily recalled dreams seem to happen in the later cycles of REM—those between the sixth and eighth hours of sleep.

Psychological testing has taught us that people deprived of REM sleep will lose their mental coping mechanisms and eventually border on insanity. It seems that, during REM, there is important physiological work being done by the brain—this is in addition to the more imaginative psychological work. Think about your brain as a computer hard drive for a moment. A nice new hard drive zips along fairly well. Over time, the disk gets cluttered and data gets harder to find. There is a program called "defrag" on most computers that finds displaced pieces of information and either places them properly in the system or lets go of them altogether. This seems to be an important aspect of the need for REM sleep, and also of dreams in general.

While exhaustive clinical evidence is unavailable, there is anecdotal evidence that certain behaviors can effect the REM state. Physical fitness and lack thereof can effect the vividness of dreams (this may be related to what is called "runner's high," a term related to long-distance runners). Physical activity stimulates endorphin releases in the brain. These hormones create the feeling of security or euphoria, which can effect the dream experience.

Taking certain diet supplements may affect the dream experience also (Caution: check with your doctor or pharmacist before taking such medications). St. John's Wort, an herbal medication dating from the time of the Crusades, contains ingredients that stimulate SEROTONIN production in the brain. Ginseng and other ephedrine-containing supplements may effect the dream state also. What all these seem to have in common is a mild stimulant effect in brain chemistry which can increase REM activity.

See FOUR STAGES OF SLEEP

SCIENCE OF DREAMS

Dreams have been treated with scientific curiosity by the MEDICAL, psychological, and metaphysical disciplines. While all of these fields have invested tremendous intellectual energy in dreams, none has been able to conclusively define the limits of dream science. Dreams are universally real in the sense that all persons experience them, yet dreams exist in a radically subjective way that cannot be tested by the scientific method. The best that science can do is to determine that dreams do occur—physiologically—and to measure the various BRAIN ACTIVITY that occurs within the sleeping subject.

SEROTONIN

Serotonin is a brain chemical that provides an environment for the transmission of favorable brain impulses. People who suffer from depression often lack an adequate supply of serotonin to maintain a favorable mood environment.

SLEEP DEPRIVATION

The universality of sleep and dreaming among the human species has led to significant inquiry into what happens if we try to do without it. These experiments have included total sleep deprivation and REM-specific deprivation. In most cases, the experiments have been pretty gruesome affairs that pre-dated the ethics that oversee the treatment of human laboratory subjects these days.

The deprivation of REM sleep has been measured most specifically among RATS. In laboratory experiments with rats in which they were subjected to REM-sleep deprivation, the rats became severely stressed. This presented itself in two ways. The first indication that there was a problem was the rats' relationship to food. Without any predictability one way or the other, the rats would either begin to fast or to gorge on large quantities of food. The second manifestation of stress was with the rats' relationships with each other. In many cases, they became very aggressive—fighting with each other, often to the death.

Sleep deprivation experiments have included both ANIMAL and human subjects. The animal subjects often died within a week or two of complete sleeplessness. The cause of death was usually some version of a stroke or hypothermia (the inability to maintain body temperature).

Human subjects have gone as long as 11 days (264 hours) of complete sleeplessness in controlled environments. Longer claims exist, but lack the documentation needed to be fully verified. These are genuinely grueling accounts. (The popularity of sleep deprivation may have begun with radio celebrities doing wake-a-thons and dance-a-thons back in the late 1950s and early 60s.)

However, what happened to the subjects could hardly be described as good-natured. After about 100 hours, subjects would become noticeably irritable, and then move gradually into severe paranoia. After about 150 hours, the brain would produce hallucinations similar to those experienced under the influence of LSD, schizophrenia, or opium usage. BRAIN ACTIVITY seemed to parallel REM-stage behavior, but these bursts of electrical energy were occurring in the waking, CONSCIOUS lives of the subjects.

The initial effects of these experiences were slept away in one extended rest period of 12–16 hours. Upon waking, subjects would resume a fairly normal schedule. However, the long-term effects of sleep deprivation, including acute depression, could last from three to six months. Presumably, had these experiments continued, death would likely have come to the human subjects as it did the laboratory animals.

SLEEP PARALYSIS

During the REM stage of sleep, the larger muscle groups of the body enter a condition of mild paralysis. This apparently is a natural defense mechanism employed to prevent the sleeper from injuring him or herself. Sleep paralysis can create particularly unsettling dream images if one becomes LUCID while dreaming and recognizes the vulnerability of their circumstances as being "paralyzed."

Sleepwalking

Also known as "somnambulating," sleepwalking is sometimes associated with dreaming; but it is actually a non-REM event that occurs in Stage 4 deep sleep. It is this fact that explains why sleepwalkers never seem to recall their excursions.

Sleepwalking is most common among younger persons, but it has been reported occasionally by adults (usually, adults blame sleepwalking for late-night trips to the refrigerator—claiming that they weren't responsible for eating a large piece of cake that was meant for the next night's birthday dinner).

Some people have even reported sleepwalking to their cars, getting in, and driving somewhere. Others have reported sleepwalking miles from their homes. Cases like this are extremely rare, and there are usually extenuating circumstances that may explain such activity.

Subconscious

This is a level of the mind that exists just below a person's CONSCIOUS mind. This is where undifferentiated stimuli are taken in and filed by the brain (for example, when walking down a busy street, all the stimuli that your conscious mind can't handle enter your subconscious). It is also the storage place for all of your accumulated knowledge.

Items in the subconscious mind can almost always be accessed at will.

Superego

In Freudian psychology, this is the part of the PERSONALITY that acts as the moral conscience; it internalizes the rules of society to govern good and bad actions. This facet of the personality is the counterpart of the ID and it holds the appetites of the id in check. The superego is interesting in its role as the "good angel" sitting on our shoulders, appealing to us to choose right over wrong. In dreaming, Freud held that the superego generally was overpowered by the id. This was because the Superego needed the assistance of the EGO to hold the id in check, and the ego is usually knocked out when the dreamer is ASLEEP. Often times, dreams are particularly troubling not because the dreamer is being untrue to themself, but so overtly true to themself.

TALKING WHILE ASLEEP

Because the most intense dreams occur during REM stage, which is a form of Stage 1 sleep and has similar BRAIN WAVES to that of waking, sleepers sometimes speak out loud in reaction to their dreaming stimuli. Most researchers say that talking while asleep is a symptom of some sort of UNCONSCIOUS distress.

THETA BRAIN WAVES

Theta brain waves are characterized by a state of heavy relaxation. During waking hours, theta wave activity occurs at moments of daydreaming or intense relaxation. Theta waves are also common among CHILDREN during waking hours and may explain the extraordinary capacity for imagination which they display. The effects of some mind-altering DRUGS can include increased theta-wave activity.

Dreaming is a Stage 3 transition between REM and deep sleep. Some dream researchers have theorized that perhaps dreaming is occurring in this sleep stage as well, but with less accessibility than the REM stage.

TRIGGER EVENTS

A trigger on a gun sets off a process whereby the force necessary to shoot a bullet is released. Similarly, there needs to be a stimulus that can act as a "trigger" to instigate a dream.

Trigger events, as they're called, are as diverse as you can possibly imagine. The brain's enormous capacity for receiving and storing information, on CONSCIOUS, UNCONSCIOUS, and SUBCONSCIOUS levels, allows virtually millions of images to vie for the attention of the dream state. Trigger events can be divided into three broad categories: PERSONALITY issues (things that are happening in your life), cultural issues (things that are happening around you), and instinctive knowledge (things that are part of the entire human condition).

UNCONSCIOUS

This refers to the part of the mind that does not enter a person's awareness. It is the part of the mind that a person simply cannot access, yet it likely contains more information than both the CONSCIOUS and SUBCONSCIOUS minds combined, and it does affect a person's behavior in many different ways.

VALUE OF SLEEP

The human body is an incredible machine. The intricate systems that keep it going do amazing amounts of work each day. In order to last as long (relatively) as it does, the human body requires regular maintenance: sleep. This is an essential period of time for the body to regain energy and to dispose of unnecessary waste products in the system.

During sleep, all the body's systems slow down—the rate of metabolism decreases to its lowest point; the blood pressure drops and the pulse rate slows; nerves become less sensitive to light, sound, and even pain; body temperature drops slightly; and breathing slows down and becomes irregular. There is also evidence that suggests the brain takes advantage of sleep to jettison unnecessary electrical energy and replenish memory systems.

The average newborn infant sleeps nearly twenty hours per day, usually consisting of three- to four-hour intervals that are broken up by hunger pangs. As the baby—and the stomach—grows the hunger pangs come farther apart and less sleep is required. After the first year, the child will sleep about twelve hours per night, plus another hour or two during daytime naps.

The adult human sleeps an average of eight hours in every twenty-four-hour period. However, the amount of sleep an adult needs varies from person to person—the main requirement being that the person feels well-rested upon waking. It is a common perception that older people need less sleep, but this isn't necessarily true. It is a fact that many older people's waking problems—physical and psychological—stem from inadequate or poor sleep. (It is an unfortunate catch-22 that many people's physical and psychological problems also cause sleeping problems.)

Modern science continues to perform research into the reason the body sleeps and the value that sleep provides.

book 2

◆

Dream Images

D ream images and icons are countless. Yet, the number of different meanings that each of those images has conveyed—to all the different people who have dreamt them—is even greater.

Encyclopedias have been published with the presumption of defining thousands of dream images with very specific and prescribed definitions. The problem with this method of dream analysis is that it ignores the fact that every dream's interpretation is unique to the dreamer. In fact, the images and icons that combine to create a dream are a product of the dreamer's individual life experiences and MEMORY. Consequently, every person has their own personalized database of potential dream images and icons, so to define dream images for everyone's consumption is impossible.

The approach offered in Book 2 is quite different. We intend to help you learn how to approach the meaning of dreams and their images in new ways. Rather than provide prescriptive meaning to hundreds of common images, we will instead encourage you to look inward and find the meanings for yourself. If in fact dream language is formed by the visual images and emotional transactions of your life, then it follows that the best and most meaningful interpretations will flow from the same source.

In the movie *Citizen Kane*, the millionaire's dying word is "Rosebud." This utterance inspires a search that lasts the length of the film. Finally, a sled bearing that word is discovered. Why did it mean enough to a dying millionaire that upon his passing it was the most important object he could name? Monetarily, it was virtually meaningless to a man with millions. However, because it was a gift from his father at a time when his father seemed genuinely interested in his son, the sled meant everything to the dying man—love, innocence, youth, etc. (Another old man may dream about a sled at a critical moment in his life and be set upon by a number of bad feelings; especially if he had had a bad sledding accident in his youth.)

This is the stuff of dream language! Prescribed definitions of dream images are often meaningless at best and distracting from the truth at worst. In contrast, the emotional hurdles and victories, the relationship struggles and resolutions, and the objects that mean the most to you because of your unique story as a human being all combine to create the person you are. Because these things mean the most to you, they are the images and icons that build your interpretive framework for the world. When you dream of these things, only you can prescribe their meaning.

Consequently, the entries in Book 2 are written in a rhetorical style designed to encourage your reflection. These questions are intended to direct your thinking toward what is significant about the objects and transactions of your dreams. More importantly, how do you feel about these things and how do they correspond to other events in your life?

Book 2 also includes discussion of many emotions that are common in dream events. Since the meaning in our lives is derived largely from emotional transactions, it follows that dreams and their meanings are likewise concerned. Many times, it is not the objects of a dream that give pause, but the emotions. Upon waking, you may remember a dream that featured only common objects, but felt peculiar as you recalled it. Perhaps this feeling is more important to your ability to understand the dream than the symbols that combined to create it. Regardless of how the dream images and emotions are put together, your mind has told you a story. Usually, it is a story of how you feel about yourself in relationship to yourself, others, and the world.

The key to using this directory of images and icons is to appreciate the metaphorical value of the images as they relate to your self-awareness. The goal of all these entries is to inspire your own deliberation process. Only you can know the meaning of your dream vocabulary. If you do, in fact, believe that your dreaming means something more than an electrical storm in the brain, then the meaning lies within you. If you are willing to deliberate, you will be rewarded with insight and a strong sense of meaning for your waking life—thanks to your dream world.

ABANDONMENT

Watching a child realize he is alone is a heartrending event. In a moment, he goes from content to worried to panicked. One of our most primitive fears is the fear of being separated from FAMILY, friends, or society. In dreams, being abandoned can have several connotations that derive from psychological or physical experience. The primary interpretive question is: "Who abandoned the dreamer, and why?"

Being individually abandoned by a significant other can represent a feeling of insecurity in a relationship. This may reflect concerns about the feelings of another towards you. Are you genuinely receptive to the idea of being loved and valued, or do you view another's affection as a "put-on"?

Perhaps you view yourself as lovable as you are known, but fear that more revelation about you will lead to isolation. This could be especially true if there is a TABOO experience being kept secret from the person who has abandoned you (e.g., marital infidelity). Dreams of this nature may be RECURRING if as a child your parents extended only conditional affection towards you.

You may see yourself as completely abandoned. This can represent a major sense of being unable or unworthy to fit into society. In this type of dream, you may not be alone in a physical sense, but lack connection with the people around you. Self-esteem issues, taboo experiences, or your ability to receive love should be areas of investigation.

People who view themselves as completely abandoned within a dream often find themselves lacking connection in many day-to-day relationships or experiences.

Lastly, you may see yourself as ritually abandoned. This dream experience finds others leaving you for "your own good."

Where have you left "unfinished business" in relationships with others?

Conversely, have others left your expectations unmet or altogether unrecognized?

ADOPTION

Being adopted yourself. Adoption themes in dreams often occur at significant points of transition or crisis in life. Being adopted in your dream can mean either that you have no human connections at the moment or that you require additional connections to remain a viable person. Dreams of this nature may occur during geographic moves, job transitions or uncertainties, or prior to marriage. Crucial questions exist concerning who adopts you, what the relationship is like with them after adoption, and whether you feel glad, ambivalent, or uneasy about being adopted. A pre-marital dream may include something like this one (reported by a 24-year-old groom-to-be):

> *"I'm sitting at a card table with people I don't know playing a game I don't understand. They are trying to teach me, but don't speak English. I get up to leave, but they take me home and treat me as their son."*

The dreamer may see himself as ambivalent about fitting into family rituals, but feeling enough acceptance from his new extended family to overcome his concerns.

Adopting another. Obviously, the gender of the dreamer has much to say about this dream. Clinical evidence shows that men and women share equal responsibility for infertility disorders. However, women tend to internalize more ANXIETY about child-rearing and may feel a need to adopt to resolve that archetypal task of life. Discerning the current status of the self in the life cycle and external circumstances of the woman would be important.

Does infertility run in your family tree?

Are you currently planning to become pregnant, but are concerned that you may not?

For both genders, adoption may revolve around a very benevolent view of the self as provider. More and more people find their motivation in an ethic of making a difference in just one life. As such, the quest for justice is shifting from the hero(ine) in the white hat who saves the town to the good person who helps one person less fortunate.

For men who adopt others with ambivalence, there can be questions of virility or competence at stake. Who you adopt, and why, could be important to uncovering the meaning of this dream.

Is there a significant bonding or separation occurring in your life that may be creating some unease below the surface of your emotions?

Do you feel a need for emotional support that is going unmet or that you are finding new avenues to meet?

AIRPLANE

Being a passenger in a plane. This dream can be mundane or remarkable, since some people are ambivalent toward FLYING while many others hold an irrational fear of flying. In America, it is a well-known fact among football fans that announcer John Madden never flies—he travels around the country by bus. Many people share his aversion, even those who dream of flying. In this case, it is an attempt by one part of the psyche to quell perceived irrationality in another part.

Dreams about flying as a passenger may hold a great sense of adventure for the dreamer. This can be due to the journey, the speed, or the destinations available through air TRAVEL. Also, it may be due to potential dangers, such as hijacking, which the dreamer may heroically overcome.

Piloting a plane. Dreams about flying in a plane as the pilot vary tremendously. Is the dreamer a competent person either in sleep or waking? This may indicate a sense of control over circumstances.

Does the plane crash? This may reveal a sense of inadequacy or incompetence.

Who are the passengers on the plane? This may reveal who you feel responsible for in life, with your flight skills revealing your sense of how well you are fulfilling those responsibilities.

If you are piloting the plane, are you competent to do so or are you overwhelmed by the responsibility?

Do the other passengers accept, ignore, disdain your presence?

ALARM CLOCK

If you were given $84,600 per day, how would you spend it?

This is how we view time. It is a precious commodity that seems impossible to acquire sufficiently.

As a symbol. Alarm clocks in dreams are often a reminder of our limitations. These may be reflections of actual problems (such as running out of time), symbolic of poor time management, or completely conceptual (such as failing to complete a life-cycle task before that cycle ends). This alarm clock could appear in the dreams of someone who is perceiving their time on earth as "growing short."

Use in Dream Recall. Studies indicate that REM takes place with regularity about every ninety minutes through sleeping time. Dream recall is heightened from 20% to 70% or more when patients are awakened during dream time. By setting your alarm clock to go off either six hours or seven-and-one-half hours after going to sleep, it is likely you will have more vivid dream recall.

Is the clock a hopeful symbol (e.g. "at last the time has come"), or a fearful one ("time is running out")?

ALONENESS

There is a pronounced difference between being alone and being abandoned. Being alone can be an intentional choice by the dreamer. This usually means finding a time for personal reflection and inner growth. The waking equivalent is the cocooning phenomenon. People are staying home more—regrouping and rebuilding their inner strength.

Aloneness may herald transition or rites of passage. When we move from childhood to adulthood, there are habits, attitudes, and relationships that are left behind. This void can create an image of aloneness. Dreams like this often present themselves as the dreamer traveling somewhere alone.

Who is separating from you, and why, in waking life?

Is this mutual, at your initiative, or another's wishes against your will?

See ARCHETYPES, CARL JUNG

AMPUTATION

Amputation of Self. Whittling away at oneself in a dream state is not unusual. Many people find themselves acquiring different forms of handicaps in dreams. Often, these can be associated with perceived physical weaknesses or self-destructive psychological patterns. The reason for the dream amputation, method of amputation, and ANXIETY caused by the amputation should all be given some thought. The result in the dreamer's life as far as inconvenience or further liberation deserves attention as well. Also, the dreamer should give consideration to the role of the amputated body part in waking life.

Amputation can also have a religious, moral, or ethical connotation pertaining to behavior. Followers of some sects view their bodies as their own worst enemies in terms of the ability to adhere to particular social or religious codes. Christians, for example, believe the words of Jesus when he stated that it was better to chop off one's own hand and enter Heaven than to send the body to condemnation intact. Many people, from a variety of faiths and other guilt structures, carry that sort of IMAGERY in their SUBCONSCIOUS.

Amputation of Others. Understanding the amputation of another's limbs in your dreams is very much dependent on their relationship to you. Amputation of a loved one's limbs may show an area where you feel violated by that person.

Amputation of a co-worker may be wish-fulfillment for the desire to handicap him or her for your benefit. Amputation of a limb that grows back readily could reflect a sense that no bad thing ever seems to beset that co-worker or adversary.

Amputation of a stranger likely represents some sort of uneasiness you may be feeling toward the mass of humanity you deal with daily.

AMUSEMENT PARKS AND CARNIVALS

As settings for dreams, these are ambiguous places. It seems as though amusement parks often include elements that we consider to be the best and worst in life. Many of us have enjoyed these places tremendously, but have also seen, smelled, or actually experienced the consequences of overdoing it: vomiting. Carnivals also include a very wonderful or frightening collection of personalities. These personalities may intimidate us at times. Sometimes the fright comes from a figure we love, such as a parent who doesn't really enjoy the carnival, but endures it for the children.

Eventually, the illusion of the idyllic FAMILY outing is transformed to an angry scene. Who are you with in the carnival and how do you experience the time there?

Finally, carnivals are full of out-of-control experiences. Being out of control can be ecstatic and wonderful. In these instances it may remind us of a sexual experience. However, it can be terrifying to people with fairly rigid waking boundaries. Spinning and riding fast are two chaos images often associated with carnivals. Ferris wheels reflect times to remove oneself from the midway to a quieter perspective, unless one is afraid of heights.

In what way are the rides metaphors for your life? In other words, how is your life like a rollercoaster, merry-go-round, or other central feature of the park?

Perhaps there is a ride pronouncedly missing that you want to experience but cannot—what is that a metaphor of and why do you desire it so?

ANGELS

> *"Jacob wrestled the angel, and the angel was overcome."*
>
> Bono, U2, *Rattle and Hum*

With the tremendous interest in angels these days, it is not surprising that they are becoming frequent characters in dreams as well. Pictures of angels, stories of angels, and a popular spirituality of angels have put the images and imaginations of angels in our collective UNCONSCIOUS.

The word "angel" literally means "messenger." Often, delivery of a particular message in the dream is the role filled by these beings. As the needs arise, they may provide additional help to the dreamer beyond simply delivering information. Since so many RELIGIONS and contemporary worldviews have made room for angels in their view of the universe, this topic needs to be broken down a little more. JUNG had room in his worldview for "spirit guides."

These were apparitions that shared both knowledge and insight. This insight came as dialogue. Consequently, the Jungian angel was something of a spiritual mentor. Religious angels have usually served more as ambassadors. They come with specific information, but not much dialogue. They are dispatched for specific purposes. Revelation, not dialogue, is the mission of the angel in this context.

Beginning with popular literature of the 1970s, angels have become more involved with tangible needs of this world. Tires are repaired, oncoming traffic is diverted, and rickety homes are preserved from the weather by angels. This seems to be a reflection on the growing interest in finding a reliable help in a malevolent world.

Angels also have become, in a sense, the sort of instant wish-granter that the character "Kazoo" was to Fred Flintstone in *The Flintstones* TV cartoon show. Kazoo was a green alien being who appeared when Fred needed help—he provided free favors and magical tricks. Some folks dream of angels helping them out in this way. In this sort of case, the dreamer may be turning toward an actual friend in real life to give them something.

Many angels in dreams represent help from an unknown and unseeable origin to survive a difficult situation. The dreamer is turning out into the unknown, expecting help from beyond his or her actual means. This could be called "wish-projection."

Finally, the angel may be what the name implies: a message.

To discern which type of angel you have in your dreams requires some energy on your part. Does your worldview include the possibility of such beings? If not, you can probably move into wish-projection pretty easily.

Did your angel speak or act mysteriously without verbalizing?

If the angel spoke, what was the content?

If the angel merely acted, what was the nature of the action?

What area of your life seems to be needing a special solution that exceeds your resources? Do you feel emotionally unsupported in one of your personal quests or spiritual struggles?

ANGER

Who are you angry at?

Why are you angry?

What is the outcome of your anger in your dream?

Being angry in a dream often represents an emotion we want to have in waking and will not allow ourselves to experience. This reflects the fact that anger can be destructive and sometimes ends up being treated as a TABOO in our PERSONALITY. The fact that it comes out in dreams may be attributed to the ID.

People who dream of being angry often have difficulty expressing the emotion constructively in waking life. Anger is a reaction to a perceived threat. As such, anger reflects our feeling that we are being denied what is ours by necessity or by right.

Dreams that contain anger may often serve as an insightful beacon into our waking relationships. Sometimes, you may find yourself dreaming of being angry at someone who never angers you in waking life. This may simply be an indication that they are not perfect; a sort of check that reminds you that they are human.

ANIMA/ANIMUS

These are terms that JUNG created to describe the opposite-gender self that lives within each of us.

The anima is the feminine component dwelling inside a male's UNCONSCIOUS mind.

The animus is the masculine component dwelling inside a female's unconscious mind.

In dreams, this opposite-gender self can be a helper or an antagonist. These dream figures can appear as translations of persons we meet with whom we have a tremendous sense of romantic love or platonic camaraderie. One of Jung's interpreters held that the anima/animus character was only understandable to those who have known true love.

However, our opposite-gender selves may reveal to us negativity in ourselves or negativity we perceive in dealings with the opposite SEX. It is important to note that sometimes, when you dream about a person of the opposite sex, they may be representing your own inner self. Carefully consider all persons of the opposite sex in your dreams as a possible appearance of your own anima/animus.

What do these STRANGERS teach you about how you view the opposite sex—do you fear, lust for, or despise these strangers for any apparent reason?

ANIMALS

Animals in dreams can take on almost any conceivable character or symbolic role. From some of the earliest recorded human dreams, animals have revealed much about the meaning of a particular dream. This includes dreams of personal insight or circumstances, and also dreams of revelatory content. Animals can befriend us, talk with us, chase us, eat us, or just be there in the dream to either comfort or bother us. Animals often appear in dreams for very personal reasons, and have to do with your own experiences with them.

How you experience an animal in both waking and sleeping is central to its meaning. This includes both how the animal actually behaves in your dream, and your waking stereotypical attitude about the animal. This is important because the two may be juxtaposed.

Consider a DOG. Dogs are often considered to be loyal and friendly. However, many people have a deeply rooted FEAR of dogs. Dogs also have stereotypes that are opposites (for example, "man's best friend" versus "call off the dogs"). People with a deeply held fear of dogs may experience a dog dream that validates the fear one night and contradicts it another time.

What the animal is doing is also central to how the dream is interpreted. Are you being CHASED BY ANIMALS? Eaten by animals? Talking with animals?

Farm animals are not too unusual in dreams. However, they seem to be less common than they were in more agricultural times. Grazing farm animals generally reflect a sense of being provided for adequately. In early dream history, grazing animals were taken as a sign that prosperity and calm were coming to, or prevalent in, a land.

Killing animals is a more unusual dream theme that divides into two general areas: killing by necessity, and killing arbitrarily. Killing out of necessity could be a hunter-provider ARCHETYPE dream or a survival dream. These dreams often reflect a sense of responsibility for the other characters in the dream or of a need to prove oneself. Dreams of killing animals arbitrarily may reflect either wish-fulfillment, anger projection, or frustration with a social TABOO. Wish-fulfillment and anger projection have much to do with how you perceive the animal you are killing.

Does this animal have any representation for you among persons in general or do you characterize a specific person as "an animal" when speaking of them?

The social taboo of arbitrarily wounding or killing animals has become a criterion for evaluating antisocial behavior in people. Consequently, it is not surprising that in dreams this would be a sign of taboo frustration. Again, what the animal represents may be of significance to you.

Starving animals hold significance in agricultural societies and Native American spirituality. These animals often reflect a concern or foreboding about the adequacy of needs being met the future. In the past, starving animals were a reflection or anticipation of famine periods. Starving animals may also be metaphors for relationship transactions in which you participate.

Common animals' stereotypical perceptions that may appear in dreams as metaphors for yourself or others (listed as "good"–"bad"):

Cat: *quiet, independent–aloof, disengaged*

Cow: *provider, gentle–easily intimidated*

Dog: *loyal, friendly–consumptive, aggressive*

Horse: *hardworking, useful–strong-willed, independent*

Mouse: *quiet; diminutive–unable to assert power*

Ox: *hardworking–dumb*

Pig: *clean, smart–gluttonous, dirty*

Rabbit: *fast, gentle, fertile–timid*

See BEAR, BIRDS, CATS, DOGS, ELEPHANT, FISH, FOX, OXEN, RATS, WOLF

APOCALYPSE

See END OF THE WORLD

ARCHETYPES

An archetype is a way of seeing oneself in a dream experience. Many people dream at one time or another of doing something heroic. We all know what a heroic action is by a sort of mystic human understanding of goodness and sacrifice. This mystic understanding is the archetype-the event of being a HERO is an archetype experience.

There are many archetypes in life. CARL JUNG formulated these out of his studies of human beings and mythologies around the world. In many ethnic and religious backgrounds, there are myths that embody the ultimate version of various archetype experiences. An example of a hero myth may be Hercules or Sinbad.

We are prone to see ourselves as archetypal figures at transition points in our lives. Change generally brings about anxiety and self-reflection. Going from education to the work force, singlehood to marriage, or childless to parent are some archetypal transitions.

ASLEEP

Dreams of being asleep are not unusual. After all, it is the actual state of your body while you are dreaming. However, dreams of being asleep are not usually dreams of being at rest. SLEEPING is one of our most VULNERABLE circumstances in life. When you are asleep, your cares are disarmed, your ability to defend yourself is limited, and your care for others in a practical manner is practically impossible. Dreams of this nature often reflect either our great ease or a sense of violation in life. How you awake, and who wakes you up, are important elements to consider.

BABY/CHILD

As an object in dreams, a baby or child represents something that requires great care and attention. The meaning is at issue regarding whether it is your original responsibility or one that has been passed off on you by someone else.

These dreams may also have wish-fulfillment content for women who are in their childbearing years. For men, the dreams may be ANXIETY-related, especially if you are sexually active without wanting to experience the consequences of FATHERING a child.

BALDING

Losing hair or becoming suddenly and completely bald are two common dream events. Often dreams of this nature reflect concern about your attractiveness or sexual virility. If you are forcibly shaved during your dream, this may be a concern over sterilization, as hair often plays a significant role in male gender identity.

For many men and some women, the loss of hair in dreams may also reveal ANXIETY about growing old. Even if the dreamer is not showing signs of balding in waking life, he may lose his hair in an age-anxiety dream.

Yet another possible interpretation of hair loss in a dream is the feeling that an illness of some sort may be imminent.

BEARS

The appearance of a bear in a dream is a good example of dream interpretation as being culturally shaped. For most of us, bears are not very good companions, and they represent ill-temperament. The exception is in Native American traditions. For the Navajo and Crow Indians, the bear is a father or grandfather figure that possesses wisdom and knowledge of the sacred.

BEATING

Are you on the giving or receiving end of the violence?

What other persons are involved?

Is the beating apparently deserved?

The emotional themes that accompany this type of dream are feelings of domination, victimization, control, and anger. The extent and results of the beating are also important to discern. Is the beating a simple fight, or is the goal that of death?

If you are the aggressor, the chances are very high that you have unresolved fear or ANGER feelings that need to be expressed. The object of your beating personifies the source of these feelings. If your victim is unknown to you, refer to STRANGERS.

If you are the victim, odds are only about fifty-fifty that you will know your attacker. Many times, we are beaten by strangers in our dreams. These strangers may reflect either particular relationships (boss, spouse, etc.) or general fears. However, it is not uncommon to be beaten by archetypal figures. We may be beaten by older members of our same gender during times when we feel our identity is not well-accepted in the world.

BED

Dreaming of being in bed may be an indication of a LUCID dream event. This means that you are aware of being ASLEEP in a dream state. Somehow, your mind is accepting the limitations of your sleeping condition. However, the bed can also be a place of laziness, sickness, death, or sexual encounter. If the bed feels like a symbol for any of these metaphors, the dream may be saying something about how you perceive yourself.

FREUD would be inclined to see the bed as a womb, as well. Indeed, the covers pulled over the head on a chilly morning can make the bed a utopian haven against a difficult world.

BERYL (AQUAMARINE)

Mineral and precious stones have historic meanings based on their color, value, and rarity. Geology and various crystal structures have significance in the New Age movement, which has renewed interest in these materials. Beryl is a crystal that represents courage and tranquillity. Dreams that include this stone may reflect material gain, or they may reflect self-esteem and inner calm given by another as a gift to you.

BIRDS

If you have ever seen the movie *The Birds* by Alfred Hitchcock, you will understand at once that birds receive mixed reviews in the human saga. Birds have often been perceived as troublemakers and omens of bad tidings throughout history. To have the birds of the air pick the flesh off your bones was an awesome sign of judgment in the ancient Near East.

Ravens, crows, and vultures could share in this task. However, the gift of flight has retained a sense of majesty for birds as a genus, and certain birds in particular. Note that the phrase "Soaring on EAGLES' wings" has been a sign of hope for twenty-five centuries.

The visual acuity of many birds (i.e. the eyes of a HAWK) also conveys positive perceptions, while ravens and OWLS are also stereotyped as vessels of wisdom in myth and literature. The ability of some birds to speak places them in a special category as far as non-human creatures are concerned. Some people may be characterized as bird-like in your dreams. If you speak with birds in your dreams, you probably have some communication issues to consider. This is true even when the birds do not speak in reply. As with other ANIMALS, the bird and its underlying image in your experience are crucial to discerning the meaning of your dream.

In addition, persons whom you characterize as being particularly wise, predatory, or visionary may be represented to you in a bird form-not necessarily as a bird with that person's head or face, but more as a metaphorical appearance.

BIRTH

The birth event is the one sacred event that virtually every CULTURE holds in common. Not surprisingly, it is one of JUNG's archetypal selves-the self creating life for another. Since it is an ARCHETYPE, there are lots of other dream images that lead back toward birth and life. WATER and OCEANS are the two significant ones. Many cultures embrace the symbol of water as crucial to life. Many times, women who intuitively know that either they or a friend may be pregnant will dream of water. This may be related to the "broken water" images of pregnancy.

Emerging from a CAVE or isolated place as a new self is a Jungian version of birth themes.

In this sense, birth is not limited to biological events, but also includes the advent of additional facets of PERSONALITY or self-awareness in your waking life.

FREUD held that entering back into small rooms or caves was symbolic of the womb. This could herald a desire to return to MOTHER, be nurtured, or experience the mother's power as a protector in certain situations. Since all of us have been born, we have feelings about it for better or worse. We may feel as though life has been a fortunate or an unfortunate experience. Either way, these feelings play into our birth dreams as either positive or negative experiences as well.

How is the birth for the dreamer? Women may experience birth dreams out of either desire for or ANXIETY toward pregnancy. In this case, the MEDICAL, social, and sexual histories of the dreamer would be very significant. There may be moral, religious, or medical factors that make a pregnancy either desirable or dangerous. Examples may include a young woman who is sexually active against her moral or religious teachings or, a woman trying to conceive, yet unable to do so. In these cases, a guilt-producing deed may be construed as causing the birth or lack thereof.

Women who see themselves giving birth under positive circumstances may be affirming themselves not just in birth, but as archetypal women. They are able to see themselves as competent within their gender to complete the traditional roles of the gender. While this sounds incredibly sexist, it is true in the sense that all of us see men and women as particular and individual persons with strengths and abilities. It's what makes an archetype an archetype.

BIRTHDAY

There are two ways in which the birthday dream is experienced.

The first is that everybody knows it's your birthday. There may be an actual party, or just a common affirmation and celebration (See HOLIDAY).

The second birthday experience is a darker image—you know it's your birthday and everyone forgot. It's an indication of the struggle for significance. Who you encounter, their apparent ignorance about your birthday, and their reaction to your news (or to your non-verbal, cloying attempt to clue them off) says a lot about the scenario. It may be that you feel overlooked in your relationships with others, or insignificant in general. If you are unwilling to tell, it may be that you are wanting more attention from the dream characters than they are providing. If, on the other hand, you tell them and they gush with apology, there may be a sense in which you feel they are operating at a relationship deficit with you over some matter. In the dream, did they give you a gift upon finding out it was your birthday? What was it?

BISEXUALITY

FREUD was a great advocate of the bisexuality of all persons. It was no surprise to him when he studied dreams in which romantic content existed that was contrary to the dreamer's usual sexual preference. Many times, this romance is a form of "mirroring." Mirroring is the desire to find affirmation of a particular aspect of yourself in a particular sort of relationship. The romance contrary to your usual preference should be set aside initially in order to discern what sort of affirmation you may be seeking from this liaison.

Another possible reason for a dream that involves bisexuality for a typically heterosexual person is that the ANIMA/ANIMUS is flexing itself.

BLESSINGS

Although the word is something of an antique in many circles, the idea of a blessing is a powerful one in the human experience. Consequently, giving, seeking, or receiving a blessing are important dream events. Many times, dreams include some kind of conveyance that will fall into this category. The idea of a blessing was central to many ancient CULTURES. When preparations for death entered its final stages, the dying patriarch or matriarch of a family would convey last wishes or hopes for affirmation onto members of a household. This was a deeply spiritual act that conveyed peace or power onto the next generation. To be overlooked or rejected during the blessing was a sign of disfavor or judgment. These things can come across in your dreams based on the subjects in them and the amount of reverence you have toward them.

In more contemporary times, we can look at these blessings or conveyances in terms of complete versus incomplete relationships. Especially with parents, the blessing or absence thereof carries with it the perception that the relationship did or did not fulfill an expectation of love, nurture, or support.

Receiving a blessing is a sign of closure and ultimate acceptance— finally, the bygones are bygones. No matter what the past provided, hope prevails. Blessings of this kind often include well-wishes, the promise of sufficient resources to succeed in life, or an affirmation of the person as being competent and capable.

Giving a blessing is an act of benevolence. It may reveal how the dreamer sees him or herself in their life cycle or in relationship to the blessee. To give a blessing is to see oneself as a source of help, spiritual power, forgiveness, or encouragement to others. Depending on who is being blessed, it may reveal that someone in relationship to you is not receiving adequate resources for their needs.

Seeking a blessing may reveal a sense of imbalance in a relationship. The dreamer may see himself or herself in a deficit situation with no apparent resolution. Images of this type may indicate that the dreamer is seeking a monetary inheritance or a chance to bury the hatchet in a relationship. In either case, the seeking may take a very humble or aggressive form, based on the dreamer's relationship to the source of blessing.

BLINDNESS
See LOSS OF SENSORY ABILITY

BLOOD
Blood in dreams is rarely a well-received image, unless it is connected with an ANGER object. The blood of another in this case may reflect seeing oneself as ultimately victorious. Most times, blood represents depletion, INJURY, or DEATH. This depletion may be physical, or it may reflect the loss of other essential resources, including emotional or financial assets.

Blood can have a kind of direct meaning as "life source." In this regard, blood may be seen as a metaphor for becoming one with another person—this type of feeling is conjured from our exposure to Native American "blood brother" images.

Blood also may serve as a sacrificial metaphor—as in the sacrificial lamb or other ANIMAL . It also may have occult implications for persons involved with such practices. Draining, drinking, or drawing and/or writing with blood are practices of this nature. Many genres of cult literature often include this type of reference.

Whose blood are you seeing in your dream?

Can you discern who caused the bleeding?

Is the presence of blood accompanied by a feeling of threat?

BOATS

Depending on your experience with them, boats can represent riches, TRAVEL, isolation, danger, romance, or complete and utter frustration. Rowboats and canoes are often found on fairly placid lakes and streams. In dreams, they may be way out of context on the high seas, therefore implying a kind of broken peace. Normally, the setting of the boat says much about its symbolic meaning.

Different types of boats may vary in meaning, but possible options include isolation, danger, escape, and romance. Sailboats often appear in similar environs as rowboats, but tend to mean either riches or frustration: sailboats can be very affluent and romantic to the dreamer, however, being dead in the WATER for lack of wind is another option.

Power boats often show a sense of power, control, wealth, competition, or travel. Danger is not often a problem, except in cases of failed motors.

Sinking boats can reveal a fear of water, drowning, or incompetence. More often, they are a metaphor for feelings about a particular aspect of life. To determine this, look at who is on the boat or conspicuously absent from it. Also, see if the reason it is sinking, which may seem nonsensical, is available in the dream.

Is the boat one that you recognize?

Is the general feeling one of happiness and leisure or one of fear and ANXIETY?

BODY

Who you are in your dreams says a lot about your body image in waking. Many times, you experience your body in dreams as just a regular version of you. However, another time you may see it as idealized or disfigured. These feelings about your body may be communicating how you perceive yourself or how you think others perceive you, for better or worse. Often, how you think about your body reflects how you think about yourself as a whole person.

When an experience of body perception is central to a dream it is worthwhile to analyze the origin of your feelings about the body perception or image. At times, our bodies will dramatically change in dreams to acquire various mystic properties. These include walking through walls, flexibility increases, or changes in height and shape. These are often just problem-solving techniques. However, they may also reveal a sense of limitation from one's body or power over one's body.

Other times, we or others in the dream will transform from a human form into something else. Transitions of this nature can be absurdly funny, or a little frightening. Sometimes, we will adopt a human body that fits the needs of the dream circumstances. This is the ANIMA/ANIMUS experience at work in the self. Other times, we can adopt an ANIMAL body to achieve a particular goal or character attribute. These events reveal areas where we feel either strong competence or distinct weaknesses in our character.

Does your sense of body seem similar to that of waking life?

If changed for the worse, does your body completely prevent you from succeeding in the dream, or does it merely make things more difficult?

BOSS

The boss relationship can be translated from dreams in two ways:

1. A significant relationship from some other area of life—spouse, SIBLING, parent, or friend—may become your boss. If someone from another corner of life becomes your boss, it is likely that you feel that person exerting too much control over

your life. It is easy to allow constructive relationships to become controlling at times. You may experience this dream in your usual worksetting, or in some nonsense environment. The place where you and this "surrogate boss" work together in this dream says something about the area of influence in question.

2. Conversely, your boss may become a sibling, spouse, or someone other than a vocational supervisor. If your boss is squirting into your personal life through images of some other, more personal relationship, it may be time to assess your work. Workaholism is the great debilitator of many homes. If your employment is fulfilling other roles reserved for other persons in waking life, it may be time to assess the emotional invest-ment you have in your work. This dream can be healthy in the collegiality it reflects, or as a warning sign for the drain work is putting on your emotional resources.

Finally, if you dream of your boss in the worksetting, you probably are stressed out by your job for any number of reasons. Dreaming of your job in general—particularly if the dream is unremarkable and takes place in real time—usually indicates that you are feeling over-worked or are behind at work.

BOUNDARIES

Although we rarely dream of boundaries per se, we often encounter uncrossable FENCES, immovable GATES, and other non-traversable obstacles. A Freudian approach would be to discern what might be gained by overcoming the barrier and then attempting to associate that gain with a TABOO event. If you have any helpers to get you over, through, or under your obstacle, they may be co-conspirators in the violation—or, your joint conquest of the obstacle may be the taboo in itself. Depending on whether the taboo is ANGER, SEX, or another violation, you may need to look closely at your feelings about what is on the other side of the fence, across the river, or whatever the obstacle is.

It can be an eerie feeling to encounter a boundary where either you feel unable to go past or your dream companions keep reminding you that nobody goes over there. It may be that the perceived threat or inability to cross the boundary is the central message of the dream.

Perhaps you see yourself as needing to move through a transition into a new self-awareness. In this case, the boundary may reveal what is hindering you. This is especially true if you are traveling too heavily to cross a river, or have companions who will not cross with you. If you have dream companions helping you with whatever boundary you face, it may be worth heeding their dream advice. Often times, we feel that a fence must be crossed when in fact the protection they provide is important.

While boundaries may feel constricting at times, the psychological pain of attempting to cross every boundary in life can cause great problems that could have been avoided by knowing when to stop.

BRIDGES

Bridges are interesting symbols in relationships. We often speak of "crossing" and "burning" bridges as representations of the opportunities and challenges of life.

Does the bridge cost anything to cross?

Is it a secure or precarious bridge to cross?

Is there a known destination, or is it a bridge to an uncertain future?

Do you have particular feelings about yourself as you cross or upon completion of crossing the bridge? Your answers to these questions may reveal a transition you perceive in your life and your feelings about it (See JUNG).

The act of building a bridge is another way to encounter bridges in dreams. (Are you building the bridge to create an opportunity or to escape from trouble?)

The destruction of a bridge is yet another bridge encounter. (What are you becoming separated from and how do you feel about that separation? Are you participating in the bridge destruction or being victimized by it?)

BUILDING

A building can represent dwelling, business and commerce, sexuality, or your own body awareness. These dreams often are interpreted by who is in the building or what happens to the building. For example, a destroyed-building dream may accompany the loss of family and friends or a time of ill health. A full building may mean business is good, or fertility is imminent. A building that is affected by a Freudian phallic symbol—any symbol reminiscent of the male sexual organ—may be an image of womanhood or sexual liaison.

BUS TRAVEL

Traveling by bus is considered by many to be the most uncomfortable means of transportation. Indeed, bus terminals are often very small, and reveal an interesting cross section of society.

Bus travel can also be very time-consuming, although it allows a fuller experience of the country. You may feel inefficient or unable to afford better means when you dream of travel by bus. In defense of busses, the passenger camaraderie is very high, especially on long trips or packaged tours. Who your dream companions are during the bus trip should be considered carefully, as well as your interactions with them. It may be that you have collected a valued set of friends for a journey of particular shared interest. If this is the case, finding a common thread amongst either the people or the sights would be useful.

BUYING

Purchasing can be a very powerful event in life. If you don't believe this, think about people you know who gain self-esteem or a sense of accomplishment from shopping. Participating in commerce is a validation of personal autonomy in many ways. It can also be destructive. In a consumer-driven CULTURE, many people find themselves drowning in debt. This debt can be an all-consuming drain not only on financial, but on emotional resources as well. Consequently, dreams of buying may be a psychological warning as easily as an affirmation.

To interpret a dream of buying requires the dreamer to think about what was bought, why it was bought, and how it was bought—cash, credit, check, or good looks. Dreaming of buying on credit may reflect a desire to acquire or control, or it may reflect a warning. In exchanges of this nature, the object bought should be closely considered. Buying staple items on credit may reflect a deep-felt insecurity about one's circumstances and future. Buying luxury items could be an attempt to compensate for inadequate self-esteem or wanting to strengthen one's public stature. Trying to buy items (or food) without MONEY may reflect a sense of incompetence concerning financial or other matters. It may also reflect a sense of unmet needs in emotional transactions.

What and who are you buying for, and from whom? If the merchant is known (e.g., spouse, business associate), the goods are essential, and the end user is yourself, you may feel that you are not fulfilling your end of the bargain in a relationship.

Being able to buy items without money is a powerful projection of control, public acceptance, or a sense that you are owed much favor. In these cases, the items purchased and the identity of the seller will provide major clues to the meaning of the dream.

CAMERA

Dreams where cameras are important often reflect a desire to stop the action, gain additional information, or capture hidden meanings. Are you taking specific pictures, or are they random?

Are you photographing people, places, or objects?

Is the nature of your photographing recreational or are you trying to capture something in particular on film, such as evidence? It may be that your life is going by too quickly for you to appreciate the nuances of it.

CAMPING

Who are you camping with, how do you feel about them, and what are the physical surroundings like?

Another real question is how are your accommodations and did you plan to camp or just end up in the middle of nowhere without provisions?

Most archetypal HERO-quest journeys include a time of testing in a man-against-nature conflict. As such, it can often symbolize a time of purification to get back in touch with the EARTH.

CANCER

See DISEASE

CANDLES

Candles often reveal a sense of mystery, romance, or SUPERNATURAL guidance regarding the setting in which they appear. The candle can also be a symbol of providence or security as it may illuminate circumstances. If the candle has an unusually large flame, the FIRE may be the central image.

Do the candles have a ceremonial feel to them? If so, other aspects of the dream may be requiring reverence.

Is someone else holding a candle or candles? Often a symbolic gesture by a dream character-such as holding a candle-will indicate that they are there to lead you.

CANYON

Being in a canyon, abyss, chasm, or pit shows the dreamer as being somewhat trapped. However, in some settings, this kind of experience may lead to a place of initiation and transition. It may just be a place of beauty and rest for others. The Grand Canyon is a favored spot for many people who dream about it long after visiting. In this regard, the canyon is just a staging ground for other relationship transactions in the dream (for example, the peace provided from vacations or from experiencing natural beauty).

CAPTIVITY

Dreaming about being imprisoned, locked in a room, or restrained against one's will can be a powerful dream image. What is especially notable about this type of dream situation is how we react to the circumstances. At times we may try to escape, but other times we may just acquiesce to, or even cooperate with, our captors. Much of this depends on who is holding you captive and why. If you are cooperating with a familiar captor, it may be that you feel that person's control over your life to the extent that you have no choice but to be a part of it.

Freudians may be inclined to argue that the captivity, especially if in a small room, reflects the repercussions of a dominant MOTHER, or a return-to-the-womb type of captivity. This is a nurture-versus-power conflict. You may even experience a captor who is not your mother, but who treats you with a mixture of power and sympathy.

Jungians may be inclined to see the captivity as preventing transition to another level of maturity in the Self. In this case, the captors may represent those who have the most to lose from the growth of the prisoner.

Political captivity in a dream is a powerful image of the self against the world. Being held hostage in this way reflects the cosmic struggle of good against evil. The dreamer may see himself as a victim of circumstances beyond his or her control, or as a sacrificial offering for a conflict or cause. Many times the cause is less defined, but the dreamer may have companions or friends as co-prisoners-in this case, the relationship with the other(s) is the key element to interpret.

CARS

Often times, the car is simply the best mode of transportation within a dream. In that case, the rest of the dream is more important than the car itself. However, if the dream includes significant data about the car, that image may be worth a deeper look. There are numerous car images in our dream lives. These may include accidents, being a passenger in a car, buying a car, or driving a car.

Accidents usually reveal perceived threats, vulnerabilities, or anxieties about the well-being of those we love. They may also reflect a sense of being out-of-control or unable to protect others sufficiently. Dreams of this nature can also have a strong PREMONITION feeling to them that inspire additional caution the following morning. DÉJÀ VU may be a very powerful element, as well, if the accident occurred on a road often traveled. Heightened sensitivity to careless habits might be a good idea following an accident dream.

Being a passenger in a car may indicate that you feel the driver has control over your destiny. The driver may even be a public figure, such as a celebrity or politician. In these instances, your feelings about the driver and how trustworthy he is can be significant.

Buying a car is often a wish-fulfillment or problem-solving dream. These dreams reflect a desire to acquire something that is beyond your means in waking life. If you are in the market for a car, your dreams may actually be trying to help differentiate the best choice.

Driving a car is roughly the opposite of being a passenger in one. However, the passengers may reflect persons to whom you feel an acute sense of responsibility. Again, they may be figures from almost any area of your life. What is important is how you relate to them and how you all agree or differ on your destination.

Castration

Dreams that include a traumatic removal of a valued possession may reflect fears about virility and castration. Often, our gender identity is tied to objects of special importance to us. Consequently, damage, destruction, or removal of those objects in dreams is an assault on our gender security.

To dream of castration may also reveal other types of power struggles in your life.

Who is performing the castration?

Is it an accidental occurrence, or is it somehow ceremonial?

Cats

Cats have several commonly observed meanings that translate pretty easily between waking and dreams. Traditionally, cats have symbolized intuitive or magical powers. The former may be a herald to trust

INTUITION. The latter may be a fantasy on your part to acquire witch skills or to investigate occult matters.

Of course, your own cat may simply appear in your dreams as a member of your daily life.

CAVE

If you ever watched the old *Kung Fu* TV series, you may remember the powerful beginning sequence: Grasshopper (David Carradine) is in a cave. He seizes the smoking cauldron and burns the tiger and dragon images onto his skin as he carries the cauldron out into the sun. Upon doing so, his initiation is complete and he is an official Taoist monk.

The cave is the archetypal place of initiation. Caves are the first and most sacred of human dwelling places. As such, people may often feel a primordial sense of attraction to caves in their dreams. Initiation is the Jungian term for becoming a Self in the transition from childhood to maturity. Jung contends that there are rites of passage that need to be completed. The cave is often the place this is done.

For much of human history, caves have been sacred places of shelter from the world; the place that became the extent of a person's kingdom in the face of uncertainty and peril. While the cave itself may not be a central image any longer, we have many metaphors for it. These include small rooms with a sacred or significant object of our past in them, small bedrooms or studies, basement workshops, or other places of solitude and silence. There is also something in such a space that confronts you—not necessarily in an endangering way, but an existential one. This grappling is the business of the cave. To make peace with the object of your grappling is the act of initiation.

If your dream includes leaving the cave, you will probably feel a new unity with the world upon your departure. It's a far cry from being disillusioned; the peace you feel comes from a fuller sense of participation and belonging in the cosmos.

CELEBRITY APPEARANCES

As the media continues to create stronger icon status for people in the news, it is not surprising that lay people are dreaming of them as well. It is not at all unusual for people to think they "know" particular public figures and so to experience them in a dream. Dreaming of any particular celebrity often reveals a fantasy for friendship or romance. These dreams may also show a sense of being a peer or equal to that celebrity as if to say, "I can do that, too."

A second aspect of this phenomenon is living vicariously through a celebrity. In this instance, people will assume a peculiar sense of participation with a public figure's success and notoriety.

Another variation of this is becoming a celebrity yourself. This may include performing with other celebrities while achieving your own icon status. This kind of notoriety may be showing you your own giftedness (or sense thereof) in a particular area, or it may be intended to encourage you to pursue a higher ambition for yourself.

Of course, because today's media completely inundates the public with images and rumors of celebrities, they may appear in your dream simply as extraneous static.

CELLULAR PHONE

Neither FREUD nor JUNG had anything to say about cellular phones. However, as they become more prevalent they are obviously making their way into people's dreams. Cell phones have changed from being a symbol of status to a symbol of security. We feel a sense of connection to our resources when the cell phone is nearby. If your dream

includes a cell phone, you are probably seeing yourself as connected—
or desiring connection with additional opportunities.

There also may be a sense of wanting to change one's social status
to necessitate use of a cell phone. Try to discern who you are calling
and under what circumstances, as the phone may have a lot of symbolic lifeline or security image to it as well.

Does it feel like a social crutch in your dream, or a helpful tool?

Is it tying you down . . . ringing incessantly and keeping you from
experiencing a sense of peace in your sleep?

CHASED BY ANIMALS

This kind of dream is common among children. Often, it reflects a
deeply held fear of the animal doing the chasing. However, it may reveal
an ANXIETY about something completely separated from the animal
kingdom. In cases like this, it is important to think about what is chasing
you and what your experiences have been with that particular animal.

For example, if a RELATIVE whom you did not particularly like had
a German shepherd DOG, you may dream about being chased by the
dog. This may reveal either the desire of the relative to obtain your
attention and affection, or it may validate your fears and anxieties
about that person.

If you often use animal characterizations of people's personalities,
this may be particularly telling. (He's a bear, she's a momma bear, he
works like a horse, etc.)

CHASED BY OTHERS

Depending on who the others are, it may be useful to determine what
common relationship exists among your persecutors. You may feel
indebted to them or simply hated by them. The former may include

people with whom you feel an emotional or financial indebtedness. The latter is a throwback to the old schoolyard scuffle. You may feel that particular co-workers are angry or jealous and are seeking your life or expulsion. If you are chased by STRANGERS, this may have more global implications for how you see yourself in the world.

During different seasons in life, many people experience a sense of not fitting in, or of being driven away. This feeling may come immediately prior to or immediately following a geographic move into a new region of the country. It may also occur around other times of transition such as marriage or a career change. This type of dream usually reflects acceptance ANXIETY. In dreams where you are being chased, the emotion of the dream is often as important as the objects and images of the dream.

Did you feel your life was threatened?

Did you feel that you could have turned and faced the chaser with relative success? These questions will help determine the interpretation of such dreams.

CHASING ANOTHER

Chasing another person you know in a dream may be a sign of needing to protect that person from themselves. Many times people embark on paths that seem illogical or even self-destructive. The impulse is to chase them down and try to redirect them.

Another common chasing dream revolves around heroic behavior. You are chasing someone to right a wrong committed against you or another. You may not directly know whom you are chasing, but you know their relationship to someone else you love and value—be it their BOSS, a criminal who has victimized them, or some other antagonist. If you can't remember why you are chasing someone, try to concentrate on the emotion that the chase aroused.

CHILDREN

Children are fascinating characters in dreams because they reflect so honestly our own thoughts and feelings. Children are often afraid of what is worth being feared, have deeply held senses of right and wrong and show reckless abandon in both likes and dislikes.

To dream of being befriended by a child can be a complex event. If you know the child in waking and dreaming, this may reflect a wish-fulfillment or projection. If you do not know the child from your waking life, he or she may be a reflection of yourself at a particular time in your past. The main puzzle piece to discern is the nature of your activity and relationship with the child.

Parenting a child can also be a simple wish-fulfillment dream or something more complex. Parenting a child may be a way that your brain is working out some difficulty in your own relationship to your parents or another relationship of responsibility.

Parenting can also be a power projection dream. There may be a relationship in your life where you feel out of control and want to bring it back under control. Since most of us have felt our parents exert emotional power toward us at different times, we are now doing like-wise in the dream relationship.

The converse of this is dreaming of yourself as the child while other figures from your life exert power in different areas. You may have dreamt that you were playing dress-up in the office and your co-workers were all regular adult figures. In waking, you may in fact experience them as more powerful than yourself or even excessively powerful.

CHOKING

Choking is a physical event in sleep for many people who suffer from sleep APNEA. The tongue relaxes against the airway in deep sleep, actually stopping normal breathing. However, people who suffer from apnea do not dream of choking more than others.

Choking may be a symbolic revulsion dream or a deprivation dream. Are you choking on food or being forcibly strangled? The source of the food or the food itself may be a symbol for a revulsion you feel in waking life. If you are choking on a hot dog, Dr. FREUD will see you momentarily. If someone is choking you, why? It may be that either you threaten them or they are depriving you of what you need to be effective in the HOME, workplace, or other setting.

CIRCLES AND RINGS

Circles and rings are archetypal symbols. They can manifest themselves as circular rooms, the magic circles of shaman or other soothsayers, circus rings, or even circular driveways.

While circles are usually positive dream symbols, it is important to note the characters that accompany them and the emotions that surround them.

Did you experience the circular object yourself, or watch others doing so?

Was the circle broken or complete?

CLIFFS

Cliffs are majestic, dangerous places. If you are on cliffs in your dreams, you probably feel your life has a combination of these two qualities. Determining which one is prevalent depends on who is with you, or why you are on the cliffs. The thrill of the danger may be the allure of the cliffs, depending on your companionship. Is there a secret crush or forbidden love with you on the cliffs?

Dreams of cliffs may lead to that falling sensation that wakes you up. The cliff, in this case, may be a metaphor of your own CONSCIOUS-NESS at that moment.

If your cliffs are on the seashore, you may be conjuring something out of the ocean or expecting to see something out upon the ocean. Dreams of this nature may reflect the ARCHETYPE of fertility or creative power.

CLOTHES

"The clothes make the man."

Clothes are an extension of how we see ourselves. If your clothes are praised or jeered, this may reflect the self-esteem curve you are currently riding.

Losing clothes may indicate a feeling of vulnerability. If you don't believe this, strip in the mall and see how assertive you feel. It may also reflect a sexual or exhibitionist fantasy.

Acquiring clothes can be a mixed event. Who hasn't gotten a gift of clothing that later became a story of bad fashion lore? However, acquiring clothing for yourself that fits perfectly and makes you feel powerful may herald a positive transition in self-esteem or perception.

Sometimes, you may acquire clothing for special purposes or clothes that carry with them magical powers. In this instance, the clothing may represent a search for cosmic providence or protection.

COLORS

Most of the time, we dream of colors because visually we live in a colorful world. However, when those colors become prevalent or unusual in the dream, they may be an interpretive object in themselves. This is especially true if an entire dream setting in is different hues of a particular color or if a significant object seems unique for its coloring.

Since many colors have archetypal feelings and emotions attached to them, the approach taken by JUNG is often helpful. However, it may be that a particular color transcends a Jungian meaning because of an experience you have had with it. If Jungian types do not fit, try freely associating significant objects from your waking life with the same color as the dream object for meaning.

COLOR	POSITIVE MEANING (NEGATIVE MEANING)
Blue	*nobility or tranquillity* (depression)
Black	*power* (death or mourning)
Brown	*Earth, nature* (scatological)
Gray	*neutral* (passionless, death)
Green	*fertility, renewal, wealth* (greed, envy)
Red	*sacrifice, sex* (carnality, taboo sex, humiliation, physical injury)
Orange	*adventure, change* (forced change, disruptiveness)
Purple	*royalty, positive personal growth* (injury)
Yellow	*enlightenment,* (cowardice, illness)
White	*purity, wholesomeness, sacred ritual* (emptiness)

COMPASS

Dreams about a compass, the universal symbol of direction, often involve either getting back on track or trying to discern what course should be set for the path ahead. Or the compass may have been found or given to you by a mentor figure of some kind. Checking out the mentor and her or his relationship to you should be a central concern of the dream.

COMPUTER

The computer has become a symbol of access to knowledge and

power. It also has become a ball and chain. The good thing is, we can work anywhere thanks to internet connections and laptop computers. The bad thing is, we can work anywhere thanks to internet connections and laptop computers.

You are either on the verge of excelling at work, or you probably need to quit working such long hours.

Was the computer simply background furniture in your dream, or did it play an integral part?

Was the computer more powerful than you are used to, or was it causing you problems?

COURTYARD

For some reason, many people have buildings with courtyards or atriums in their dreams. This may just be so much scenery, as we tend to like such things architecturally. Often times, these dreams reflect a desire to return to a more renewing or living place. The courtyard can also be a womb image. As such, it can represent you getting back to your life source. It may be a sense on your part of MOTHER power coming into the situation that has brought you to the courtyard. In these cases, you may be looking at the courtyard as a place of nurture or interference.

CREATURES OF MIXED OR UNKNOWN ORIGIN

Did you watch *Godzilla* right before bedtime? A lot of our unknown creatures come from visual images out of horror films. However, they may possess power or destructive potential that hits at the core of our being. In these cases, we are confronted by a sense of angst or loss from unknown dangers through these creatures.

There are some mixed creatures that are more playful, however. These creatures may be combined characterization of favored friends or pets, or may come from favorite literature or mythology images. In this case, the images are positive for us.

CROSS OR CRUCIFIX

This powerful religious symbol often carries with it either comfort, judgment, healing, pain, or a desire for protection. Obviously, how the object enters the dream and what effect it has on the dream plot is very important.

The symbol can have either great attraction to the dreamer or revulsion and avoidance. To avoid the cross may indicate either judgment, shame, ambivalence about traditional values, or a MEMORY-dodging CONSCIOUSNESS. This memory-dodging is a defense mechanism to prevent looking all the way into the implications of choices or experiences tied to religious symbols in your life.

On the positive side, the cross can feel very redemptive or provide a sense of security. Many religious icons operate as a "positive TABOO" for us. Just as dark taboos are symbols, practices, or icons we do not mess with out of fear, certain positive symbols carry positive taboo power. We are secure because of the power of the symbol.

Christians who encounter the cross in dreaming may experience a sense of inner healing, renewal, or reconciliation in the dream.

Who is with you when you encounter the cross and what are the activities immediately prior to or subsequent from the cross experience? These questions may give clues as to whether the cross is an internal healing symbol or external one for broader reconciliation.

CRYING

Weeping in dreams is not at all unusual. This is often because of the emotional power carried by the images and persons you are encountering. Weeping in the dream is generally separate from actual physical tears forming. It is more often that weepy feeling you get in your heart when a particularly moving scene is played out before you. The best advice is always to go with the dream. Emotional releases and revelations can have a very cleaning effect on the psyche and should be embraced whenever possible. However, you should try to determine the TRIGGER EVENT that caused the emotion.

Did someone else make you cry directly?

Were you crying for a particular reason, or was it for a general emotional release?

Did the tears make you feel ultimately better or worse?

DANCING

Dancing can be a powerful psychological or spiritual release for people. Many primitive CULTURES view dancing as a sacred, as well as recreational, event. Dancing before religious icons has been a symbol of praise and sacrifice to divinity for thirty centuries or longer. Often these dances were done to elicit favor or providence from the gods.

In contemporary culture, dancing is more recreational as an offshoot of mating ritual. All this is a fancy way to say we dance in hopes of getting lucky. As such, dancing has taken on more sexual connotations for many people.

If you are dancing alone, this may be a regression to a more sacred understanding of dance. Some people use metaphors like, "I'm dancing as fast as I can" to illustrate their sense of relationship to the world. This may include dancing alone or dancing individually for an audience.

Dancing with others may include a sense of uncoordinated participation with the world around you, depending on the dance and nature of clothing. Do you fit in well? Another variation on dancing with others is moving through diversity in relationships. This may be especially true if you are considering beginning a romantic relationship among several choices of partner.

Others dancing for you may indicate your perception of them, especially if the dance has flirtatious or overt sexual content. This may reflect either your feelings of desire for them or a sense of their desire for you. Dreams of this kind may strike the dreamer as crass or exhibitionist in nature.

If you are dancing alone, is the style of dance appropriate to solitary movement, or are you dancing in a waltz pose without a partner? Perhaps you feel as though the others are not following your lead or fulfilling their half of the deal in a relationship.

If the dance and music seem incongruent, or if you are dancing without music, are you doubting the appropriateness of any facet of your life or relationships?

If others are dancing for you, is it sexual, performance, or ceremonial—and why?

DARK ROOMS, ROOMS WITHOUT EXITS

The room without exit may be a womb image. As such it represents either MOTHER-nurture or mother-power conflicts as you discern whether you are satisfied and safe to be in the room, or unreasonably restrained from your other objectives for the moment. Do you want to get out of the room, or is the room a haven against potential dangers in the world?

Is the room pleasant or painful as a space in its own right? These are central issues to identify.

Does the darkness of the room inspire peace and rest or fear and disorientation? Peace and rest may indicate sanctuary or maternal reassurance. Fear and disorientation may show mother-power or personal loss in an archetypal shift of awareness or threaten shift in roles.

DATES

Many times in dreams, dates and numbers are used as a signal to identify something from the dream that will translate to waking life. In Book 1, TRIGGER EVENTS and parallel process were discussed as two influences on dream events. In dreams, dates may be clues to guide you toward a time or event that is serving as the trigger for the dream.

DEAD PEOPLE AS LIVE CHARACTERS IN DREAMS

Dead people who appear alive in dreams have three general categories of participation: cameo, resolution, and judgment.

Cameo participation is a little eerie in recall, but not particularly noteworthy in the dream itself. In these cases, the dreamer simply sees a dead person intact and living, just hanging out in the dream scene. Often there is little direct participation in the dream per se. The dream image probably is tied to an activity that the dreamer and dead person once participated in together. Most likely, there is a latent sense of missing the person that made the dream appearance possible.

Resolution participation usually involves a specific action with the dead person. In this case, the dead person's presence is central to the unfolding storyline. Either you lack something they need or they act in a way to provoke emotion (positive or negative) from you. In either case, the transaction or inability to complete it revolves around some deficit that needs resolution in the relationship. These dreams may carry a sense of judgment or joy, depending on whether or not the relationship transaction is resolved.

Judgment can often involve the dead person as a dead person or zombie. These dreams are particularly troubling as we often see ourselves as unable to reverse of complete the necessary actions to salvage a situation.

What traits did the deceased embody during their lives (i.e. Uncle John was a saint; Aunt Agnes was mean as a snake)?

Was their behavior in the dream consistent with or contrary to their general behavior in life? Perhaps you need to look more closely at the true PERSONALITY of the deceased and how they were characterized by others.

DEAFNESS
See LOSS OF SENSORY ABILITY

DEATH
Death can appear in dreams in many forms ranging from the NEAR-DEATH EXPERIENCE to wish-fulfillment projected on others. It may seem to be terrifying, or almost joyful in its sense of power.

The near-death experience can be either a psychological phenomenon or a physical one. The physical phenomenon comes from LUCID dreaming in a NIGHTMARE condition. You may become aware of the body paralysis of the REM state and feel powerless to defend yourself in the dream. This can create an overwhelming sense of vulnerability to the threatening circumstances of the dream and a near-death experience.

The psychological facet is part and parcel of feeling endangered by your circumstances. This danger may be tangible or merely sensed in the dream. If it is tangible, the source of the danger is the area for interpretive work (whom, why, how, and what has endangered your life?). If the danger is merely sensed, it may symbolize ambivalence concerning a soul's transition into facets of self-awareness you may not want to completely embrace.

There is also a spiritual near-death experience. People who participate in actively seeking OUT-OF-BODY EXPERIENCES in dreaming may feel themselves unable to, or prevented from, returning to the body. These dreams are powerful images of how we sense the cosmos or spiritual realities impacting upon our lives.

Was the death a sudden deprivation of life or a release from the struggles of it? Moreover, as you became aware of dying, was it threatening or peaceable?

Death of self, loved one, or stranger. Dying in a dream is not too unusual, though if it happened with regularity our waking lives would probably begin to feel a little unstable. Often, derealization (see MOVIES) accompanies death so your dream can continue with your observation. Otherwise, death is the wake-up point.

To die yourself is very troubling. Most people have not invested much emotional energy in preparation for death and feel that death is a strong enemy to be avoided. Being confronted with death is a place that is uncomfortable. By the way, how did you die in your dream and do you assign responsibility to anyone for your death? These are important questions.

The death of a loved one may be the result of numerous factors. You may feel genuine ANXIETY for that person's well-being. The death may be more symbolic than that as you struggle with the reality of your love for that person as weighed against repressed ANGER towards them. Finally, it may herald the passing of the relationship if the loved one is romantic and not familial in connection.

The death of a STRANGER can be the development or transition of different aspects of the self. Consequently, it is often useful to decide how you knew the stranger and whether you seemed deeply moved or only casually concerned with the death. It may be that the randomness of life in the central concern. In this case, looking at who else in the dream is concerned with the stranger's death and your connection to the fellow mourners is important. The death of a stranger may symbolize stereotypes that need to be rethought or explored as a means to a greater self-understanding. Are you being confronted with situations where your attitudes about others are being challenged?

DEMONS

Demons are interesting dream characters. Whether you view them as psychological constructs or ontic reality in your view of the cosmos, their presence is a significant statement. The meaning of the demons revolves around their power relative to other major characters in the dream.

Demons may have seductive or violent power in a TABOO relationship to the dreamer as either a nemesis or helper to the cause of the dreamer. In these cases the dreamer sees him or herself as helped or hindered by SUPERNATURAL POWERS in the accomplishment of a moral or personal conquest.

If a demon is helping you complete a task, it may say something about how your task is viewed morally either in your SUPEREGO or in the structure of the spirit realm. If a demon is thwarting your progress, this may reflect your perception of evil working against you in your life. If the demon is threatening others who are important in your life, you may be struggling with how to protect or provide for others in a world perceived as hostile.

If the demons are helping you acquire something you hold as taboo, some self-examination concerning motives may be appropriate. Are they powerful in an alluring or repulsive way?

DEPARTMENT STORES AND MALLS

The department store is the personification of capitalism. Many people enjoy just wandering through stores and malls to experience the numerous choices. However, they can be a little overwhelming.

Dreaming of these places reflects a feeling of having choices or even too many choices. It may also be a reminder that you have not been careful with your money of late.

Depending on your status as a potential buyer (see BUYING), being in a mall may reflect your sense of power or competency given the choices you have. If the choices all reflect items you would find in a waking-world store or mall, the items you are most drawn to may be the objects of central meaning in a dream. The salespeople you are bumping into may be significant if they are familiar. Perhaps you feel as though you owe somebody something or someone expects particular actions from you.

Are the items that you want missing or available in abundance? This may be a metaphor of the balance, or lack thereof, in facets of your life.

Are clerks unable to assist you in finding your needs? Perhaps you are looking outside yourself for growth that can only come from within.

DIAMONDS

The diamond is a crystal of riches, romance, and strength. It is the hardest and most valuable stone. Dreams containing diamonds may be a wish for wealth or a reflection on the futility of riches.

Do you perceive others as substantially more or dramatically less well-off than yourself?

Do the diamonds inspire fear, embarrassment, or boasting on your part towards others?

DINING WITH OTHERS

The act of social eating is an interesting mixture of sensuality, personal interaction, and just plain survival. In dreaming, it is usually re-markable for the camaraderie that accompanies it or the method of preparing the meal.

The dinner table has always been central to the family myth. We see one another and communicate the most around the dinner table. Even in families where communication was vague or non-existent, the dinner table was the central, or only, place of meeting. In dreams, these eating events may include characters who have long since passed on, or who you may have only met through pictures. The people eating the meal together should always be examined to see if anyone is notable either for their presence or absence.

What is being eaten is also worth examination. In some families, particular dishes become associated with the family identity in general or particular members of the family. These may include foods no one particularly likes or good foods prepared by someone nobody particularly likes. The point is that FOOD becomes a symbol for our lore and story as a family.

Of course, a nonsensical meal or method of preparing may also accompany the eating event. This may reflect either the absence or presence of particular characters or a lack of knowledge given a prepa-ration that is outside the family's traditional menu. The symbol content of the food (liver, who died of liver trouble?) or persons involved with particular foods should be associated through the MEMORY.

Is the dining situation a friendly one or even a celebration?

Is the food very unusual or otherwise remarkable?

Does the fact that you are dining with certain people in your dream merely provide a setting for those characters to address other issues?

DISEASE

Curing diseases may be a projection of your benevolence for the world. Many of us want to feel as though we are good people who have something to contribute. Disease and the cure thereof allow us to feel power to influence the outcome of other's lives.

Getting a disease could be revealing of a self-defeating lifestyle choice if the disease creates a particular handicap. If the disease is transmitted from a particular person, you may be ambivalent about their influence in your life. If the affliction holds TABOO quality, for example, AIDS or other sexually transmitted disease, there may be internal ANXIETY about the moral quality of your life. Getting a disease can also reflect a fear that is either rational (family history) or irrational (news story as TRIGGER EVENT).

Is the disease peculiar in that it is only apparent to certain persons or only comes over you in the presence of certain others? The body often symbolizes the emotional content of relationships.

Are you embarrassed by the disease and its consequences, or do you tell others about it?

DISFIGURED OBJECTS OR PEOPLE

We are used to the modern proverb "it's all screwed up" as a metaphor for situations and relationships that fail to meet our expectations. Dreams of this nature often reflect our verbalization of people or things that fail to fulfill our needs. How many disfigured people or objects you encounter in your dream is an indication of what facets of your life are not meeting your expectations.

Can you ascertain how the object or person came to be disfigured?

Does the disfigured object continue to work, or does the disfigured person seem unaware of what you are seeing?

Disproportionate objects

Woody Allen, in the movie *Everything You Ever Wanted to Know About Sex (But Were Afraid to Ask)*, gave us a breast as big as a house. This breast was a terrifying and consumptive thing. Yet breasts receive so much attention many times, it is hardly surprising that they occupy tremendous perception power in our world.

In dreams, certain objects may assume unusual proportions. This significance often reflects the importance of the object to the dream story as well as the emotional dimensions of the object. Emotional dimensions refer to the importance people place on others, on things or on situations. For example, it is often difficult to help people perceive the emotional power of family members. If you ask them to draw their childhood house—apportioning rooms based on the amount of influence and memories they have about the places—the emotional dimensions of the home become clear.

Many times, people have attached emotional dimensions to very positive or very negative experiences that alter the dimensions of those objects in their SUBCONSCIOUS perception. A spouse who feels emotionally chastised may dream of oversized silverware, reflecting the dimensions of a spoon used to give spankings in childhood.

Distant sounds

Distant sounds can be beautiful and frustrating. In dreaming, they may just be rounding out the scene in the SUCONSCIOUS. For example, dreams of beaches or BOATS may include requisite sounds effects such as waves, fog horns, or BIRDS.

Sometimes, distant sounds can create a foreboding feeling as well. Some sounds, such as THUNDER or shouting, may be frustrating because they appear without an apparent source in the dream. These sounds can be alluring and cause you to search, or create a warning that circumstances are changing. Sometimes, you may feel that the sounds are a distinctive message you should be able to understand.

These sounds are sometimes just for us, other characters in the dream may not be hearing them or responding to them at all. Sometimes, the message is clear to others, but obscure to us. In waking, you may be feeling a disparity between others about a situation they feel is dangerous that you have assurance about or vice versa. You may also perceive others as more perceptive than yourself and be looking for their input in your current circumstances.

Are you often accused of not listening well by a boss, spouse, or partner?

Do you feel that your life has an ominous, undistinguished danger lurking on the outskirts of it?

DIVINE COMMUNICATION

Dreams allow awareness from somewhere other than the CONSCIOUS mind to enter into our range of perspective without the prejudicial judgment of EGO blocking the potential of larger reality. More directly, the best time for the divine to reach humanity is when we're not so busy being ourselves.

JUDEO-CHRISTIAN, Tao, ISLAM and HINDU RELIGIONS all have significant appreciation for the dream as divine reality penetrating the consciousness of humanity. However, ideas about divine figures taking initiative in relationship with humanity vary widely within world religions (see Book 3).

What can be said here is that dreams that seem to include revelation from beyond could be treated as divine revelation itself, or as some sort of revelation from your own deepest values. In other words, don't be too concerned with the media through which any powerful message comes, or don't overanalyze the messenger. Let the message be the medium.

DIVORCE

Divorce is an excessive commodity now days. A first grader recently said, "My parents haven't gotten their divorce yet." Unfortunately, divorce has translated from a social TABOO to a rite of passage.

Often, it symbolizes ANXIETY concerning insincere commitment from a partner or underlying resentment toward a partner. It may be represented by other significant persons in your life going through the divorce as a displacement of your anxiety over the matter.

Do you have relationships that are very tiring or emotionally draining? Perhaps you are wanting to get someone out of your life, but lack the diplomacy skills to address the situation.

Do you feel excluded from or cut off by past friends over a current disagreement?

DOGS

Dogs can be great friends or frightening adversaries. In dreams, the friendly dog may be a representation of a trustworthy relationship or intuitive affirmation of it. The wild dog may represent a nagging, ongoing struggle with a seemingly irresolvable conflict. (Of course, either case may just be a replay of a life situation starring a real dog that you know, either friend or foe.)

Do you want someone who is unfairly persecuting you to "call off the dogs"?

Is there a relationship in your life where the loyalty is at question or is especially pronounced?

DRUG USE

Drug use in dreams is often a sign of TABOO violation. Drugs have powerful social symbolism attached to them that makes it difficult for a drug-user to feel good about himself or herself as a user. The exception is use of drugs in spiritual preparation. In certain Native American groups, the use of peyote as dream preparation or during a dream is associated with journeying to find one's self and life vision. As interest in Native American spirituality increases, some people may dream of themselves as participating in sacred rites.

How does using drugs affect your relationship with others in the dream?

Do you fit into or become excluded from a particular group?

Do you feel guilty or good?

Effect of drug use on dreams. Drug use affects the brain by enlarging the time spent in Stage 4 deep sleep and shortening REM-phase dreaming. Since certain drugs are CONSCIOUSNESS-altering, they may cause dreamers to feel expanded consciousness prior to going to sleep. However, drug use ultimately disrupts sleep patterns with negative results.

EAGLE

The eagle is an important Native American symbol, as well as having a place in the ancient literature of Greeks and Hebrews. All these images exist in our common-day lore on roughly equal terms.

The eagle is a symbol of great wisdom and vision in the lore of Navajo and Crow Native American legend. As such, it is often associated as a sacred emblem that sets the dreamer apart for special uses by the Great Spirit.

In Hebrew and Greek literature, the eagle is a symbol of power. Given its great size and strength, eagles were able to remove even small livestock from the herds. This gave the eagle a persona of majesty, power, and fear.

To dream of the eagle is to be spiritually validated as a person of great wisdom and insight concerning both this world and the spiritual realities beyond the comprehension of this world.

EARTH

The Earth has numerous symbolic roles in dream language. "Mother Earth" and "Mother Nature" are idioms used to describe the Earth as a source of life. In dreams, this often translates to the Earth as a source of our being. Other dreams of earth include worry over having a home, being outcast, or "chaos dreams" involving the END OF THE WORLD.

Dreams that include fear of environmental destruction may appear because of news garnered from the daily headlines.

EATING, WATCHING OTHERS EAT

The act of eating can be very telling in a dream, or it can simply stand for basic survival.

Did you acquire your FOOD in the normal manner or in some unusual way?

Is the food recognizable to you or is it something you've never had?

Watching others eat may reflect a deficit concerning your own material or emotional needs. This may be from a pity-party perspective or from the view that others are gluttonous. In this case, it is worth it to ask who you are watching eat and why haven't they invited you to join.

What style of eating is prevalent in the dream? Grotesque gorging and gluttony may indicate excess in your life or the relationship you share with other eaters.

Is the food consumed with great ritual and sacred decorum? This may indicate a sense of providence or divine guidance in an aspect of life.

ELECTRICAL SHOCK

Electrical shock and other energy emanations are often associated with trying to cross a TABOO line or some other kind of punishment. Sometimes the energy is not from a traditional source (i.e., cattle prod, electric fence, stun gun), but is rather the projection of power against us from another dream figure. Probably because of the paralyzing power of electrical shock and the invisible nature of electricity, we feel invisibly restrained or unable to move. The taboo we are violating may be obvious, such as trying to enter a place that is forbidden or it may be more general, trying to assume too much personal power in the cosmos. Either way, being confronted by electrical or other energy metaphors can be a jolting dream event.

Did you notice where the shock came from, or did it surprise you?

Did the shock hurt or disable you, or was it merely a nuisance?

ELEPHANT

In the Zulu CULTURE, the elephant is the symbol for wisdom, patriarchy, and sacred relationships (similar to the BEAR or EAGLE in Native American culture). It is important to notice that geographically different cultures find symbols within their own contexts to convey universal themes of human concern.

Also, most western cultures revere the elephant as powerful and possessing a strong memory. Because of our common acknowledgment that elephants have powerful memories, to dream of an elephant may be an association with the act of MEMORY—this may point to something forgotten in your life.

EMERALD

Giving or receiving emeralds may represent an act of BLESSING. Emeralds as crystals are appreciated for their spiritual and intuitive growth powers.

END OF THE WORLD

The radical annihilation of the world is a theme that seems to recur in many of the world's CULTURES, cults, and RELIGIONS. Sometimes there is a subsequent reordering and renewal of the world that includes a particular group being placed in supremacy. Other times, there is a mystical translation of chosen inhabitants into a structured paradise. Another option is unrelenting chaos and loss of this world without recourse.

Sometimes, the PREMONITION feeling that you get after these dreams leaves you feeling very eerie. You may be unsure (or fairly sure) that what just happened in dreamland may be about to happen out in waking life. The means may be different for any given dreamer depending on your worldview, but the feeling is roughly the same—that time seems short for this world.

There can be several different approaches to seeking meaning in this dream. The origins of these approaches are in personal psychology, cultural tensions, and religious or spiritual revelation.

Feeling dramatically out of control in your personal life can trigger APOCALYPSE dreams. This may be caused by hormones in adolescence, the death of a loved one (especially parent), or divorce and other significant relationship losses. The ending world is an escape mechanism to avoid dealing with a world so dramatically changed by new circumstances. This world-ending dream often features the dreamer alone amongst generally unrecognized figures. This reveals that all people close to the dreamer are gone.

Cultural cues for world-ending dreams come out of a collective angst about the frailty of our planet or the human race. Angst is concerned about what might not be, as in radical non-being of the self, planet, etc. These dreams may be triggered in times of global hopelessness and unpredictability. A millennial change generates this kind of dreaming for some people. Damaging news about the earth, global warming, and cosmic collision potentials will do it for others. Economic uncertainty will create angst for some people. Whenever instability or insecurity become themes of cultural awareness, apocalyptic dreams increase. Interpreting this type of dream asks, "How is the world ending and who is to blame?" This dream may be a calling for you to protect yourself against a risk that is beyond your comfort zone, become more involved in a particular cause, or to think again about the rationale of your fears.

Religious or spiritual revelation that heralds the end of the world is a powerful image. Usually, the dreamer will see some significant icons of their faith initiating or withstanding the destruction. Another scenario is that adherents to the mysticism are identified in a particular way and survive the destruction because of their association. In these dreams, the world is often reordered. Many times, these dreams will accompany a time in the dreamer's life when he or she feels that the entire world is against them and only their association with something larger than themselves can provide a resolution to the struggles being faced. (Or, they may just be receiving an oracle about the conclusion of this world. . . .)

ESCAPE

To escape from someone or somewhere is often indicative of needing to uncover new potential in the self, or to drop bad habits of the past. This new potential comes from incorporating the next order of ARCHETYPE into the CONSCIOUS.

Escape can also reveal either a BIRTH experience metaphor, or that one is discovering self-imposed limitations and is seeking to overcome them.

Whom you escape from, how much violence or argument it requires, and the reaction to your escape all contribute to determining the meaning of this type of dream.

EXTRAMARITAL AFFAIR
See INTERPRETING SEXUAL DREAMS

FAMILY
See RELATIVE, FATHER, MOTHER

FATHER
Fathers are interesting dream figures. They may be presented numerous ways and can create many feelings through their presence. Psychological research has shown that your perception of your father has the most impact on your perception of any higher beings that you may believe in.

As a result, dreams about fathers are often dreams about POWER, presence, and love. Power is often the first experience we have of our father—he is all-knowing and all-seeing. Discipline is a by-product of this. Fathers may often be present in your life in unusual or sporadic ways depending on your family. Such dreams may create the feeling that perhaps all is not settled in the world.

The appearance of your father may indicate warmth, strength, or the lack of these things in their relation to other aspects of the dream. Also, the appearance of your father if he is deceased probably has to do with unresolved issues (these usually can be deciphered based on the other aspects of the dream).

The most important things to note in dreams that feature your father are: the circumstances surrounding his appearance, others in the scene, your normal relationship with him, and any peculiar aspects to his presence

FECES

It was observed in an internet chat room one time that, "No matter what goes wrong with your children later in life, someone, somewhere, will blame it on potty training."

In fact, that approach to psychotherapy is one of FREUD'S most lasting contributions (after penis envy). This is made all the more interesting by Freud's own scatological struggles, as articulated in his biography (*see Book 3*).

For many people, the feces have been a portend of good fortune or wealth. This may include the actual conveyance of wealth or the desire for such a "find." In either case, the interpretation reverts back to Freud's own feelings that the feces were perceived by the infant as being something they created and therefore something valuable. The true surprise would be if an adult person awoke from a feces dream feeling particularly at ease with a sense of well-being.

The origin of the feces and means of discovery are both important issues to discern in the meaning of the dream. For example, if the feces comes into the dream through direct biological means, who it belongs to and your interaction with it—visual only, cleaning up, etc.—may say much about your relationship with the other characters.

If it is simply discovered, or known about without actual visual participation in the dream, then the possibility that another's influence is upon you is troubling. At this point, it is conceivable that the dream could relate to money if your influence is far reaching, or if others are odorously impinging upon you.

FENCES

Fences may be symbols of personal separation in a negative sense, or protection in a positive one. These meanings are often derived from specifically who the fence is separating us from. If you can discern a feeling about what may happen if the fence were traversed (would it be better or worse), that may tell the role the fence is playing in the dream.

Fences can also be a source of BOUNDARY. This is true if there is a sense that the fence cannot be traversed.

What are the boundaries of your life in relationship to other characters in your dream? Perhaps you want to change those boundaries and move a relationship in a new direction. If you are alone at your fence, perhaps you need to or are protecting yourself from others more or excessively.

See BOUNDARY

FIRE

Burning is a tremendous fear many people from many different CULTURES hold in common. However, it is often simultaneously associated with purification. To pass through fire intact is to see oneself as becoming purified. However, being burned may indicate that one perceives life as extraordinarily threatening and painful. If a particular object is on fire (house, car, etc.), this may symbolize over-commitment to it or fear of a world without it.

FREUD found fire to be a symbol of male power. In this case, fire may indicate control over a circumstance or a struggle to feel that way, depending on whether the fire is controlled or not.

Do you question your own morality at times?

Are you seeking cleansing from a bad experience?

Do you perceive your own life is about to go through a significant transition that requires spiritual preparation?

FISH, FISHING

FREUD held that small fish represented the male semen. Medium-sized fish (logically enough) were CHILDREN. Fishing poles were a symbol of the phallus.

Other dreams about fishing may resolve around seeking provision for your needs in life, desiring to find something that seems "below the surface," or looking for primordial instincts, if Darwinism is your worldview of choice.

To dream of fish may simply be a dream of nourishment, or lack thereof. It may also point to a sense of adventure or TRAVEL.

FLOOD

See WATER, END OF THE WORLD

FLOWERS

Flowers are a universal symbol of beauty. To discern a particular meaning, the COLOR of the flowers may be as significant as the flowers themselves. This is especially true for flowers of unusual or nonsensical colors such as green roses. In a dream it would not be surprising to get green roses from a dear friend. This would happen if you are dating your friend's heartthrob in waking life or you sense jealousy from them concerning your romantic attachments.

Consequently you may have acquired knowledge about flower meanings that your SUBCONSCIOUS is now accessing to illustrate a point. This can be especially true if you are given flowers by or are giving flowers to another.

Do particular flowers have special memories for you due to childhood, the death of a loved one, or a prom date or wedding?

Here are some common reference points for particular flowers:

Lilac	*Poison, illness, death*
Daisy	*Indecision about feelings, giver illustrates issue of concern*
Orchid	*Sexuality, sensuality*
Rose	*Red=Love, Yellow=Friendship, White=Purity, Black=Death*
Lily	*Renewal, springtime, resurrection*
Narcissus	*Self-love, personal reflection*

FLYING

Without Assistance. Flying in a dream is a fairly common, but very powerful event. Flying events seem to be divided among those who fly spontaneously in their dreams and those who have a LUCID dreaming event and choose to fly. In either case, the dreamers report powerful feelings of freedom in the flight.

Flying as a spontaneous event often includes some special effort, like flapping one's arms, to get going. However, many people experience flight as soaring by a mysterious, jet-like POWER. These events are precipitated by a strong desire to TRAVEL or an imminent danger that requires ESCAPE.

Flying as a lucid dreaming choice is often of the levitation variety. These dreamers simply choose to fly because, in the reality of their dream, they know they may. This may be related to astral projection or an OUT-OF-BODY EXPERIENCE that some people undergo.

These flights allow dreamers to transcend circumstances and acquire a more favorable or safer perspective. What prompted the will to fly—danger or euphoria—and where did the flight lead?

Nonsensical Means. In addition to flying independently, dreamers may fly on bikes, cars, boats, or other non-airborne equipment. These flights are generally brought about by circumstances where the current means of travel suddenly became inadequate or endangers the dreamer. A good example of this type of flight would be a bicycle that becomes airborne rather than be struck by a car. This dream may reveal a dreamer that sees dangers as inconsequential. It may also be a HERO dream.

FOOD

Food, like eating, is a powerful image. Foods may be scenery, or may be central images in the dream. Who prepared the food can also be an important detail to understanding what it means. For example, if there is a bowl of potato salad like Aunt Sally used to make and she has been dead for two years, Aunt Sally, or her personal influence, may be important to dream insights.

Excessive amounts of food may herald fertility, gluttony, or wealth. (How did the excessive food get into the dream and how did people in the dream react to its presence?) It may be that you or others have divergent views of what constitutes excess or gluttony. Provision and fertility often go hand-in-hand: you may dream of needing more food than another because you believe you have additional responsibilities. It may be that the food was acquired simply because the means existed to acquire it—this can mean wealth or benevolence, depending on what becomes of the food.

Fresh food may be a sign of renewal. This can present itself as needing to get fresh food (take a sabbatical), having fresh food (feeling as though this is a renewing place you're dreaming of), or harvesting (being in touch with nature or feeling proud of work you've accomplished).

Spoiled food is a sign of waste, excess, gluttony, or mismanagement. These dreams often carry a sense of repulsion for the loss, order, or appearance of the food.

Have you ever struggled with your weight, food as a comforter, or an eating disorder such as bulimia or anorexia?

Were you put in uncomfortable positions because of food and others forcing you to eat unwanted items or unsatisfactory quantities?

Do the foods in the dream correspond to significant persons in any of these emotional transactions?

FOREST

Forests can seem magical, daunting, majestic, sacred, dangerous, or phallic. Forests exist in a dream context as something to be enjoyed, embraced, avoided, or traversed. These ideas are central to the interpretation.

If a dream is spontaneously set in a forest, then the forest should be considered as a peaceful, benevolent setting or a more dangerous setting. These dreams say something about how the dreamer is experiencing their waking environment.

If the forest is somewhere to go, then who goes in and for what purpose (to acquire or avoid something) is prominent. If it is a singular journey made to acquire good, special powers or wisdom from a forest-dwelling hermit, then the forest is a place of trial and transition. A forest as a hiding place may show that the dreamer is reacting against a feeling of being overexposed to technology and modern business. The desire is for a time of renewal and the majesty of silence in life.

A mixed-couple (in either gender or orientation) journey may give credence to Freudian analysis. Forests can be very romantic places that open us up to desire and potential.

In waking life, is the forest a symbol of peace and rest, being lost or overwhelmed by choices, or discovery?

Do you feel life pressing in on you so densely that you are "unable to see the forest for the trees?"

FOSTER PARENT OR CHILD

You may be trying to work out special needs that someone in your life has for extra care and nurture. Or you may be trying to find a source for these attributes in your own life.

See ADOPTION

FOX

The fox is a predator of great cunning and wiles. As such, to dream about the fox is to see oneself as either possessing or being victimized by such attributes. The focus on this symbol should be your sense of fear or kinship toward the fox. Whether you like or dislike the fox will determine the representation of the world and your relationships in it. If the fox is an adversary, the object that the fox is trying to take from you may be revealing.

A fox appearing in your dream should indicate that the qualities you most associate with a fox are somewhere at play in your life; either by you against someone else, or by someone else against you.

Is there someone else in the presence of the fox that shares its qualities?

Is there another person in the dream who seems to be approaching you with caution?

FRUIT

Fruit can be a symbol for femininity, harvest, or decay. However, it could just as easily fall into interpretations of FOOD. Therefore, how the fruit was present in your dream should be carefully considered.

Did you offer fruit to someone, or vice versa?

Did the presence of a particular kind of fruit in the dream correlate to an appearance of that fruit in your recent waking life?

GARDEN

Dreams about gardens may be metaphors for your perception of your life. Well-ordered or over-run, productive or dying on the vine, such dream images reflect how we feel about ourselves.

Often a garden makes up the setting for a dream in which other factors take precedence; however, the fact that your dream takes place in a garden is also significant in a minor sense.

GARNET

This is the crystal of focus and order. Finding or being given jewels of this type may indicate resolution of difficult circumstances. Another scenario may be peace and clarity of mind in the circumstances you are facing.

GATE

Think of the gate in larger terms as an opening in a BOUNDARY or secured area where one is not normally allowed access.

Is the gate locked or unlocked? Do you have to open it or is it opened for you? Depending on your answers, these questions may reveal some level of tension concerning an opportunity that may exist for you.

What is inside the gate: a building, a sacred or TABOO place, or a place of tranquillity and safety? You may see yourself going to such a place alone or with a helper for some kind of ritual experience.

If you go through the gate with somebody, it may herald that a relationship in your life is moving on to a different level (for good or bad).

Are you at a loss for opportunities, or do you feel prevented from making progress towards a particular goal? The gate may reflect potential progress, or the hope thereof, depending upon where it leads in your dream.

GHOSTS

A ghost may represent something that is gone but not forgotten—or something that is almost forgotten but that you simply cannot release.

The appearance of deceased RELATIVES usually tells of unresolved issues. In these cases, you should pay particular attention to the surroundings, the other characters present, and any unique aspects of the apparition.

GIFTS

What is given and to whom? This may indicate a relationship equity being worked out in the dream—a conveyance that attempts to equalize the relationship or symbolizes the nature of the deficit in the relationship.

On what occasion is the gift given? If there is a particular event connected to the giving—birthday, holiday, etc.—it is valuable to see what the particular expectations of the event are. Whether or not the gift is appropriate to the expectations will say much about the event.

It may be that a gift is expected and none is available. This may reflect an inability to meet the expectations of others or of others to meet yours.

Another possibility may be that you are not understanding the expectations of others.

See BLESSING

GOLD

Gold is the universal symbol of purity and wealth. The acquisition of gold may be a display of POWER or wealth. The source of the acquisition as a conquest, gift, or discovery is important.

Equally important is the sacred element that comes into play. How is the gold used and what kind of wealth or power does it represent in the dream? It may be that you get a golden helmet, similar to Don Quixote's. This is an archetypal form of sacred power for completing a mission or HERO quest.

Did you find, lose, give, or receive an article that is made out of gold?

Did the object make you feel better or worse?

GOD: JUDEO-CHRISTIAN

Two great moments in the history of God images have occurred in pop CULTURE recently. The first was George Burns befriending John Denver in the film *Oh, God!* The more recent one is James Earl Jones dispatching special orders to Roma Downey and Della Reese in the TV show *Touched by an Angel.* In the first instance, God was approachable and grandfatherly, while in the second He became much more daunting and powerful.

God images in dreams are very diverse. Often, it is not God as a direct visual image that you encounter, but something that is known to contain a projection of God's power and presence (religious icons, a bible); or it is simply a sensation that some high-powered entity is present. Many times, the object or presence will somehow illuminate us to a providential solution to a problem that is confronting us in the dream. Other times, the symbol may block progress as a warning. This may be especially true if we are being confronted with a choice that is luring us towards a TABOO experience or relationship.

In these dreams, the content of the revelation should be of primary concern. The presence of God, even as a dream image, is not to be taken lightly. Many times, our waking EGOS prevent clear awareness of the full supernatural possibility of God. Yet, while sleeping, we may be more receptive to direct communication.

Discerning authentic spiritual content should be the concern of the dreamer. Does the Higher Power that appeared in your dream match up with your view of a Higher Power in waking life?

In military parlance, there are authentication codes for messages to insure that an impostor is not compromising official orders. You should probably employ this type of authentication process before accepting the possibility that you were, indeed, visited by your Supreme Being in a dream.

Checking the content of the revelation for consistency with the character, nature, and intentions of God should be thoroughly explored before acting on any dream revelation.

Did the image of God frighten or threaten you? Consider actions or thoughts in your life which may warrant such policing.

Was your dream guest trying to tell you something? Consider points of confusion in your life to determine if the dream was one of guidance.

GODS: GREEK, NORSE, ROMAN

Various gods such as these figures often represent idealized desires, obstacles, POWERS, or relationships. The presence of the god figure often comes as a superlative. Some examples of this include: Thor as the most strength, Zeus as the most wisdom, and Eros as the greatest sexual desire. We may either encounter these figures directly or feel ourselves as persons occupying their bodies or adopting their attributes.

These experiences show us important features of ourselves as agents of action in the world. We are confronted by these superlatives and are either thwarted by them or become more self-aware in who we need to be in the circumstances and relationships of life. If you are a student of mythology, it may be useful to investigate your dreams for themes of power, problem-solving, and self-awareness.

GROCERY STORE

The grocery store is a place of necessity, compared to the department store of diversity and choices. To dream of being in a grocery store may be to dream of acquiring sufficiency for one's needs. What is important is to look at whether or not the grocery is a good option for acquiring what is needed.

Does the grocery store fit your needs, or do you really need auto parts or some non-food item? This may indicate that you are looking in the wrong place for answers in your waking life.

Do your fellow shoppers seem at ease or harried, and is there a sense that there "isn't enough to go around?" This may indicate ANXIETY over finding a mate, locating the right job, or some other limited commodity in the waking life.

GUNS

Dreaming about guns and interpreting these dreams depends greatly on your attitude about guns. There are many people who are comfortable with the life-and-death POWER of guns and use them recreationally. Whether the dreamer is a recreational target-shooter or hunter, guns may not have much significance apart from what is being shot at or who is hunting with you.

However, for others who are more awed by the gun's power to cause death, the gun is a TABOO symbol. Dreaming about guns from this context reveals a sense of being deeply threatened by the environment of the dream or persons in the dream. The gun may represent a nearly desperate need to reassert personal control in the situation or to find personal power in relationship to others.

HATS

Hats as noteworthy objects in dreams are not too common. A hat can be seen as an extension of POWER and influence in the dream. Removal of the hat by another can be taken as an invitation to confrontation. Giving a hat to another may be considered a romantic wish-fulfillment projection.

Also, the presence of a hat may be related to a dream of perceived BALDING.

In some cases, the hat is simply a reminder of another event, such as a sporting event involving a professional team, or an activity like skiing or FISHING.

HAWK

Hawks are interesting dream figures. They aren't quite EAGLES, but they definitely rank above the crows. Like the eagle, hawks are common symbols in many CULTURES.

Native American dreams revere the hawk and eagle the way the Greeks revere Zeus and Hermes. The hawk is the warrior-visionary while the eagle is the sacred wisdom and power.

To dream of hawks is to see oneself as engaged in, but outwitting, opponents through the ability to perceive more completely. It may also be a dream of providing adequately through skillful acquisition or insightful maneuvering.

Do you see yourself as soaring with the hawks or pecking with the pigeons in waking life? This may be wish-fulfillment or concern over the direction your life is heading.

HELICOPTER

The helicopter is an interesting object in our CULTURE. Originally, it was thought that the helicopter would replace the car someday. However, prices never came down, leaving the helicopter as an icon of wealth or authority. Since the Vietnam War, helicopters have become more associated with conflict than commuting.

To dream of a helicopter probably means that you envision yourself in a situation of potential hazard or needing to be "whisked away" from your present circumstances. The former would be expressed in a helicopter as a means of ESCAPE. The latter equates images of romance and wealth.

HERO

Because our dreams are our own creation, it is very common for a dreamer to experience the role of "hero" within a dream. Usually this is a sign that the person is very confident in life in general, or in a specific aspect of their life which is addressed in the dream. The fact that you are the hero in a dream may arise soon after you have accomplished something. It is even better to have such a dream just before taking on a challenge of some sort in your waking life.

The fact that you may find yourself enhanced with incredible skills or superhuman POWERS is noteworthy.

What special skills did you have in the dream?

Were there any recognizable people in the dream? If so, their presence may indicate the area to which you should attribute the dream's implied meaning—business, home, or leisure pursuit.

HOLIDAYS

Holidays are interesting dream settings because they have so much meaning in our waking lives. They can be positive, as in instances of favored memories of family and traditions. They can also be traumatic, in terms of unmet expectations, loss, or absence of loved ones.

How the holiday comes into the dream story is important. If the dreamer knows of the holiday all along, then others' perceptions and participation in the holiday are important to consider.

However, sometimes everyone knows about the holiday except the dreamer. The dreamer may not be able to adequately prepare for or be able to participate in the holiday. This may reflect ANXIETY about the expectations of others and the willingness to fulfill those expectations. Sometimes we fall short because the expectations are inappropriate; not because we are incompetent. Either feeling or interpretation is an option.

Do others seem prepared for, appropriately excited about, and connected to your understanding of the holiday?

Are the gestures of celebration appropriate?

Do you feel fulfilled, bemused, or empty after the dream?

HOME

A lot of things can happen to your home in a dream. It can be built or purchased, destroyed by the weather or war, or conquered or overrun by invaders. Most dreams about homes occur when there is transition, instability, or significant growth occurring in waking life.

A home overrun is often reflective of instability in the dreamer's relationship to the world. Feeling overwhelmed is not unusual. However, if overwhelmed is the chronic condition of your life, then being overrun by a particular sort of person or ANIMAL may reflect the source of waking ANXIETY.

The home destroyed may come with geographic relocation, financial pressures, DEATH, or DIVORCE. In these dreams, the home is being "pulled apart" or somehow losing its ability to provide safe haven. If this dream is occurring in your life, it is worth looking at what influences are stressing your life and the effect they are having on your waking life.

A home built is an expansive view of what is happening in your life. Perhaps you are feeling an upswing in your job or financial base that will allow you to acquire additional opportunities. Perhaps a relationship is or will be changing from dating to nesting. In any case, the home-building dream should be considered a positive one.

Because homes are often a symbol of feminine influence or the womb, interpretive questions arise logically from transitions.

Are you or your partner pregnant and needing a "nest" for the expected progeny?

Do you feel a need to involve yourself in a significant relationship with another?

Do you feel rootless or too set in your ways?

HORNED ANIMALS

The horned ANIMAL may represent a male power figure in your life, or, if the horn is nonsensical, it may be a displacement of another person's power (or your perception of unearned power that is being wielded by another). The goal is to discern your feelings about the animal and whether you see any relationship between the animal and individuals in your waking life.

If the horned animal is a nonsense creation, such as a horned dog, it may indicate sexual tension in a relationship. Do you feel as though someone close to you has mixed motives for being in a relationship with you?

Another scenario is feeling threatened by another's power to impale you. You may sense this as being a sort of sexual-penetration ANXIETY, but the general indication of power and intimidation is more satisfactory.

HOSPITALS

Hospitals really bother us a lot. We are exposed to them at many levels in our own lives and through media and entertainment. Whether you are the patient or the visitor, no one wants to be there. Yet to dream of a hospital is not uncommon.

As often as not, hospital dreams have little to do with sickness. However, in many hospital dreams, we have good reason to be there. They break down into dreams involving the emergency room, general care, intensive care, being unable to leave, and receiving nonsensical treatment in them.

Emergency room dreams have more to do with the well-being of significant persons and relationships than the emergency room itself. Many times, people involved in emergency room dreams are worried (excessively) about the people coming to see them or the person they are going to see in the hospital.

General care dreams reflect our sense of needing or being needed by others. Differentiated from the above dream, general care dreams do not reflect a crisis-level ANXIETY, but more of a dependent lifestyle. The relationship in a hospital is a one-way flow from care-giver to patient. This is a picture of dependence.

Intensive care is a place of danger and, at times, release. We all understand that the really sick people are there. It may be that you are needing to let a person go, especially the chronically ill. It may also be a place that reminds you of someone who has already passed.

Being unwilling to leave the hospital may show that you are ambivalent about facing the world independently. For the nuisance that the hospital is, it is also a place of intense care and support. The nature of your illness may be a metaphor for the aspect of your life where extra care and support are needed.

Receiving nonsensical care in the hospital is often a way of working out or illuminating unbalanced needs or demands in life. Everybody is paying attention to something you feel is unworthy of notice. Or, conversely, nobody will treat you for what you perceive to be the true problem. This can be truly funny if, for example, you acquire a large growth that strikes you as perfectly normal, but concerns others. It may become an object of obsession for numerous doctors, some of whom you may recognize as a boss from work, a romantic partner, a peer from some sort of leisure pursuit, etc. The darker version of this is feeling genuinely ill and being unable to receive treatment for it.

HOTELS

Hotels are great places. A cheap hotel is the epitome of tackiness and indecency, while a nice hotel is the picture of elegance, wealth, and romance. To dream of a hotel usually brings you to one of these two poles of awareness. Either you are hiding—out of guilt or adultery—or you are basking in the POWER of wealth or romance.

A third option may come from how connected you feel to the world. If the hotel is a residential or transient hotel, you may feel insecure about your economic condition or the relationships that govern your life.

Do you have or find a room, or is there "No Vacancy"?

Your feelings of inclusion, separation, or identification with others may be connected to the hotel event in the dream.

INCEST

Don't panic if you have an incest dream. If you recall a dream like this, the images can be daunting, but they do not necessarily refer to sexual activity or abuse. Take a deep breath and process the images and the situation carefully. Incest may consist of a feeling of romantic or sexual love between family members, as well as actual sexual relations. But it is more likely an indication of less complicated affections.

The ANIMA/ANIMUS self (which we may recognize as brother or sister, but which in actuality is a representation of ourselves) may be the object of our affections—in which case the presence of "incest" is simply a confirmation of self-respect or a sense of attraction toward a quality that we ourselves possess.

Other times, we may be recapitulating old experiences in light of new romantic interests. Many young children go through a time of articulating a desire to marry the opposite-gender parent. This is a natural expression of what FREUD calls the Oedipus and Electra complex.

It is important to evaluate how you feel about the dream in waking. If there is an overwhelming body awareness that corresponds with a dream of sexual violation, and if it is recurrent, you may want to consider profession intervention.

INCOMPLETE RELATIONSHIPS

TRIGGER EVENTS can be a little frustrating because they conjure dream images of persons or events that we had closed the books on in waking life. It is important to remember that ignoring or removing attention from the past is not the same as healing it. If you have a dream that is particularly powerful due to the memory it conjures, look at what event in current life is parallel to the relationship that is conjured in the dream. It may be a warning that you are heading for another experience similar to the one you have experienced in your dreams.

The punchline is that these relationships do not "automatically" resolve themselves. Our dreams can be a place where we are shown the need for completing these tasks.

INFECTION

The unique element of an infection dream is that it may have developed from a specific injury to a specific body part. The location of the wound and how it was infected are central concerns to interpretation of this dream.

Did the wound come to you randomly, from your own actions, or from another person?

Does the infection carry a sense of fatal dread or just discomfort?

INFESTATION

Being overrun, even by a desirable commodity, is an undesirable experience. Even good things can get carried away. Many times, we feel as though our lives our out of control. In dreams, having an infestation of a particular person, object, insect, or ANIMAL may be a pictorial representation of feeling overwhelmed.

If the infestation comes from a positive event, it may be a warning from your SUBCONSCIOUS that other necessary obligations are being neglected due to your consumption by a singular activity. If the infestation is a categorically negative image, such as RATS or mosquitoes, it may be that your life is getting severely undermined.

Is the infestation happening in your home, car, or other intimate place?

Are there any others present?

INJURY TO VARIOUS BODY PARTS

Becoming incapacitated by injury during a dream is fairly common, especially if you perceive yourself as operating out of a power deficit in waking life. Many times, people feel as though advantages lie outside themselves or with others, and see themselves as "handicapped."

The cause of the injury (means and inflictor) tells a lot about the significance of the injury as a dream symbol. If the wound is self inflicted or accidental, there may be a sense in which you are tripping yourself up by engaging in self-defeating behaviors. If the wound is inflicted by someone else and is intentional and malicious, others may be preventing you from reaching your potential.

Of course the wound, its care, and the consequences from it also mean much. If you continue dreaming after the wound occurs, what are you unable to do that is normally classified as an "essential" activity?

Are you able to repel the attacker and treat the wound successfully?

INTIMACY

Intimacy is one of the primary dream emotions. Many times our dreams include elements of intimacy with others whom we desire, or intimacy that escapes us. These dreams reflect our desires for connection to the others in our world. Intimacy with others is not always a synonym for sexual desire in this case. Rather, it can be the feeling of emotionally connecting with others, or, feeling unable to do so. The central interpretive questions are: Do others respond to your overtures for intimacy? Do you seem unable to connect as deeply as you would like? Do you not feel the urge to respond to another's advance for intimacy?

If you dream of romantic intimacy without being able to fulfill it, there maybe unarticulated concerns about your self-esteem, since one's sexual attraction is important to one's sense of overall confidence.

Are you feeling as though people care about you? Or is your love, platonic or otherwise, unrequited? Insight into this dream may become more apparent as you consider whether the object of your desire is a parent figure, CHILD figure, or romantic interest.

IRON (COMMODITY)

Iron is traditionally held as the ore of judgment or power. Thor's hammer was made completely of iron. When Thor wields his hammer of iron, the power is fearsome. If a person is characterized as iron fisted, they are powerful and dictatorial.

To dream of iron can mean a dream of being judged or sitting in judgment of others. Either way, the iron object is the power icon for whoever is in control of it.

It may also have to do with the building of a HOME, or thoughts about building a solid foundation with regard to career, relationships, or general perspective on life.

IRON (HOUSEHOLD OBJECT)

The iron is a pretty mundane item and a generally despised chore. Feeling a little like Cinderella, you may be wondering if your life will ever be exciting. The iron can also be a symbol of conflict or servitude if the ironing is not for ones own benefit.

Usually, a dream involving ironing is just a mundane dream that may cause you to realize how mundane your life has become and possibly encourage you to try something new.

JOKES

Jokes are funny because of the element of truth contained in them. In dreams, we may access our own sarcasm or humor about our circumstances. However, we may have characters in our dreams that make jokes that we do not find at all amusing. These may reflect our own

ambivalence or a need to lighten up because we are not enjoying ourselves as we could.

JOURNEY

The longer one's life, the more apparent it becomes that life is not a destination, but rather a journey of searching for meaning, understanding,
and ultimately happiness. While we don't necessarily characterize our
dreams as journeys, there is a sense in which our waking journey is
sometimes affected by our most powerful or memorable dreams.

Many dreams include needing to TRAVEL from A to B before
progress is made in completing the dream task. Many times, this traveling is the challenge. The elements may be uncooperative or contrary.
Traveling machines may be magically powerful or nonsensical and
unreliable. Sometimes, we are simply walking across a field, down a
road, up a hill, through the forest, or along the CLIFFS on our journey.
The environment around us along the way can be familiar, strange,
friendly, anxiety-ridden, and a host of other possibilities. The purpose
of the traveling and the companions along the way can be significant.

The journey is often a symbol for trying to find what is needed to
bring life into equilibrium. This is the task of finding one's place in the
universe. It could also be characterized as the archetypal search for the
most authentic self. In either of these metaphors, there is the idea that
our souls tend to be a little restless at times. The journey is the task of
finding out what the soul needs to quiet that restlessness.

In waking life, this is played out by the "I need a change" feeling
that crops up every now and then. The process of individuating yourself from the expectations and influences of others conjures feelings
along these lines. In dreaming, we often travel alone, leaving others
behind by choice or necessity, to find what our next task is.

Along the way, who we meet and what we partake in may reveal much about where our individual struggle is in the waking, CONSCIOUS self. We may encounter STRANGERS with whom there is an adversarial relationship or a romantic one. We may encounter mystical strangers who unlock unknown powers within us or withdraw particular powers from us. In either case, the journey is our personal goal, and how we experience others during the process says much about the relationships of our waking world.

Is your destination known to others, or held in confidence?

Do others invite you to accompany them, vice versa, or are you on a solitary trip?

Can others direct you, or are you traveling to an unknown place? Answers to these questions influence the meaning of the dream in your life.

JUGGLING
Most of us go through seasons of life that create the feeling of juggling—having responsibility for more objects than we can reasonably handle.

If you successfully juggle alone, or for no particular reason, this may reflect the desire or feeling that you actually are controlling numerous facets of your life. Often, we are juggling publicly and being judged for our success in doing so. In these juggling dreams, the audience is key. Perhaps the audience consists of people to whom you should be delegating tasks or from whom you feel unreasonable expectations.

Who is watching you juggle, and what is your relationship with them in waking life?

How well are you juggling, and how does the audience react?

JUNGLE
The jungle often hides itself in the density of its own matter. As such, it

is a place of great complexity and unknowing. For many of us, the metaphor "it's a jungle out there" describes the unpredictability and potential threats of our world. To be in a jungle usually means you are on a quest for treasure, sacred knowledge, or other things kept in deeply covered and generally inaccessible places.

The danger that you feel about the jungle is also the reason that things of value are kept there. The difficulty in acquiring riches or wisdom heightens the appreciation of them. (Dense urban environments can be a metaphor of the jungle as well.)

In your waking life is the jungle a symbol of all that is wrong with human progress or the place where danger lurks? Some people perceive the jungle as the beauty of undisturbed nature while others feel it is a haven of mystery and danger.

Who is with you or brought you to the jungle?

What are you looking for?

Jury

If you dream of being on a jury, you may feel that an important decision needs to be made in your life, or that you need to help a friend or loved one make a decision.

If you find yourself on trial before a jury, you likely are experiencing some sort of pressure or judegement form others in your waking life.

Keys

Keys stand for POWER and access. To lose one's keys in a dream is to be out of control or lack the means of access. It may symbolize that you feel unable to acquire what is needed to complete a task or obtain access to persons or knowledge.

To find your own keys is to assert your own power in a given situation. You have the ability to be "captain of your destiny," so to speak.

What is most interesting is to find a key that previously had no meaning for you. This is especially important when the key has no direct use, but "feels" as if it might be important. In a dream like this, you are probably searching for options to identify new potential within yourself or in relationship to others.

Who was with you when you found the key and with whom did you share the discovery in your dream? There will be numerous clues in the answers to these two questions.

KIDNAPPING

Kidnapping is a powerful image for us because it includes strong victimization and loss-of-power issues. Someone who is kidnapped goes from being in control of their own destiny to being completely in the hands of another.

If you are dreaming of being kidnapped, the obvious questions are: "What is the condition of your captivity; and by whom are you held?"

If you cooperate with your captors, you may be wanting someone to take control of an untidy section of your life. However, you may feel as though your autonomy has been so severely compromised that you lack the ability to manage the situation.

If your captors are somehow familiar, this may reflect a sense that life has entrapped you. Where did your abductors take you and how? Your SUBCONSCIOUS may be showing you an area where your life has become excessively entangling to your autonomy.

It may be that somehow your kidnapping allows you to separate from your environment and start again. Perhaps you are wanting a second chance and do not have the courage to take one. By having yourself kidnapped, you have an excuse to act or behave unusually and blame you captors for it.

KISSING

Kissing is often associated with youthful love. It is teenagers, and not parents, who kiss until they are weak in the knees on the escalator in the mall. You can be kissing another, watching others kiss, or experience that "I'm about to be kissed" moment.

Kissing another is often wish-fulfillment or sexual acting out. The wish-fulfillment may not be to kiss per se, but to experience the youthful energy of love. Kissing in this sense is the desire for the awakening of passion, not necessarily the passion acted out.

Watching others kiss may be a sign of knowing too much about them personally or participating in their lives at too personal a level. The exception here would be if you are watching your partner kiss another, which is an obvious herald of infidelity or a desire for voyeurism in the relationship.

The "about to be kissed" moment is an interesting one. Often, it occurs as we wake up. This is the dream that may most accurately reflect a desire for actual passion with another. The reason we wake up is the TABOO feeling that perhaps, while we want this, it would not be beneficial to actually participate in it.

Is the kissing comforting or threatening to you?

Is it something you sought after, or was it forced upon you?

Is your general experience repugnant, romantic, or passionate?

LACTATION

Lactation is an interesting dream symbol since it is uniquely women who participate in this activity in waking. Dreams about lactation may reflect archetypal gender identity concerns. A woman who dreams of this may see herself as fulfilling a mothering role. This may be literal, as in wish-fulfillment, or figurative, as in mothering a man in a romantic relationship.

Some women have ANXIETY about their ability to provide adequate milk after childbirth. In these instances, dreams of feeding a child may be visualizations of these concerns.

LADDER

The ladder may indicate access to high places in this life or access to special places in the universe. It is also sometimes an object you fall from when you have dreams that include the falling sensation.

The central idea of a ladder is gaining special, albeit precarious, access to other places. Such access often carries with it the possibility of a dramatic loss of ability or favor with the prevailing influences of the situation.

If you are in a situation that requires you to obtain a ladder, it may be that you see yourself as inadequate in your current means. The limitations of height and gravity are acutely felt in this world. If your dreams do not offer you the possibility of FLIGHT, the ladder is often the only solution to the problem.

LAUGHTER

In dreams, we may feel emotions and responses to them much as we do in waking life. This is especially true about very funny and very sad events. Dream laughter may often come from a deeper level than waking laughter in that our emotional expressions are often more outward and unrestrained in a dream.

The interesting part is that dream laughter may also be very inappropriate. Since we often dream of ourselves as archetypal caricatures, we may laugh with a diabolical twist; whereas in waking, ANGER would be the more expected response. This sort of unchecked laughter can usually be an expression of the ID.

If you experienced laughter in a dream, did others laugh with you?

Did you laugh at something inappropriate? Did you feel ashamed or somehow empowered by laughing at such?

LEOPARD

Spotted ANIMALS are interesting symbols because of their nonconformity to a uniform color. Often we may see people as spotted or as leopards if we suspect them of shiftiness or insincerity.

To see a leopard mauling a kill, especially if it makes eye contact with you, likely means that you have been dealing with someone who you do not trust, and that you should take stock of recent dealings with that person and others like them.

LIGHTNING

Lightning in dreams is a pretty flexible image. Some people enjoy lightning and therefore desire it as a background effect. Others are frightened of its POWER and unpredictability. However, there are many power metaphors that merit attention.

You may find yourself in possession of lightning as a resource for dealing with problems. This type of lightning is an asset for handling frustration that could be characterized as a wish-fulfillment. Dream logic: just blast it out of the way.

Lightning may also be a warning in your dream. If you have fears about lightning in waking life, a person whom you are with or a building that you enter in your dream may cause a lightning effect. This is the mind's way of offering a dramatic visual warning. There may be an element of judgment involved, as divine wrath is often envisioned as a lightning bolt (personified in the Greek god Zeus and the Norse god Thor).

What did the lightning strike, and did anyone get severely injured?

Where did the lightning come from, and at what point in the dream?

LOSING AN OBJECT OR PERSON OF VALUE

The things we value most often serve as an extension of our self-awareness. A favorite HAT, CAR, or relationship reflects a part of how we feel about ourselves. Therefore, the loss of such an object in a dream is significant. It is equally significant whether you actually own the object in waking or not.

If the thing lost is an inanimate object, what does it symbolize for you? Examples would be jewelry, favored clothes, or pictures and family heirlooms. In losses of this kind, the indication may be that you are nervous about losing an expensive or important new object in your life.

If a person is lost, the first question to ask is, "Who?" It may be that you have questions about your commitment to another or their commitment to you. However, it is not to unusual to be looking for a STRANGER.

Why are you searching for this person?

Do you find this person? Where?

LOSS OF A SENSORY OR MOTOR ABILITY

Usually, this is a very symbolic event in a dream.

A 34-year-old man reports:

I dream of being in a situation where I need to act resourcefully to help a STRANGER avoid danger. Suddenly, I go blind for no apparent reason! It is very frustrating.

Becoming suddenly impaired in this way is different than being injured in a physical accident. The lights just seem to go out without explanation. With a dream like this, it is questionable whether or not the dreamer feels competent to fulfill his duties in waking life. However, this can also refer to his reluctance to accept the challenge of the HERO self.

Seeing oneself as a hero is kind of daunting, and the fact that it is your dream doesn't mean that you will necessarily and easily assume that role. Suddenly, the awareness of caring for those to whom you have no obligation is quickened. It's a hassle. Many of us can barely fulfill responsibilities to the people around us in ordinary situations.

Another scenario for loss of a sensory ability is to exchange it for something or someone else. The old saying, "I'd give my eye teeth for . . ." articulates the human willingness to exchange one ability or attribute for something else of value. There are many times when our minds use the principle of exchange to help us verify the relative worth of relationships or objects.

There can also be a distinct martyr image attached to this kind of loss. This is especially true when the dream includes loss of ability through some potentially painful means. The loss may be seen as an exchange for something that was gained during the dream or in waking life.

LOST FEELING

Many times, life feels like a JOURNEY. Not surprisingly, in dreamland, the journey becomes confused. This may be a simple reflection of a dream that did not make sense or a dream story that did not seem to go anywhere.

However, there are two ways to become lost, both of which say a lot about how we view ourselves in waking. First is being lost because you have choices and lack the ability to know which one to make. This may include dreams of driving a CAR, mall dreams, amusement park dreams, or other dreams where opportunities become uncertain. The other version of feeling lost is isolation, or a sense that motion is not leading to progress. Which image of feeling lost most accurately conveys your awareness in the dream?

If you are lost due to choices, you may be at a point in life where you are unsure of what you want. This may include vocational, relationship, or personal values that seem "up-for-grabs." It may also reflect an inability to see where a particular choice will take you if you make it.

If you are lost due to motion that does not lead to progress, you may be pretty ambivalent about whether your waking life is meaningful. Your ability to feel effective in life is being compromised in some area that needs a little examination.

See ABANDONED, ALONE

LUGGAGE

Talk of "emotional baggage" has become very common nowadays. This contemporary term has given rise to a new way of experiencing relationships with yourself and with others. Dreams of cumbersome baggage often represent a life that is too cluttered, or one that lacks reasonable emotional BOUNDARIES.

To dream of a mysterious piece of luggage may indicate something that is hidden, such as a secret or an idea.

Does the luggage in your dream seem to get in the way?

Are you very nervous about losing a piece of luggage that you are carrying around for no apparent reason? This may mean that you should take stock of things that you are holding onto—maybe there is something that you can safely dispose of that will lighten the load.

LYING

Lying is supposed to be a TABOO experience. Early human history held lying as a sacred act of transgression that was not just interpersonal, but against the gods, the fates, or the cosmos. However, sociological research has found that the lie is losing much of its taboo power. Many people are adopting a fast and loose attitude with the truth in order to fulfill or protect their self image.

Thus, interpreting dreams about lies depend a lot on where you stand with the truth in waking life. If you feel ashamed to lie, the lying dream may indicate that you are being less than genuine in a particular facet of your waking life. This may also indicate guilt in a transaction that has been ignored rather than resolved.

If you are fairly comfortable lying in waking life, then your dream is probably showing you a weakness in some area that needs to be compensated. How you choose to do this will be your business. Quite probably, you are more concerned about how others perceive you than the actual appreciation of yourself for who you are. This is especially true if your dreaming lies are being discovered.

Are you regularly lying to a particular person in waking life?

Do you find yourself exaggerating the truth or outright lying to win acceptance from others in waking life?

Do you feel others are intentionally deceiving you concerning their motives or intentions?

Is there an inner self that you feel would not be embraced if people knew you too well?

MAGICAL POWERS

One of the great things about dreams, especially LUCID dreams where you are aware of dreaming and can practically control the outcome, is that you can acquire unusual powers. These may include almost any conceivable ability needed to solve the problem at hand. The problem is that you may lose them without explanation at a critical moment.

The acquisition of magical powers may come from a number of sources. You may simply conjure them from within yourself. You may be given an article of clothing that contains special powers, or you may find a rock or other object that projects power into you. The implication is that you can solve problems with available resources. However, this may simply be a WISH-FULFILLMENT dream to dispose of problems without working through them.

The loss of powers is often a reality-check dream. While you may think you have power in your dream to do great and glorious things, the truth in waking is that problems do not always solve themselves. There may be a level at which your mind is concerned about your waking bravado in certain situations.

The "magic" you experience could be a sign that you are struggling against the most reasonable outcome of a particular situation. Often, we are unable to appreciate the logic or simplicity of a given situation because of our desire to "work" it.

What is the nature of your magical powers in the dream—physical or mental?

What do you use these powers to accomplish?

MARATHON RUNNING

The marathon is the archetypal struggle of the self to accomplish something beyond the limits of the human body. Many times, we dream that we are competitive, which is a sign of competence. However, other times we lack the ability to be competitive, because in our dreams, our waking limitations often accompany us. This may be particularly true if your colleagues and associates run in the marathon also, but more effectively than you.

Why are you in the marathon? Are you able to run it competitively?

Are your competitors familiar to you, or strangers?

MARBLE (STONE FIGURINES, BUILDINGS, HALLWAYS)

Marble in architecture is the premiere ostentatious element. Often, marble is reserved for dwellings of authority and POWER (government, big business, stately mansions, etc.). If you are fortunate enough to occupy the building, it may be that you are feeling a special allegiance with power structures. If you are occupying a corporate or government building, it may be a representation of power that you feel in daily living. The people who come to visit you in these structures are central to understand the meaning of the dream. If you are living in a marble mansion, you may be on the verge of a successful business venture.

If you are visiting these places, note the feeling they arouse in you.

MARBLES (GLASS OBJECTS)

Childhood toys and stereotypical childhood games often illustrate the childlike approach you take to many relationships. To understand the marble dream, think about how well you play and how high the stakes are in the dream.

To dream of a game of marbles, or many other childhood pastimes, can mean an attempt to return to innocence. A key element is who is playing with you.

Are you playing with childhood friends, or with someone you've only known as an adult?

Does the game feel like a fun activity, or is it a competitive challenge?

MASKS

Dreaming of wearing a mask is often a dream of how you want others to see you. A twist on this theme is that you may be afraid others are perceiving you without knowing the real you. It may be that the mask attaches and removes from your face, depending on whose company you are in. Also, others may be conspicuously placing the mask on you to give you an identity that you are uncomfortable assuming. Or, they are wearing the mask themselves to deceive, frighten, or amuse you.

If you are wearing a mask, who is in your presence and what is the mask like? Ask the same questions if others have the mask.

MEDICAL PERSONNEL

Living in the age of technology, we are much less dependent on spiritual figures and much more on technical professionals. Consequently, if you have discord in your psyche, it may present itself as a medical dream.

Dreaming of medical persons takes on three general types of presentation: you as patient, you as medical professional, and you receiving nonsensical care from medical persons.

As patient, you are wanting someone to fix where it hurts. In dreaming, this is often a feeling of powerlessness or irresponsibility regarding matters in your own life. The area of physical discomfort probably symbolizes an area of emotional discord. This can be as obtuse a connection as you can imagine.

If you are the attending doctor or nurse, you may not know your patient, but you see yourself as empowered with the knowledge and skill to bring about healing. If you know the patient, so much the better. The dream may reflect a care-giving or supportive role you fulfill. The presenting symptoms of the patient may allude to a facet of the relationship where you may need to give additional attention.

Receiving nonsense care from doctors or nurses frequently falls into the category of being unable to communicate. Either others are not understanding your needs or you feel unable to articulate your needs. You may be experiencing a very lop-sided relationship in which your needs are going virtually unmet.

A romantic liaison with medical personnel is another dream scenario that often occurs. In dreams of this nature, you may be wanting your romantic interest of waking life to be more attentive to your personal needs. Or you may just be one of those people who gets crushes on doctors and nurses and are experiencing some dreamland WISH-FULFILLMENT.

A doctor may also appear in your dream as the person who is trying to save the life of someone close to you. This character is likely a projection of yourself, in the sense that you want to be able to help someone in need.

Does the doctor seem to ignore you or is she unable to understand your questions?

Does the doctor assure you that everything will be OK?

MEDICINE MAN

The medicine man is a figure that you may dream of in a literal sense, but often encounter in dreams of archetypal awareness. The figure of the medicine man is the figure of sacred knowledge, spiritual power, and healing that speaks not only to our bodies but to our souls.

As such, many dream characters—STRANGERS as well as some FAMILY members or friends—may fulfill this role in the dream. The medicine man encounter is an encounter with the wisdom of the universal SUBCONSCIOUS. There is something eerie, yet reassuring; safe, yet a little unnerving about the medicine man. The encounter often leaves us looking at the world a little differently for the presence of the medicine man. The important thing to remember is that this character's role is to be a ritual connection of past and future—physical world and spiritual world. As such, dreams concerning the medicine man often reveal our position at the intersection of these influences in our lives.

Do you see yourself as a healer-guide for others in your family or community?

Is the medicine man character (you or another person) benevolent, powerful, or TABOO in comparison to mere mortals in the dream?

MESSAGE RECEIVED IN CODE

The dream plot often is forwarded along by very unusual events (e.g. suddenly the room turns blue and everyone disappears). Other times, a cryptic message works its way into the dream event.

Often the code is symbolic rather than alpha-numeric, though it can be either. Other times, it is a riddle. Whether or not you can decode the message becomes the dream conflict.

If you can decode the message, does it mean anything to you? It may make perfect sense to you, but mean nothing to others in the dream, or vice versa. The point is that the message was decoded, showing insight. The relative meaning lies in whether or not the insight can be appropriated by the dreamer.

If you cannot decode the message, you may be experiencing life as incomprehensible at some level. This dream reveals that truth of your CONSCIOUS life. The key is to look at who in the dream serves as a source of knowledge about the code.

Who gave you the message?

What was the reaction of others is when they learned of the message?

Are they worried for you, nonchalant, or joyful?

MESSAGE SENT IN CODE

We all go through times of struggle against the world. In these times, we are inclined to hold our cards pretty close to our chin. In dreaming, this may be expressed as sending coded messages or communication.

Privacy is a tenuous feature in this world. The need for human association calls us toward exposure, while our need for personal security draws us to pull the shades. Consequently, we simultaneously expose and cover through coded communication.

This dream may reflect a feeling that only one or two people in your life can comprehend your deepest thoughts and fears. Another scenario is that you are looking for a safe way to express guilt. A third option is that others cannot comprehend your meaning.

Who is the message for and why did it need to be coded?

Did the receiver understand the code?

Were you in captivity, spying, or trying to conceal your meaning in a public forum for other intentions?

This may indicate that the code is a metaphor for a deeper sense of relationship you share with certain others in your life or profession.

MIRROR

In dreams, mirrors can reflect directly, reflect with additions or deletions, or serve as a doorway into another reality as in *Alice in Wonderland*. The mirror is troubling because it shows us plainly what is before us, forcing us to interpret and evaluate whether or not we like what we see.

If the mirror is inconsistent—by adding or deleting images—it is a projection of perceptive versus actual reality. In this case the dream may be a herald that you are misinterpreting the motives of others by not accepting them at face value. (Who or what is being added or deleted from the mirror?)

Finally, the mirror as a doorway to another world is usually a fantasy created by the SUBCONSCIOUS. As Alice discovered when she went through the looking glass, the mirror is a metaphor of possible worlds. Does your dream mirror function as a GATE or access out of one BOUNDARY and into another possible world?

What is more desirable or more threatening about that world?

MISSING APPOINTMENTS

Many people live and die by the desk calendar these days. Ours is a time-conscious, time-driven CULTURE. Most of us have more things to do on our schedules than we can comfortably manage. These pressures have created an environment where missing appointments and scheduled events is a constant threat.

Dreams to this effect are common. One of the TRIGGER EVENTS for these dreams is the nagging fear that we may not get it all done as we should. Our ANXIETY about appearing competent to others is fragile and often assaulted in dreams.

Another interpretation of this dream is missing an opportunity. Life invites participation in more than could ever be accomplished. Every invitation comes with the promise that this event could change your life. The changes may include relationship or career rewards.

A final scenario revolves around fulfilling the relationship obligations that already exist in your life. In this case, dreams of missed appointments may be reminding you of personal obligations that already exist. You may be missing appointments as a sign that you are not fulfilling the needs of your spouse, family, or employer.

MONEY

Money can be lost, gained, or spent in dreaming. Dreams about money are often really about POWER, control, and competency. Consequently, the larger perspective of who is interacting with you around money and what your role in the transaction is are important features of the dream.

Many people who dream about money are controlled by it—the desire for it, the lack of it, or the inability to control themselves with it. This last category is seen most clearly in money dreams experienced by people who are drowning in debt.

If you gain money in a dream, note from whom and under what circumstances. This may be a dream about BLESSING. The gain of money in this instance is more a gain of emotional power and renewal through a completed relationship that no longer depletes the soul.

You may see yourself as having great wealth to dole out to others. This is often a symbol of needing to convey blessing onto others. The true need is rarely financial, but a need to help others.

Losing money for no apparent reason is the picture of being unable to control oneself. The lack of control may actually be in the area of money, but it may also be the inability to restrain oneself from overcommitting resources emotionally or otherwise.

In your waking life, how do you perceive and value money? In some families, money is an object taken for granted, in others it is a powerful symbol of control, influence, or status. Whether or not you have money problems, money dreams could reveal feelings about your relationship with power.

MOON

The moon is often an archetypal woman image. In many CULTURES and religious orders, the moon is identified as a MOTHER figure. This is true in Native American, African, Christian, and Eastern literature and lore. The moon dream may come with or generate an intuitive feeling that someone in the inner circle of your life is pregnant.

Another moon scenario is a product of the twentieth century. Specifically, the desire for space TRAVEL. These dreams can be based on either the scientific desire to experience the event or the spiritual desire for absolute separation from the churning, tumultuous human experience on EARTH.

The moon can also evoke feelings of magic and mystery.

MOTHER

Dreams that include your mother can be extremely varied in meaning depending on your relationship with her and particular situations at any given time.

Did you perceive your mother as omniscient and all-loving at a particular phase of childhood?

Has your mother's relationship with you included POWER struggles or inappropriate intrusions into your affairs?

Have you lost contact with your mother (either by DEATH or by choice) and left some issues unresolved?

The answers to these questions will help decipher many of the images that appear with your mother in your dreams.

MOVIE

Attending. What kind of movie do you go see and with whom? If this is among the most memorable dream images, you may be trying to initiate or resolve a relationship issue by watching others portray it. The movie plot will often provide guidance on how to do this. Even if the movie is a film with nonsensical or overwhelmingly destructive events, your SUBCONSCIOUS chose it for some desire that lurks below the surface.

You may be searching for a vicarious substitution for a life you consider mundane. In the film, what particularly (un)satisfactory events are portrayed by whom and how do those events parallel your own life?

Starring In. One of the strangest feelings to have is the dream that includes watching yourself in a movie. For starters, you are two places at once—watching yourself and being in the movie. While sometimes your dream logic says, "oh yeah, this is a film I am in," other times it fails you. These turn into dream events that contain an OUT-OF-BODY EXPERIENCE.

In either case, there is often a sense of derealization of whatever is occurring in the movie plot. There can be several reasons for this. One is to lower the psychological pain of a dream. Since you are watching yourself in the dream, you can reinforce your defense mechanism even in the subconscious state by saying, "It's only a dream." Another is to allow you to evaluate the events more objectively. Insight requires self-awareness. Self-awareness requires being able to discern your power and action in the world. The movie makes power and action more observable.

The other version of the movie dream is simple wish-fulfillment. "Hey, you oughtta be in pictures." So you are.

Is your life so good or so bad that at times you wonder when the dream will end? These feelings in waking life can create derealization in dreaming perceptions.

MOUNTAINS

The mountains can be a place of majesty, danger, or ritual sacred land. You may just like being in the mountains and dream of them for that reason. They may make you feel good about nature, rebirth, and being alive.

Also, the mountains may be a something to cross alone—either by choice or because you find yourself there for some unclear reason. You will want to consider who said good-bye when the JOURNEY started, why you left, and what you expected to encounter in the mountains of your dreams.

The mountaintop experience has long been a idiomatic expression for the best life has to offer. Are you searching for or unable to attain a particular success in waking life, or do you feel you have ascended to that height in a particular area?

MURDER/SUICIDE

Causing DEATH has very diverse meaning depending on who dies, why and how they die, and what interpretive framework seems to fit the death. The changing ethic of death in our society may also begin to effect death in dreams. In recent years, the assisted suicide and euthanasia movements have begun to effect dream presentations of death.

The ID is often revealed as a mass murderer in dreams. This is because ANGER and aggression that cannot be displayed publicly works its way into dreams of wish-fulfillment. Recently, stress has been popularly defined as "choking the life out of someone." Fortunately, the id can do for you in dreaming what the rest of you would like to do while you're awake.

If you killed a stranger, you may well have been trying to assault a facet of your own PERSONALITY that is particularly troubling, self-destructive, or shameful to you. By killing the stranger, you are showing your desire to excommunicate this bad aspect from your life. This can be valuable.

It may have been that you killed yourself. Of course, you may not necessarily intend to kill your whole self, just a part of it.

The worthiness of killing yourself in a dream stems from the fact that a pathological tendency or troubling behavior pattern in your personality needs to be resolved. For example, there is never an appropriate time to steal from another. Consequently, if that is part of your personality at some level, your dream life may try to kill it off by projecting the negative facet onto a stranger (representing yourself) who you then dispatch.

However, what is not worthwhile is killing a part of yourself in order to ignore it. Each of us has shadows of our public selves that we hope are pretty well hidden from the perception of others. We often criticize those around us who are most like us in many ways. These shadows need to be accepted and constructively dealt with so they do not turn into pathologies. The act of committing suicide in a dream should be taken fairly seriously. This act says a lot about how you are perceiving yourself and your value as a person. If you continue to have such a dream, and the thoughts of suicide run through your waking mind, it may become more than symbolic. If this happens, you should seek out someone you trust to discuss your life with.

MUSEUM

Places that collect artifacts provide pictures of our past and the persons, events, or activities that have influenced us most. Regardless of what museum you visit—history, art, wax, or special interest—the artifacts or with whom you are viewing them will indicate a facet of your waking life needing attention.

If you are in a history museum, the objects may all point towards a branch of the FAMILY tree. The way you feel about the artifacts you view will undoubtedly reflect your feelings about the situation or people illustrated in the dream. You may be shown that you need to do some repair work.

What pride or embarrassment do you derive from your "history" as a human being and member of a family?

A wax museum may reveal that you are dehumanizing people in relationships. This can be positive, if you have given away too much power. However, often it is a negative sign that you are treating others as objects without regard for their humanity.

The art museum can be a restful place or a place of recounting life experiences both good and bad. You may not be in any of the paintings or you may be in all of them. Depending on your exposure to art, you may view only a particular genre or artist. However, what you view is showing you truth about yourself.

MUSIC

If everyone had their own personal background music, interpersonal relationships would be a lot easier. If you didn't like someone's music, you would know to avoid them. If a love song was playing, you would know what to do; heavy metal likewise. It is not unusual to have background music in dreams. We are used to having music on television or in a movie set the tone of a particular scene or character.

An interesting phenomenon is when you compose music in your dreams. It may be very telling regarding the emotions present in your dreams which, in turn, can help you decipher the meanings of the images.

NAGGING

One of the reasons we respond so strongly to dream content is because it often is an exclamation point rather than a period. Dream statements exist in the superlative as often as not. This is especially true of the interpersonal relationships—some are revealed as the best; others as the worst. Over time, no interpersonal event is more draining than the nag.

Who is nagging you and why? Some dreams include the nagger as a caricature of nagging, and the droning eventually becomes funny. Other dreams create a symbolic avoidance of a person because of a fear of nagging. The final version of the nag is the forward, ongoing sapping of your emotional strength through the dream story.

There may be a facet of your waking life where you have chosen denial as your modus operandi. Nagging dreams may be a specific attempt to draw you back into dealing with it.

More often, the dream is about a person that you are taking too seriously or not seriously enough. The interpretation depends on your waking relationship to the individual, the content of the nagging as it reflects actual waking priorities, and your honesty in the relationship.

Are you meeting the expectations of others responsibly or do you feel inherently inadequate?

Are others directly criticizing your inadequacy at certain levels?

NATURAL DISASTERS
See END OF THE WORLD

NUDITY
Exposure in dreams is a powerful event. Often times, people report dreaming they are nude or dressed only in undergarments. These dreams often reveal the vulnerability that lies just below the surface of our more confident selves. This vulnerability comes from the self that we hide from others. The hiding may be CONSCIOUS, such as TABOO behavior, or less conscious, stemming from a general sense that if you were fully known, you would not be fully accepted.

The peculiar thing about these nudity dreams is that they often are a reverse of the fable *The Emperor's New Clothes*. If you recall, the fable included two tailors who persuade the emperor to stand naked before the throne while his subjects pretend to admire his "new clothes." A young boy finally states what everyone knows, but is afraid to say: that the emperor is naked.

In the underwear or nudity dream, you know that you are under-dressed, or undressed, but everyone else seems to take it in stride. Once you begin reacting to your state of undress, then others begin to notice and judge what is seen.

Your SUBCONSCIOUS may be growing weary of maintaining the facade that is the waking, public self. It may be time to evaluate the relative worth of hiding versus revealing additional facets of yourself. This may be general in nature and apply to all of life, or a specific person or relationship that requires more honesty.

Of course, there may be an exhibitionist sexual overtone to this dream that is wish-fulfillment or fantasy.

Do you consider yourself open towards others, or are you concerned about "covering" adequately?

What are your feelings about your own body?

NUMBERS

Numbers have many means of access into dreams. The most common is through objects. For example, sometimes you have stones in your hand. Another time, a STRANGER may give you stones. How many stones does the stranger give you?

Another means of access to numbers is through time. This time could be generalized in that it feels like about one hour. You may look at a digital watch and see an exact time, maybe even a nonsense time. It may be a particular date. In any case, the occurrence of numbers in dreams is an interesting study.

While numerology is a field of study in itself, there are general conclusions that can be drawn about dream numbers that may be helpful. First, you need to ascertain how the number got into your head in relationship to the dream.

Adding the digits together and discerning a difference between numbers, squares, and cubes is another way to handle numbers in dreams. Our minds are capable of pretty tricky internal math, given the chance. The problem with math and waking life is that able minds are talked out of successful math efforts due to common misconceptions and other illogical fears.

The study of numerology is a good complement to your dream interpretations, especially if numbers come up often.

NURSE

The nurse is a unique figure in MEDICAL PERSONNEL dreams because of the romance attached to the helping professions. Sometimes nurses are even portrayed as ANGELS. Aside from the romantic component, nurses often functions as extras in other medical or sickness dreams.

OARS

Oars are an archetypal sign of "man against nature" struggles. It is our labor against the elements that represents what we are striving toward. To dream of rowing a BOAT or anticipating to do so is to dream of your struggle against circumstances. You may be feeling overworked or outright overwhelmed by trying to keep your head above water financially, relationally, or vocationally.

Are you straining in life to make progress?

Do you feel as though you are working with inadequate support in your vocation, marriage, or other relationship?

Are you rowing against a prevailing wind of negativity or distractions from your aspirations?

OCEAN

The ocean is the place of origin for all life. Especially in Jungian interpretation, this is a place of creativity, fertility, and birth. There is also a lingering sense humans have of rising up out of the collective origins of life in the oceans. It is easy to see the Darwinian influence of these ideas. More importantly, it is easy to see the lack of connection some dreamers could have with this approach to dream interpretation.

Given the widespread popularity of boating, scuba diving, and cruise vacations, numerous people have experiences with the ocean that were not available in the past. It may be that the dreamer has one of these connections to the ocean, rather than a general perception of fertility.

For some, the ocean can impart a sense of fear and foreboding, especially if they can't swim. Its ultimate vastness, coupled with their lack of swimming ability, can appear in a dream as a reflection of some insurmountable struggle they may be having in waking life.

OLD MAN/OLD WOMAN

These are archetypal figures of wisdom or spiritual POWER in dreams. For many people, the role of the FATHER or MOTHER has been lost in society through either DIVORCE, workaholism, or some other emotional dysfunction. The psyche is prone to look for versions of this loss wherever it can create them, even out of the self.

Often times, these characters personify and validate an internal source of wisdom that has been written off by the psyche. It may be that you are confronted with a problem that escapes solution because of the most CONSCIOUS worldview you ascribe to. However, another means of problem-solving that you view as old-fashioned may be effective. The wisdom figure in your dream is trying to teach you this truth.

Do you fear or disdain either your lineage or the prospects of your own aging?

Are you ambivalent about the purported wisdom of your elders concerning life choices you are now facing?

Are you looking for or missing some wisdom that would aid your life-quest?

ORPHANAGE / BEING ORPHANED

This is often a dream of neglect, fitting in, or seeking to act with benevolent POWER in the world. Much of the meaning to be derived from this sort of dream depends on how you locate yourself within the orphan scenario of the dream.

If you find yourself working in an orphanage, seeking to ADOPT a child from an orphanage, or just visiting an orphanage, you may be seeing yourself as an agent of justice in the world—this is worthy of consideration. You may be trying to fight against injustice, or trying to compensate for acts of unfairness you have committed in your waking life.

If you appear as a child in an orphanage, the connectivity of your waking relationships is worth examining. Do you have a sense of belonging and rootedness in the world or a sense of trying to find your place?

ORCHESTRA

The complexity and beauty of the orchestra is almost universally appreciated. Even among those who do not like classical MUSIC, it is accepted that the orchestra is a very sophisticated musical machine. Dreams of being in the orchestra may reflect the feeling that you are in a place of either harmony, or profound disharmony, in relation to the world. There may be a facet of your life in which you are feeling a tremendous amount of performance anxiety. If the orchestra has a familiar conductor (a co-worker or boss, a family member, an acquaintance, etc.), the relationship between you and the conductor may reveal the area of ANXIETY.

If you are attending the orchestra, there may be romantic underpinnings involved, based on your companion in the dream. There may also be a sense of wanting respite from the daily grind of the waking world through music.

An additional interpretation is that the dream is a wish-fulfillment based on the lessons you took as a child and the inability to perform publicly as an adult.

OUT-OF-BODY EXPERIENCE

The out-of-body experience can be a dramatic one. Clinically, this falls into a phenomenon called "dissociative experience or disorder."

Often times, the experiences that create this feeling are powerfully ecstatic or traumatic. In either case, the feeling is similar to watching oneself in a MOVIE. Basically, whatever is going on in the dream is so powerful that the dreamer is separating herself from experiencing it directly. The result is a self watching the self in a moment of life. Dreams of this nature can be very revealing about the self at work in the world (see MEDARD BOSS). LUCID dreaming can also create this feeling. In lucid dreaming, the dreamer is CONSCIOUS of dreaming and may be watching herself in the dream.

Dreams of this nature may create a feeling that the dreamer has projected herself into another sphere of reality, creating a sense of astral projection. This idea has been popularized by certain paranormal studies on perceptions of reality.

Native American CULTURES view the out-of-body experience as a fuller unity of the soul with nature. As such, it is not surprising that they hold such experiences in high regard. It is in this sense that you can consider the out-of-body experience a brush with great POWER—in a world of physical limitations you suddenly have the ability to go wherever you wish to go. You have complete control regarding your place in the universe.

Conversely, another possible out-of-body experience involves a complete loss of power: seeing yourself lying on an operating table in a HOSPITAL.

Does your out-of-body experience empower or frighten you?

Do you choose your TRAVEL destination or do you simply appear somewhere through no choice of your own?

See OUT-OF-BODY EXPERIENCE in Book 1

Oxen

Oxen are the ANIMALS of agriculture and work. If you dream of oxen you may see yourself as wanting to return to a simpler, farm-based life, or that your work is never ending.

Are you bearing the burdens of others unnecessarily or unfairly?

Owl

The owl is the ARCHETYPE of wisdom in many cultures' parables. The owl is often a sign of longevity, as well as knowledge. This knowledge pertains especially to the future and the mysteries of the night. You may be seeking such knowledge or be receiving an oracle hinting that you may be in possession of such knowledge.

Is the owl in your dream mysterious or forthcoming?

Does the owl speak to you? What does it say?

PAIN

Physical. Pain in dreams is an interesting phenomenon. Sometimes, a peculiar sleeping position becomes the TRIGGER EVENT for a painful dream. It's the body's way of saying, "Hey stupid, roll over." However, the ability of the brain to produce physical stimuli that match the dream event is an amazing thing. It makes dreams that are emotionally realistic even more real.

Many times, the pain sensation is related to a particular facet of body awareness or relationship disparity. Nowhere is this more apparent than in dreams of injury, infection, and AMPUTATION where physical sensations accompany visual images. Try to recall where the pain was centered, and relate that body part to aspects of your life that are applicable.

Was the pain caused by you, another person, or an object? Was it caused purposefully, or by accident?

Did the pain feel so great as though it may lead to amputation, or was it merely a nuisance?

Psychological. In dreams, we are often faced with dilemmas that create a lot of ANXIETY for the dreamer. Some of the things we do not know directly in our self-awareness are unknown because the trauma of unmediated awareness would be devastating. If dreams cause psychological pain, it should be treated much the same way as physical pain.

Does it hurt enough to get help, or just a little bit when precipitated by peculiar actions?

How often does it occur, and is it staying the same or getting worse?

Does it interfere with daily routines because the lingering pain is so troubling?

Do you feel you have enough knowledge and resources to treat the pain yourself, or does it feel as if the pain has deep roots in your life?

Depending on how you answer these questions, you may wish to seek professional help dealing with the psychological pain of dream events.

PARALYSIS

One of the most troubling dream events, and startling physical side-effects of REM, is paralysis. Large muscle groups often become paralyzed during a dream, presumably to prevent injury to the dreamer in case the dreamer's instincts would cause a physical reaction to dreaming visuals. It can be troubling if the dreamer becomes aware of his body in a paralyzed state without being aware of the fact that the mind is still in a dream state. Suddenly stripped of every physical capacity for defense, the dreamer can experience great panic or victimization in the dream. This scenario is a troubling version of the LUCID dream. Instead of mind awareness and body control, the dreamer has body awareness and no mind control.

Hundreds of years ago, this phenomenon was observed and named "having a witch on your back." The idea was that an unfriendly spirit within the dream had pinned you to your bed. Indeed, it is not uncommon to have a sense of spiritual oppression in a dream that includes paralysis.

See OUT-OF-BODY EXPERIENCE

PEARLS

The pearl has become an archetypal semi-precious stone.

Individual pearls in dreams usually have to do with moments of personal discovery. Most people who dream of pearls understand where they come from and view the pearl as a TREASURE to be discov-

ered. However, in dreams the pearl is rarely discovered in an oyster but simply found and conveyed to the dreamer or from the dreamer to others. Usually, this is done as a metaphor for some other kind of conveyance of intimate personal knowledge between the dreamer and other characters in the dream.

Pearl jewelry is often a gift of wealth and is something associated as classical, rather than contemporary. Metaphorically, this could be contrasting old versus new MONEY.

How did you come to possess the pearl or jewelry in your dream?

Was the pearl a material possession or did it seem to have heirloom-quality emotional features to it as well?

Did you experience the pearl as a gift from the world, a gift from another, or a gift you gave to another?

Who was involved in the gift-giving? Did it seem like an event that is congruous with your waking life?

PETS

Dreaming about pets is not uncommon, as they fill our lives much as FAMILY members (and often we like them a good bit more than family members!). Dreams involving pets often provide simple companionship for the other actions in the dream. However, there may be pet dreams that are either particularly meaningful or troubling.

Acquiring a pet that you do not have in waking life is a pet dream that may reflect your desire to have an ANIMAL. However, the dream could include an element of representation if owning the pet is symbolic of some other relationship in life. What kind of pet you acquire could be telling (see ANIMALS).

The DEATH of a pet is another particular type of dream in this genre. This dream could symbolize an ANXIETY if the pet still alive in waking life.

However, if the pet has died, it could be a dream of archetypal shift or a particular rite of passage that accompanied that time in your life. You may be recalling that shift or preparing for another one as you move forward.

The third type of pet dream involves having pets that either you have no desire to own or never have owned in waking life. These dreams are important for what the animals symbolize to you in waking life. For instance, you may dream of owning a SNAKE as a pet, yet in waking life you are horribly afraid of snakes. This may project a desire to overcome or control a particular facet of your life depending on what that animal represents to you.

What role did the pet in your dream play—was it there for companionship, to impress someone, or just to shake things up a novelty?

PHYSICAL EXAMINATION

Dreams of physical examination often occur at times when we feel our lives may not be as well-ordered as they could or should be. Close scrutiny often reveals trouble where we thought everything was fine. Or, conversely, it reveals that we are fine when we were having vague feelings that there may be trouble.

Who did the examining and what was the nature of the problem discovered, or were you fortunate to be given a clean bill of health?

PILLOW

The pillow is a central feature of sleep and works its way into dreams at times. Mainly, it is as an object of protection and security. Many times, dreams of pillows include either numerous pillows or rooms that are like gigantic pillows. The former is a desire to experience the world as benevolent. The latter version may be defined as a Freudian desire to return to the womb or motherly protection.

Some people believe that certain stones or crystals can be placed under the pillow as part of the dream incubation process.

See DREAM INCUBATION, CRYSTALS

PLANTS

Plants are often not a specific item of dream interpretation because most of the time they function simply as background scenery. The exception to this rule is when a particular type of plant is identified in the dream.

Plants that are significant are those that have historic importance in literature or your personal experience. For example, you may dream of visiting a friend who is sitting in a thicket of hemlock. Obviously, this plant is significant because of the implications of hemlock and SUICIDE in ancient lore.

Other plants that may be significant are those that remind you of a childhood MEMORY, a particular place, or a particular person. In those cases, identifying the relationship of your current circumstances with your memories is important.

PLAYING SPORTS

Individually. You may feel responsibility for your own success or satisfaction. Many times, entertaining ourselves stems from being neglected by others, so we dream of playing alone and enjoying ourselves in spite of them. Other times, it is a product of distancing ourselves from others, even if perhaps they would want us to play in the group.

Do you feel a sense of loneliness or comfort in the dream?

With Others. Dreaming of playing with others can be a symptom of your need to enhance your interpersonal communication skills. It can also inform you of the possibility that you have been neglecting communion with others, and that you need to seek more camaraderie in your life.

Was the game in the dream for fun or competition?

PLAYGROUNDS

Playgrounds are the scene of many of our most favored childhood memories. What makes a playground dream significant is who accompanies you and what age you are in the dream. It is not uncommon to have a playground dream where the dreamer is the only child among adults or the only adult among CHILDREN. These dreams usually indicate that there is a disparity between how you are acting in the world and what a more appropriate disposition would be. You may need to either lighten up or take yourself more seriously, depending on some of the distinct images in the dream.

Equally important in the playground dream is the presence of particular friends or FAMILY members. This is especially true if they have passed away in waking life but participate in the dream as living characters (see DEAD PEOPLE AS LIVE CHARACTERS). Dreams of this nature are often pointing towards INCOMPLETE RELATIONSHIPS that are either repeating themselves in waking life or need resolution.

A 44-year-old woman reports this dream:

> *I am on a playground . . . there is carnival music playing in the background. I am on the turntable apparatus that spins faster and faster. Suddenly, I vomit in front of my friends. I feel humiliated for losing control. I am very sad because I have on my favorite little girl dress.*

This dream is interesting because of the mixture of happy and sad memories. The dreamer does not report ever VOMITING at a playground in her conscious MEMORY. However, upon investigating the dream, she realizes that her FATHER is the one making the turntable spin. She feels as though she was enjoying herself tremendously up until the crucial moment. Then she realized the dress she vomited on in the dream is one she was given the summer her parents DIVORCED.

POISON

Dreams of poison often fall into general categories of POWER, SUICIDE, or revenge. Poison is a powerful image for us, as from childhood we were all taught the dangers of it.

Power dreams often involve drinking poison without consequence. Many times, the dream world provides the ability to act without concern for outcomes and to assert free will over social constraints. The poison dream can represent this, depending on what poison was consumed, under what initiative, and who watched the deed.

Suicide-by-poisoning dreams often have little to do with suicide, but much to do with peer-pressure, difficult work relationships, or a lack of personal power. In dreams of this nature, the dream may be teaching you that a certain part of your life is self-destructive.

Finally, the dream of poisoning as an act of revenge may reveal latent or unexpressed ANGER towards the object of your revenge. Poison is a satisfying way to commit a crime because we often associate it with painful death and sneakiness.

POLITICIANS

In the media age, dreaming of things political is becoming more frequent. Since we are often exposed to the intimate details of public figures' lives, we feel we know them, even if we only know about them. Consequently, we work these figures into our dream lives when events in our lives seem to empathize with what we know of public figures.

Often, politicians, like CELEBRITIES, pop into our dreams for no reason other than the fact that we are bombarded with images of them on a daily basis. What may be important, though, is your waking-life perceptions of the politician who appears in your dream.

POLITICS

Politics and political posturing are part of our everyday lives. From office politics to national politics, we are threatened by the coercion of others, as well as encouraged by the prospect of their accolades. Being in a political dream may indicate that you feel you are having to bargain for attention, moral choices, or the affirmation of others.

You may also see yourself in competition with those around you for a limited supply of MONEY or emotional affirmation.

Did you or someone else initiate the particular politics of the dream?

POOL

Swimming in or lying beside a pool is the ultimate wish-fulfillment dream for many people. The rest and relaxation of sunning outside is a wonderful invitation. However, depending on who is in the pool, you may be missing out somewhere in waking life. Evaluating this message depends on who is in the pool and what they have in common with people in your waking life. Perhaps you need to be less of a watcher and more of a joiner.

Do you feel as though you should be "part of the action" instead of on the side, sunning yourself?

If the WATER seems somewhat unwelcoming, there may be underlying feelings that the pool represents something you are being lured into against your will. In this case, the occupants of the pool may be people whom you generally trust, but also have some misgivings about.

POWER RELATIONSHIPS AND FIGURES

In dreams, one of the central interpretive concerns is the relationship between the dreamer and other dream characters. Usually, the relative power of the dreamer to others is important to understanding the meaning of other dream exchanges. Dreams of police, military figures, possessing supernatural powers, weapons, MONEY, or special knowledge are all dreams of power. The question is, does the power reside with the dreamer or with others in the dream?

If the power resides with you as the dreamer, there are probably feelings of competence, success, and conquest (especially romantic) prevalent in your life right now, or else you are hoping for them. People over whom you assert power may represent a facet of your life that feels out of control.

This relationship becomes particularly complex in dream interpretation if you are leading others in a non-coercive way. Power is not just making others do what you want, but being able to influence cooperation through more subtle means. You may lead INJURED people, DEAD people who appear as living in your dreams, or others who are afflicted with some LOSS OF SENSORY ABILITY.

If the power is exerted by others on you, reference the entry on VULNERABILITY for more insight.

PREGNANCY

Pregnancy has two points of entry into our dream lives. The first is dreaming of oneself as being pregnant. The second is that you actually become pregnant in waking life and that TRIGGER EVENT creates this particular dream content.

In dreams, anyone can get pregnant. It is not an experience that is limited by gender or age. Generally, it is a herald of creativity, virility, or wealth. However, there are numerous underlying themes that need additional interpretation.

If you are a younger woman who dreams of getting pregnant, but has no waking intention of doing so, it is likely that you are working through an archetypal transition into a new self-awareness. One of JUNG'S ARCHETYPES is the archetype of parenting or preserving the species. To see oneself engaged in such activity is to grow from being a CHILD to identifying more prominently with adults.

If you are sexually active, but without the intention for pregnancy, your dreams of pregnancy may occur in harmony with your monthly cycle. In these dreams, there may be a certain amount of "what-if" ANXIETY that needs resolution.

A man who dreams of being pregnant himself is often in a situation where his virility or creative participation in the world is in question. This occurs most among men who see themselves as less creative than they would like to be. The dream serves as a form of compensation to illuminate the more creative facets of their PERSONALITY. Men who are pregnant do not give birth exclusively to children, but a wide range of objects that somehow support their mission in the world.

Becoming pregnant in waking life can conjure a huge variety of dream events. These range from the violent to the hilarious and almost everything in between. Since pregnancy conjures a wide variety of feelings in waking life, from euphoria to tremendous anxiety, this is not too surprising.

Other dreams that are prevalent during pregnancy include dreams of martial infidelity, DEATH of the partner, chronic health problems, birth defects in the child, losing the pregnancy through accident or miscarriage, having twins or multiples, and dreams of heightened fertility where additional conceptions and gestations occur frequently or despite prevention.

Infidelity and death of the partner dreams often are played out in response to feelings of insecurity do to appearance changes or changes in sexual relationships during pregnancy. Dreams of chronic health problems and birth defects represent negative WISH-FULFILLMENT anxiety on the part of the woman.

Dreams of multiple-order birth and repeated gestation are the most complex dreams. Often times, pregnancy is overwhelming at some level for the woman. These feelings most often stem from fear to adequately MOTHER. The onslaught of pregnancies may be a visual representation of this anxiety.

PRISON, INESCAPABLE DWELLINGS

Entrapment is a common and interesting dream event. While some would also classify it as troubling, the flip side of being stuck somewhere is relative safety from the threats of an unknown outside world. Often, this safety facet of entrapment is neglected because of our obsession with freedom.

Being entrapped is often a dream about self-awareness. As the old saying goes, "Wherever you go, you take yourself with you." As this relates to dreams, being unable to escape usually is a picture of being unable to grow or accomplish in life what you desire to do. JUNG'S theory of archetypal INDIVIDUATION may be helpful for interpreting this dream.

Entrapment can be portrayed as either an absence of choices or too many choices. The absence of choices is a one-room cell. You are alone with no where to go. Too many choices is the mansion with no exits. Wherever you go, you are still stuck. This dream indicates that while choices may exist, they are unsatisfactory for effecting the new freedom or opportunities desired by the dreamer.

Discerning the solution to your captivity may often be revealed by who your captors are or where you are being held in captivity. To gain additional insight into the prison dream, look for familiarity among the guards, the decor of the mansion, and your sense of why you need to escape. Are you just uncomfortable being told what to do, or is there an actual threat within the prison, mansion, or inescapable dwelling?

Some inescapable dwellings are protective while others are punitive. Which one are you trapped in by your dream?

In waking, did you assume a negative feeling about a place that actually provided safety and predictability in your dream?

PROBLEM-SOLVING

Problem-solving in a dream situation and solving waking-life problems through dreaming are two very different experiences. The former is a dream event while the latter uses the dream event to address waking concerns.

In dreams, you may find yourself able to solve more problems than you normally do in waking. Problems that you can solve in dreams are virtually limitless because you are not bounded by logic. Many times this can work to the dreamer's advantage. If you are able to solve problems effectively, it is a reflection of untapped competence in a particular area of your life.

The idea of problem-solving through dreaming comes from the saying, "Let me sleep on it." The EGO is designed to differentiate which ideas are allowed to enter CONSCIOUSNESS. Consequently, some thoughts are dismissed before they even get a chance for deliberation. The problem is that most of us are prejudiced by our experience to eliminate potentially good solutions to our problems. This is due to the neurosis that is part and parcel of every PERSONALITY.

By sleeping and dreaming about a particular problem, your mind accesses a broader variety of problem solving choices than it would normally have the ability to recognize. When you awaken, you may not remember the specific dream content, but the problem may be miraculously resolved.

Always take note of the methods used in your dream situations to solve problems therein. Is there any situation in life that may benefit by employing similar tactics?

PURSUIT
See CHASING

PYRAMIDS
Pyramids are structures of mystery and POWER. Traditionally, they have been ascribed with human and universal powers.

A pyramid may also appear as a phallic symbol; or as a symbol of virility, creativity, or the ability to solve problems. They may also appear as an invitation to the exotic.

Do you enter the interior of the pyramid, climb the outside of the structure, or walk around it without coming close?

Who are you with when you experience such a powerful object, and what is your relation to that person or persons?

QUARANTINE
(ALONENESS and ABANDONMENT are two other versions of this event.) In dreams, the idea of being quarantined is the idea that others are prohibited from contact with you for generally secretive reasons. This is different from aloneness (which is voluntary) or abandonment (which is malicious). In quarantine it is often for your own good that others

are leaving you alone. In these dreams it is the need to cleanse or renew the spirit that often creates this situation.

Another version of this dream is being quarantined for punitive reasons. If you are experiencing some ambivalence about your moral life, you may bring quarantine upon yourself in dreaming as a means of resolving the situation. You may be seeking a "clean bill of health" from others concerning the situation that has prompted the quarantine situation.

Basically, it is a way of testing TABOOS subconsciously. If your waking life has brought you to a place of moral uncertainty, your SUB-CONSCIOUS may govern a time of evaluation, while you dream of being separated from the person or circumstances central to the conflict.

QUARTZ

This particular stone is often described as having a harmonization effect. Dreams of it may reflect a desire for or acquisition of harmony with the world.

QUICKSAND

It is not unusual to feel as though the circumstances of life are pulling on us. Quicksand is unique in that it looks like regular terra firma until it is too late. Moreover, in waking life, the more one struggles against quicksand, the more entrapping in becomes.

In dreaming of quicksand it is important to ask yourself who or what led you into the trap. In addition, as you were sinking in the quicksand, try to recall what you were most worried about. Many times in dreams, what you are most concerned about is not the actual consequences of the quicksand crisis, but other circumstances similar to those you are currently experiencing.

QUITTING

Quitting is an event that all of us are tempted with at one point in life
or another. Whether it is home life, work, or planet earth in general,
quitting may feel like the best choice. Virtually everyone has days
when selling your possessions and buying a one-way plane ticket
somewhere sounds mighty good. However, quitting is rarely about
quitting altogether, but rather not wanting to continue under the current circumstances. Quitting is often elective as well. The quitter
doesn't want to face the consequences of resigning from life, but rather
to avoid the requisite hassles of participating in it.

In dreams, we are often granted the latitude to quit without having
to experience consequences. Rather, we can simply eliminate unpleasant facets of life in its troubling condition. This is wonderful, as quitting
dreams illuminates our most draining emotional conflicts in waking life.

Many times we quit things in life because we cannot conceptualize
solutions to our problems. However, in dreaming, our quitting usually
points to the solution to the problem. All of us have what we consider
to be feasible and unfeasible solution choices. In dreaming, there are
more choices. What you quit from and gravitate toward may be showing you resolution potentials you had not previously considered.

For example, if you dream of quitting your job, what you do next in
your dream could be a symbol for a vocational path that holds more
reward potential for you. Sipping margaritas on the beach is not very
lucrative. However, being a travel agent is a reasonable carrier path.

If you quit your family in a dream, this may be a sign that you need
to disengage for a while from significant others. This is not the same as
physical separation. Rather, it means that you may need to back away
from your usual emotional patterns to find a better modus operandi
for relationships.

Quitting life in a "Stop the world, I want to get off" type of statement may indicate that you are tired of trying. This may indicate that either life truly is uncooperative to you or that you need to assess how you address situations in life. It may be that there are self-destructive patterns at work that are undermining your ability to function.

What facet of your waking life is most dissatisfying? Is there a correlation what you quit in your dream?

RAIN

Weather in dreams is generally a detail that may be left unanalyzed unless it is particularly noticeable to the dreamer for some reason. Rain is one of these notable exceptions. The reason comes from the relationship between WATER and fertility that many CULTURES affirm. In dreams where rain and water-fertility are identified, there is usually an unique feature to the rain. This can be as mundane as a drought that is broken to rain that only falls indoors on one or two particular people.

Does the rain cause you problems of some sort or is it a welcome addition to the scene?

RAPE

Dreams of rape are dreams of violence. As a dreamer, you may find yourself as an aggressor, victim, or spectator to the crime. In dreams of this nature, your role and feelings about the others in the event are crucial to understanding the meaning of the dream. If you have RECURRING dreams of being the victim of rape, you should try to determine if post-traumatic stress is a factor in your dreams.

Being a victim in a non-recurring rape dream usually indicates a message that you are being personally violated, thwarted, or ruthlessly exploited in waking life. In dreams of this nature, the aggressor is a faceless adversary. This could be explained by the fact that people who get close enough to us in life to exploit us often are significant to us in other, more positive ways. The dream is not meant to have an actual aggressor, but simply serve as a warning that you're being overpowered.

Being the aggressor in a rape usually indicates powerful unresolved or unexpressed ANGER at someone. As with the victim scenario above, the other party to the rape is often faceless. For example, if you harbor anger towards an opposite gender BOSS, parent, teacher or co-worker, rape dreams may occur. Finding a source of unresolved anger in waking life can provide great insight into the meaning of this dream. Identifying why you are unable to express your anger in waking life will also help.

A 25-year-old woman reports:

> Even before I became sexually active, I remember having recurrent dreams of men tied down. I would force myself on them sexually. It was always against their will, and according to my power or desire. I never knew them, and often I did not even notice their faces. It is strange to me that I should have such dreams without even knowing what actual sex was like.

This woman had a deeply troubled relationship with her father. Although there was no incest or sexual misconduct, there was little affection either. The woman reports that her relationship with this parent has been very bitter and troubled. However, she notes that as the relationship improved, the dream lessened in frequency.

Observing a rape is often equally troubling. This is because of the powerlessness you feel in relationship to the victim. Many times, there is an intuitive connection with the victim or the aggressor. In either case, the dreamer may be feeling angry or exploited in waking life.

The watching is an attempt to dissociate oneself from the trauma of the event. This often allows better recognition of the relationship between aggressor and victim. Consequently, whatever psychological protection is gained by indirect participation is lost on the more complete awareness of the other characters.

RATS

Rats are almost universally despised in the modern world. Their reputation as disease-laden scavengers seems to precede them wherever they go. Some people own rats as PETS and will, of course, perceive them differently.

For most people, dreams of rats reveal concerns of becoming destitute scavengers themselves—friendless and outcast. Another potential scenario is that the dreamer feels his or her social security is being gnawed away. In contrast to theft, when all is quickly and dramatically taken, the rats gradually erode their environment.

In your waking life, do you view rats as potential pets or potential predators?

In your dream, are the rats a serious threat to your health or possessions, or are they merely an uncomfortable presence?

RELATIVES

Relatives are powerful features of both the waking and dreaming worlds. As a consequence, interpreting dreams of relatives is a complex task. There are hundreds of different possible interpretations that originate within the world of the dreamer as well as from classical psychology.

The reason dreams of FAMILY are so prevalent is that everyone has a desire to know what "normal" is, and then act that way in the world. Countless times, clients will come to therapy complaining, "I just want a normal family," or "I just want a normal marriage." The definition of this idea comes from our relatives and how well they fit into or detract from our idea of normalcy.

Dreams of family may affirm or undermine "normal" feelings about ourselves. Extended family relations are very significant in developing the family lore and ritual. As you mature and reflect critically on normalcy in your understanding of it, these rituals either affirm or work against the norms of your perspective. Who does what, why and when is often determined by influences in the extended family. The result is that we construct a family story that defines who we are in our family and what our family means in the world around us.

Relative dreams of this type lend themselves to archetypal interpretations that offer insight into how the dreamer sees him or herself in relation to the larger human community represented by the relatives. To interpret dreams of this kind, discern what relatives were in the dream and whether they are still living or dead in waking life. Many times, relatives who have passed away are alive in our dreams. Usually, one of two circumstances exist. Either the activity in the dream reminds you of a ritual aspect of the relationship with this relative, or your relationship with the relative is incomplete.

Many times, dreams about relatives are RECURRING. These can have both PROPHETIC or historic meaning. This is especially true in cases where the central characters are relatives with whom there is either emotional tension or uncertainty concerning their health. If there is emotional tension, the dream may be identifying the source of the tension to create an opportunity to resolve it. If there are particular relatives with precarious health, the dreams may resolve, or warn of, impending DEATHS in the family.

The place and occasion for the relatives' appearance in the dream are important to the interpretation of it. For example, if only the women in your family appear with you in a dream of an activity that they have historically participated in together, you may see yourself as joining with the family in new ways. There are numerous variations on this dream:

1. Not wanting to join the activity (ambivalence about traditional expectations).

2. Joining a group of exclusively opposite-gendered family members (confusion about fitting into the family on your terms).

3. Joining a group of family members with something unique in common; i.e., all bald, all with cancer, all widowed, all single, etc. (identifying with or having concern over ending up like others whom you chagrin or pity).

While family members are powerful dream icons, their meaning can be quite diverse. Often, free association is the key to discerning their impact on your dreams and the meaning of that influence.

Individual family members, especially FATHERS and MOTHERS (or representations of them) are often prominent in dreams. For better or for worse, they are primary influences in the shaping of our personalities. This includes how we respond to our environmental stimuli, as well as how we value ourselves and our inner nature.

Consequently, another significant aspect of relative dreams is what these dreams show about how our individual EGO development and PERSONALITY strength have been influenced by individual relatives, for good or ill. Personality strengths and weaknesses often express themselves in alternating generations. For example, in one generation, the father is relentless in expressing ANGER. In the next generation, anger becomes TABOO and inexpressible. In this way, dreams of the individual parent often have a compensatory effect.

Often you will have a dream that includes a particular family member in a very unusual situation for that person (for example: scuba diving with Grandma). Often in this type of dream there will be plenty of other symbols and images that point to the true meaning of what the dream has in store for you.

RINGS (JEWELRY OR MAGIC)

Rings may be symbols of covenant or commitment, as in marriage. Often rings of this type reflect our deepest desires to make or receive commitment from others or in regard to a particular task.

Rings with magical vibrations may be about acquiring supernatural POWERS.

Rings of magic drawn on the ground, such as medicine rings or crop circles, may have more to do with protection, as the ring is often the limits to which evil may approach. In dreams of this nature, you may be anxious that circumstances are pressing too hard upon you and feel that you need an intercessor.

Did you create or find the ring? Do you feel any sense of control over it?

Is there a ring that someone else is using to gain power over you?

RITUAL BEHAVIOR

When dreaming, you may feel a need to repeat particular actions or behave in an unusual way at times. This is often ritual behavior. In your dream, the behavior is often necessary to avoid or undo some evil act that may occur.

This is a reflection of the work of superstition in your life. If you are by nature superstitious, you may be getting a challenge from your SUB-CONSCIOUS to let go of a particular compulsion. Or, your superstitions may be receiving validation from your UNCONSCIOUS mind.

In your dream, is the ritual empowering?

As you compare the ritual with your waking behavior, is it comforting or troubling that you participated in it during your dream story?

RESCUING

In dreams of rescuing, you are either doing the rescuing or are in need of being rescued. If you are doing the rescuing, you likely see yourself as a HERO, shepherd, parent, or mentor to others. Who the others are, what you rescue the others from, and by what means often reveal how you see yourself within a particular network of relationships.

If you are the one being rescued, it is likely that you are overwhelmed or feeling incompetent in an important area of your waking life. The consequences of failure could be catastrophic. If your rescuer is someone known to you in waking life, it may be worth seeking his or her advice concerning particular struggles you are facing.

Is the rescue something that was expected, and so did not carry very much ANXIETY?

Was the rescue an against-all-odds type of mission? Did it fail or succeed?

ROYALTY

Royalty is becoming more of a mixed dream symbol in contemporary dreams. Three hundred years ago, it would have been a universal symbol of wealth and power. However, as we become more aware of the struggles royalty face, it is more common to dream of them in relation to our own daily struggles.

Many times our dreams are a search for persons who can identify with our inner struggles. As royalty DIVORCE, grieve, and grow-up in the public eye, we look to them as symbols to reinforce our own daily crises. Or we dream of them in an effort to attach the splendor of their lives to our normal lives.

Becoming a member of royalty is often a WISH-FULFILLMENT dream for wealth. However, if your dream includes an element of returning to the era of monarchy, the dream may also include a desire to assert oneself more powerfully in a particular area of life, whether it be in a financial or emotional realm. Looking at who serve in your court and in what capacity would be a worthwhile examination.

Entering into the presence of royalty can be another version of the mirroring dream. However, it may also be a judgment dream, if you are holding secrets in your life that undermine your ability to function openly. Nobility often served as the final court of appeals in many nations.

Does a hierarchical society please or repulse your personal sense of social order?

In your waking life, do your conversations include discourse on who is better than or less than others?

RUBY

Dreaming of rubies is often a dream of wealth, POWER, and energy. The ruby is viewed as the crystal of leadership and kings.

Are you receiving them as a gift, finding them, or stealing them?

RUNNING

Running is a traditional symbol of health and vitality in addition to being a means of fleeing potential danger. Thus running could be considered a dream of virility, as well as fear.

Usually, in a dream of running in which fear is the dominant emotion, you will find that you can either run all night and successfully escape the danger (albeit with a serious emotional drain), or you find that you continue to falter and stumble, making the object of your fear even more terrifying. In the latter case, try to relate the dream situation to a situation in your life where you are feeling incredible pressure. Sometimes a simple change of perception can solve the problem.

See CHASED

SAINTS, SACRED FIGURES

Saints and other sacred human figures in our dreams often appear as heralds of benevolence or as the "morality police." While many times these are positive dream experiences, the dreams can also leave a feeling that perhaps you are not doing all you can to be an agent of good in the world. The dream may be inspiration to involve yourself in a particular cause through hands-on work or financial donations.

The moral side of the dream is often a judgment on current lifestyle choices. When your psyche is in conflict between the desires of the ID and the restraint of the SUPEREGO, the superego can marshal symbols of judgment to strengthen its position. Often these will arrive under very peculiar circumstances. A dream of sexual desire may suddenly find the object of its desire cloaked in the garb of a priest, pastor, rabbi, policeman, or a particularly strict third-grade teacher you may have had.

If a saintly figure in your dream suddenly turns into a demon of some sort, or begins to resonate emotions that are non-traditional from such a figure, perhaps it is a sign that you need to check your morals concerning a situation in waking life.

Does the saintly figure in your dream appear as a helper or emotional benefactor, or does the character seem to be coming down on you as a law-enforcing authority figure?

SARCASM

Dreams are as open to humor as they are to any other part of your PERSONALITY. Sarcasm is a particularly interesting facet of humor that emphasizes the shortcomings of a person. Consequently, whether you initiate or are the butt of the sarcasm shows something about your place in the dream.

Sometimes, the entire dream falls into this category. The dream is almost a cruel joke played upon you. This may be a dream that sheds light on your relationships or potential in the world. This dream may occur when you are in a situation that could potentially place you in circumstances that are way over your head.

Dream sarcasm often has metaphorical meaning related to waking events and vice-versa. For example, a phrase used by others to torment you may become a central object in the dream that you either worship or loathe.

SAPPHIRE

The sapphire is the crystal of faith, peace, and good fortune. Consequently, dreams of the sapphire relate to receiving or discovering these attributes in your own life. Whether you find the crystals or are given them by another character in the dream is crucial to determining what the dream may mean. If you find the sapphires on your own, you are probably needing to plumb the depths of your soul to find the peace or spiritual insights lacking in your life. If they are given to you by another, it is a sign that some spiritual mentoring, guidance, or direction is needed in your life.

SEARCHING

Hunting for a misplaced item is frustrating. However, discovery can be a pleasant reward. In dreams about searching, whether the dream ends with or without finding the object is important to its meaning.

If the dream resolves itself, it is important to note what or who you were looking for, and how those things were found. Think about the relationship that exists between the object and who (if anyone) helped you find it. Many times, the thing that is lost in the dream reflects an area of life where we are feeling incomplete or ineffective. Finding it in partnership with others may be a cue to seek outside wisdom in the resolution of the circumstances.

A 48-year-old man reports dreaming:

> *I am looking for my car keys. They are nowhere to be found. I am turning the house upside down, yelling at my wife, and generally coming unglued. My daughter is out, and I begin to blame her. A friend of hers comes in and says I should look in the front door. I do. My keys are there.*

This searching dream is interesting because the man reported throughout counseling how anxious he was concerning his daughter's driving. The loss of control he was feeling in his daughter's life consumed much of his emotional energy. After this dream, he realized that much of the home conflict he was experiencing came from his own ANXIETY more than actual defiance on the part of his daughter. The insight produced from the dream resulted in a much more peaceable home life for everyone involved.

In an unresolved dream of searching, the dream often illustrates the need to find resolution of an emotional trauma. The unresolved search can be for an object or a person. Some common versions of the person dream include the crying BABY that cannot be found, chasing a runaway whom you cannot locate, or receiving a message that cannot be returned. These dreams may occur in periods of extended grieving, such as the DEATH of a loved one.

Another unresolved search scenario is the unfound place or item. For example, you may have a map in a dream that leads to no where. Or perhaps you simply lose an object by setting it on the table. Dreams of this nature can give tremendous insight into the goals of your life and how effectively you are actualizing them. If you are having a lot of these types of dreams, it may be that you need to examine whether your goals and your behavior are consistent or mutually exclusive.

SELLING

Selling can be presented as your employment, as in selling to others in a retail environment; or it can be more personal, as in selling your possessions. Obviously, if your waking livelihood includes sales, dreams of selling will not be unusual. Unless you sell something particularly sentimental, most of the remarks here will not apply to you.

If you are employed in selling in dreamland, the emotional transaction at work is persuasion. The object you are trying to sell may be ridiculous or an actual consumer item. Depending on which it is, this may reflect whether or not you feel you will ever be persuasive. Your clientele also is important to this dream. Do they have something in common?

Do you see yourself as persuasive in waking life, or do you need to develop those skills more fully?

If you are having a yard sale in your dream, you may be trying to creatively solve a financial problem or be feeling burdened by your possessions. If the yard sale has an element of emotional darkness, there may be financial ANXIETY involved that precipitated the need for downsizing the household. Dreams of this nature often try to show feelings of over extension. Heed them.

If you are selling items of great sentimental value, you may be seeing yourself as divesting from a particular relationship. This can happen at times of transition into adulthood or (desire for) marital separation. Many times, you do not actually perceive the emotional content of the items in your dream the way you would in waking. They are simply "extras" that you no longer wish to carry through life.

The act of selling in a dream, usually, is in the most general terms symbolic of some sort of emotional transaction that may be taking place in life.

SEPARATION

Separation can relate to ABANDONMENT, marriage, friendship, career, or geographic upheaval.

Many times, the SUBCONSCIOUS impulses of PERSONALITY are less mature in their PROBLEM-SOLVING than the CONSCIOUS, waking self. The function of EGO is to filter these impulses so they do not get out into waking life. However, since the ego is turned off in sleeping, the immaturity of the ID will have us walking away from our marriages, jobs, friendships, etc. at the drop of a hat.

Being separated is different than being quarantined, abandoned, or quitting in that it is often mutual. In dreams, other characters can be more cooperative, since it is our SUBCONSCIOUS that is controlling their actions.

Who or what were you separated from in the dream, and did it seem like a permanent or temporary condition?

Was the separation easily decided, or was it gut-wrenching?

SEX

Dreams of sex and looking for sexual meaning in dreams is something of a pastime for dream interpreters. Often, you don't have to look very far. Sexual content, feelings of love, flirtation, attraction, and nocturnal rendezvous are often very explicit in dreams.

Sexual meaning has long been a first path of inquiry in dream interpretation. This is due, in part, to the significant contributions of SIGMUND FREUD to the area of dream interpretation. However, interpreting the sexual content of dreams can be difficult. University studies reveal significant differences in how men and women dream about sex. However, when all is said and done, almost everyone is "doing it" in dreamland.

How Much? Sex during dreaming is reported as a topic of at least 12% of male dreams and 4% of female dreams. This discrepancy is generally consistent with our waking sex drives, with men doing much more thinking about the topic than women. (It is said that men think about sex far more than 12% of their waking lives, though.)

In his book *Finding the Meaning in Dreams,* G. William Dumhoff reveals some interesting data about the manifestation of sex in dreams:

Gender	Participating In Sex	Watching Sex Acts
Men	93%	7%
Women	68%	32%

This table indicates that women often separate themselves from what is going on in the dream sexually, whereas men see themselves as participants. This can be significant to understanding why it is more common for men—particularly boys—to have orgasms in the dream state than it is for women. It also reveals the conflict that many women feel about the good-girl/bad-girl TABOO.

Aside from overt sexual activities in dreams, the question of sexual images and symbols as they occur in dreams is important. Because sexuality is often cloaked in a heavy shroud of secrecy, either through childhood or throughout life, the SUBCONSCIOUS is prone to visually represent sex in a variety of ways. Freud, in his theory of the sexually driven PERSONALITY, contributed much to this line of thought.

Freud did for sexual content in dreams what Henry Ford did for internal combustion. Suddenly everyone, everywhere had dreams of sexual content. Ultimately, this led to Freud's demise in some segments of the intellectual community. Many scholars wonder if Freud was really as pre-occupied with sexual symbolism as he is purported to have been. The following is a partial list of the phallic symbols you may find indexed in a Freudian dream interpretation book:

Aerosol Cans	**Antenna**	**Balloons**
Bats	**Birds**	**Boilers**
Bottles	**Can Openers**	**Cannons**
Cigars	**Cars**	**Chalk**
Church Spires	**Cords**	**Cucumbers**
Drills	**Fishing Poles**	**Fountains**
French Bread	**Golf Clubs**	**Gophers**
Guns	**Hammers**	**Hats**
Keys	**Kites**	**Knives**
Lances	**Laser Beams**	**Moles**
Nail Files	**Neckties**	**Needles**
Pencils	**Pens**	**Pipes**
Pistols	**Planes**	**Plows**
Revolvers	**Rockets**	**Ropes**
Scalpels	**Screwdrivers**	**Snakes**
Spears	**Sticks**	**Swords**

Syringes	Tall Buildings	Telescopes
Tractors	Trains	Trees
Tubes	Umbrellas	Water Taps
Woodchucks	Wrenches	Zippers

Not to be left out, women's sexuality was likewise a source of attention and interest for Freud. The following list is far less extensive than the list for male phallic symbols, but almost as diverse:

Bowls	Children	Churches
Closed Rooms	Earth	Fruit
Flowers	Gardens	Houses
Moon	Mounds	Oceans
Ponds	Suitcases	Tunnels
Urns	Vases	Water

Interpreting Sexual Dreams. Sexual dreams are not about sex exclusively. Often they are about how we perceive people and how we think others are perceiving us. To construct a framework for interpreting sexual dreams, it is important to identify who is with us in the dream and how we feel about the experiences being had while dreaming.

Certain dreams are simply romantic. Boy and girl meet in the dream state and find themselves enjoying one another. This scenario commonly involves an attractive acquaintance and a generally pleasing environment. There is no violation of taboo, except for a sense that perhaps things are moving a little fast in the nocturnal relationship. Often, the dreamer has simply acted upon a desire for a relationship with a particular person. Freud's theory of WISH-FULFILLMENT is a sufficient explanation.

Other dreams begin to press on the boundaries of our taboos. These include dreams with sexual content the dreamer would consider inappropriate in waking, but participates in during the dream. These dreams can be very troubling. One can wake up feeling as though a rape was committed, a fidelity violated, or that innocence has been stripped away. Dreams of this nature may require some more thorough examination.

Identifying the "who" or "what" that has generated discomfort is an important first step. Was it a BOSS, co-worker, friend? Someone much older or younger than you with whom you have an affectionate, but platonic relationship? Or was it the nature of the encounter—coerced, cheating, public, or whatever—that is the most distinct feature of the dream? Who was forcing whom? Was it a STRANGER who reminded you of someone you know? Representation and DISPLACEMENT relationships are often components of sexual dreaming.

Some of these dreams indicate our own ambivalence about taboos. There is, after all, something exciting about what is forbidden. In other cases, we are expressing our own frustration with a sex life that is not satisfying. Still other times, others have violated our boundaries and we respond by perceiving them as taking unmerited favors from us.

In all of these cases, the dreams are worth noting and studying. By looking into what you may find abhorrent at first, you will see aspects of your personality and the relationships around you that have gone mostly unnoticed. Perhaps most importantly, you will become more aware of the various facets of your personality in those relationships.

SHARED DREAMS

There are two kinds of dreams that fall into this category: mutual and concurrent. In each case, two or more people dream of similar characters and activities. What differentiates them are the means by which the dreams occur. In mutual dreaming, the dreamers intentionally develop a desire to experience a shared dream through INCUBATION.

However, in concurrent dreams, the dreamers had no idea their content would be similar going into the night's rest.

Mutual dreaming is an intentional movement toward influencing dream content. This discipline allows dreamers to design psychic meeting grounds for SUBCONSCIOUS awareness of one another. This can be a seedbed for finding new facets in a relationship, from the ordinary to the sensual.

It is often quite interesting to get together with your mutual dreamer friend(s) and compare dreams. The best way to do this is for both or all of you to write down what you dreamt about the subject in question, then share the essays.

Concurrent dreams are often discovered by chance. You may be telling a friend about a dream you had, using vivid details, when all of a sudden she reveals that she had the same exact dream. This is a rare and mysterious occasion indeed!

SIBLINGS

Dreaming of siblings can be pretty ordinary stuff. If you have brothers and/or sisters in waking life, it would be expected that in dreams of your FAMILY, they would be present. The important work of interpretation comes when either your sibling is missing, or if you suddenly acquire siblings in dreamland that do not ordinarily exist in the waking world.

If your real-life sibling is noticeably absent from a dream event, it may reflect your perceptions of your family at large. While either you or your sibling may be at odds with the family, a dream of an incomplete family is a picture of fracture in one or more of the possible relationships.

Sometimes, if you are experiencing particularly strong identification with a co-worker, they will show up in dreams as a newfound sibling. If the dream solution to the new sibling is a comfortable arrangement, this may herald a positive partnership. However, this event can be a little troubling. In dreams of this nature, you may feel as though the new sibling is burrowing too far into your life and relationships.

SIDEWALK

Sidewalks define the path in most neighborhoods. In dreams, the sidewalk often feels more like the yellow-brick road in *The Wizard of Oz*, intended to help you stay on course. The sidewalk is interesting because it often leads to scenes that would not be found in a neighborhood. Instead, the sidewalk leads to MOUNTAINS, CAVES, volcanoes, etc. It often leads the dreamer to the next place in order to move the dream story forward. As nonsensical as this sort of appearance of a sidewalk may seem, it is merely a method that your UNCONSCIOUS mind uses to further the dream story (such as the use of a well-known object or person as a bridge between story elements).

It is important to recognize that dreaming about a sidewalk as a significant symbol of the dream interpretation is rare. More often, the sidewalk is simply part of a common street scene.

Does the sidewalk take you to a place that sidewalks usually don't go?

Is the sidewalk or the street that you are walking along a familiar one or is it just an ARCHETYPE of a sidewalk?

SKELETON

The skeleton is a universal symbol of depletion, DEATH, and secrets. Likewise, in dreams, it can appear in a variety of ways and reveal a variety of things. To discern an appropriate meaning requires examination of the context, and your reaction to the skeleton in the context it appeared.

The depletion scenario often occurs when skeletons are animated—their somewhat taunting presence will seem to exasperate you. Where are you when you find these animated skeletons? Combining the bones with the emotional image of the office, home, or a relative's home will indicate a facet of life where you feel as though someone or something is "sucking you dry." Interestingly, you may not be afraid of these skeletons and possibly may even enjoy them, intuitively realizing that you are related to them and don't mind being their benefactor. (In spite of the fact that you do not want to end up like them!)

Death scenarios are contrasted to the above by the complete lack of animation. Often, there is more fear associated with the discovery of the bones as well.

Upon discovery, did you know whose bones they were and how they came to be there? These dream discoveries may offer insight into a person (or yourself) who is being symbolically killed by their circumstances. This death may be either emotional or physical.

Secrets, or "skeletons in the closet," is the last scenario. Bones of this nature often appear in very inappropriate situations, but don't often generate much reaction among the dream characters. People know there are bones around, but they are not discussed in the dream. By assessing who is in the dream when the bones are found, insights can be drawn about the relationships and loose ends surrounding the person(s). If you are hiding something in waking life, the skeleton bones may appear in your dream in plain sight of some significant other in your life. The fact that that dream character doesn't seem to notice your "skeletons" is the handiwork of your UNCONSCIOUS protecting you. However, such a dream image may be a warning signal that you either need to be more careful about exposing a vice, or cut it out of your life completely.

SKILLS

At critical times in dreams, your faculties may become enhanced or limited. These include mental, as well as physical faculties. Suddenly, you find a great wealth of knowledge to resolve a problem, or acquire a skill to do so. Other times, you suddenly lose certain abilities.

Acquiring. The amazing thing about acquiring knowledge is that it is generated in your own mind in the dream. If upon waking the process used to solve the dream problem was logical, you may want to contemplate problems in your waking life that resemble the dream problem. Your mind may be accessing problem-solving skills that you have already eliminated from consideration, or never thought of in the first place.

What was the nature of the skills you received? Were they logical, practical, or completely impossible to translate into waking life?

Losing. Of course, you may forget something or lose some faculty just as easily. In dreams of this nature, your insecurity about appearing incompetent is working its way through your awareness. In the physical realm, the loss of ability might be sudden weakness or loss of a sensory perception such as sight, speech, or hearing. Sudden weakness may result from actual body awareness in dreaming, as SLEEP PARALYSIS affects motor abilities during the REM state.

Dreams concerning the loss of other physical skills, such as operating a car, throwing an object, or performing a job-related task may reflect a loss of MEMORY or oversight of a particular detail concerning a problem plaguing the waking life.

Who is with you when the skill evaporates? What are you trying to accomplish?

How does this event correspond to your waking life?

SLEEPING

Dreams of being asleep are common, as that is your condition while dreaming.

See ASLEEP

SNAKE

The snake is a difficult dream symbol because it is so widely interpreted among various CULTURES. Interpretations run the gamut from blood-curdling fear to wisdom and peace. These options are determined by literary history and folklore from different cultures, as well as personal experience.

In waking life, it is not uncommon to be afraid of snakes. For some people, this fear is disruptive and pathological, even to the point that a photo of a snake represents an oppressive threat. For these people, snake dreams are almost universally bad. If the dream includes someone who handles snakes, whoever tames the object of the fear is likely a source of wisdom and control in the dreamer's world, and may be a representation of some aspect of themselves or someone else they know.

Among Asian and Native American cultures, the snake is a wisdom symbol. The idea of wisdom comes from the snake's ability to shed its skin and renew itself. If one dreams of snakes from this perspective, it is a dream of renewal, problem-solving, and good tidings in general.

In Judeo-Christian cultures, the snake is a symbol of temptation or spiritual opposition against reaching one's goals. This concept is derived from Bible when Satan tempts Adam and Eve in the Garden of Eden in the form of a snake. Sometimes, a snake dreamt in this context will remind you of a particular person in your waking life with whom you have a competitive relationship.

Finally, FREUD and classical psychotherapy have also thrown interpretations into this "pit." The contention is that the snake is a type of phallus. The snake often embodies fear about intercourse and an aversion to it.

Coming up with an insightful interpretation for your dream snake could be tricky. What emotions are prevalent regarding the snake: fear, respect, or opposition?

What is your attitude about snakes in waking life: neutral, fearful, or friendly?

Did the snake appear when you were alone or were others with you when the snake entered the dream scene? What are your feelings about those others?

Answering these questions should lead towards a productive interpretation of the snake dream.

SPACE TRAVEL

As shuttle flights and space stations become a part of our modern vocabulary, space TRAVEL becomes more accessible. Consequently, dreams of it also are more common. This sort of dream is often simple WISH-FULFILLMENT—a desire to see the world from a different perspective. However, it can also be a dream of ESCAPE, travel or search. The purpose of the travel is obviously the key to resolving the dream. Another potential scenario for meaning concerns the mode of travel. Are you in a spaceship, or in something more familiar (like your car)?

Dreaming of space travel is a very exploratory opportunity. It can also mean that you are lost or are groping for something in a vast vacuum.

Did you want to be in outer space in your dream or did you simply find yourself there? Did you feel safe being there?

SPEAKING IN PUBLIC

Public speaking is the number one fear of the majority of adults—it even ranks higher than death! The result is that dreams of this sort are common. Rarely are they NIGHTMARES, but rather dreams of scrutiny and overcoming. Often the occasion of the speaking or the audience members will suggest something to you about an area of your life where people are looking too closely for your comfort.

Another version of this is the public speaking dream where the topic or attire is totally inappropriate for the dreamer's context. This dream is similar to the NUDITY dream in that exposure and inadequacy are themes in the dream. The dream may be an attempt to expose a weakness that you are covering up.

Was the nature of your public appearance absurd, or did it somehow fit logically with your waking life?

Did you feel a sense of high anxiety during the situation, or were you calm and forthright?

SPHINX

The Sphinx is an ancient Egyptian statue with the body of a lion and the head of a man. Throughout the ages it has been known as a bearer of POWER and mystery.

Dreams concerning the sphinx are mystery/wisdom dreams. These types of dreams may occur when there is an impasse in your waking life. Note the concurrent images in your dream and consider their relation to a difficult decision that has to be made in your life.

SPIRIT GUIDES

The use of spirit guides as a means to acquire aid and understand a larger reality has become common in recent years. In these dreams, sacred or supernatural knowledge comes from a STRANGER who seems to have mostly human attributes but also seems to possess some supernatural quality.

To dream of such a guide often reflects a deeply felt need for mentoring, direction, and support that is not being given through conventional relationship. Or, such relationships may not exist in the dreamers life, hence the need for a spirit guide.

See STRANGERS, ANGELS

SPIRITUAL ICONS

Dreaming of spiritual or religious icons often reflects either POWER or unity. We want to feel united with the universe, and icons are a good way to symbolize that identification. Other times, you may dream of being in a situation where supernatural power is required to resolve the conflict. In this case, icons serve as the vehicle or symbol of that power.

There are countless icon images available to all humans. The ones you find in your dreams will relate to your experience in life. (Some examples are: the crucifix, the full MOON, the Star of David, Stonehenge, and the Buddha.)

Are your experiences with icons tied to sacred or supernatural events that you prescribe to in waking life?

Are the icons revered or disdained by others in your dream? How do you feel about it?

STATUES

Dreams of statues are fascinating. Whether you stumble across the statues, create them, or become one yourself, dreams of statuary can be challenging to interpret, but offer great insight in return for the effort.

If you discover statues randomly, note the kinds of figures they are

and the emotions they conjure for you. This type of dream may be a version of the "SKELETON in the closet" dream. The statues may also be mythological or SPIRITUAL ICONS.

Another statue scenario is the dreamer making a statue. In these dreams, the statue often represents someone you know (or some facet of your own PERSONALITY) whom you wish to control or contain. This dream may be signaling a MEMORY that needs to be brought out in the open for resolution.

The dream of being a statue often finds its inspiration in the phenomenon of SLEEP PARALYSIS. Since we cannot move large muscle groups while dreaming, our brains assume we have become statue-like. In dream logic, it makes perfect sense. Being aware of yourself trapped in a statue often reflects that another is wielding excessive control over you.

STORY

If you see yourself as hearing or acting in a story, you probably have the feeling that others are controlling your life and making choices for you. While the narrator of the story is probably unknown to you, he or she represents the person controlling your life. If you feel that you are the narrator watching yourself in a story, this may indicate uncertainty about the choices you are currently making in your life. You are wanting to test them without consequence before acting on them in waking reality.

STRANGERS

Strangers in dreams can be very puzzling. Most often they are simply displaced persons and images that are drawn from the list of persons we know by face and name (sometimes they represent our own ANIMA or ANIMUS). Strangers can reveal a tremendous amount of information about how we are experiencing the world. Different theorists have offered numerous explanations of who these characters are and how they worked into our psyches. Organizing the cast list is a useful endeavor for interpreting any dream.

Anima/Animus as Stranger. CARL JUNG theorized that in the Self there were female counterparts to the male PERSONALITY and male counterparts to the female personality. These counterparts are psychic projections that appear to us in dreams. When a female stranger shows up in a man's dream, her behavior can be a projection of the feminine side of his personality. This is conversely true for women who dream of male strangers. These strangers don't often have SEX appeal for the dreamer, though some may. What is more common is a soul-mate friendship. Understanding these characters is helpful because we learn how we want others (particularly the opposite sex) to perceive us. The corollary is how we are afraid they perceive us.

A second dimension to the anima/animus character is the desire to express what perhaps we are unable to express in waking life. Women may have animus characters in their dreams who show tremendous ANGER to compensate for a feeling that they cannot show in waking life. Likewise, men may have anima characters who cry due to the pain of life—an emotion they may not feel the ability to indulge. These strangers are often benevolent to us. They may be helpful, protective, or supply information to solve a problem. When they are troubling, it is often because they are acting out in a way we wish we could.

Displaced Strangers. This is when your dream moves a person from one type of relationship to another. An example would be having a well-known celebrity become your brother or sister. A more common example includes boss or teacher as a parent. In addition to personality roles, emotions might get displaced. This is especially true in the case of anger or sexual attraction that cannot be expressed in waking.

Incubus/Succubus Strangers. These are stranger-lovers who appear in dreams to have sex with the dreamer (an incubus visits a female; a succubus visits a male). They often represent the extremes of the sexuality experience. Either they are idealized lovers in the emotional and physical sense, or they are demonic and repulsive lovers, employed to steer you away from a waking practice that you may know is bad for you.

Shadow Strangers. These are strangers of the same gender as the dreamer who possess the negative attributes of the dreamer. Most often, these negatives are presented in extremes. It is a very useful situation for understanding ourselves. Each of us has negative traits which we try to cover-up in our public life. Sometimes, we may even develop denial defenses in our EGOS to refute that we have downsides to our PERSONALITY. These shadow strangers appear in our dreams to show us our weaknesses.

Subway station

Being at the terminal of a transportation system (such as the subway) often indicates choices. Places of commotion and confusion often appear in dreams when choices are being confronted in life. Many times, the dream experience is a good place to test various choices with a more open mind than the waking world permits.

The initial question to ask about the subway station is: Do you have the means to ride any train, only some of the trains, or none of the trains?

Who is with you in the subway? Are they deciding which train to ride or are you leading them through the station?

SUPERNATURAL POWERS

If you have supernatural powers in a dream—flying, magic, mind-reading, etc.—it is often a dream of regaining control. Very often, you will be the only one in the dream with these powers and you will use them to work towards a particular end: escape, winning a battle, or rescuing others. Sometimes, these powers extend to or are opposed by others. In this type of case, your mind is tempering your powers with you inability to "fix" your own world completely and individually.

TABOO

One very unusual thing about dreaming is that almost any object, person, or association can seem to project a taboo power. This taboo may be either negative or positive.

A taboo is something that contains intrinsic, potentially dangerous power that may be conjured and directed against oneself or another.

Generally, the object, person, or association is representative of a moral wrong. GUNS, for example, may carry a sense of taboo POWER. So may some magical dream objects. Occasionally, a very common object may have taboo power in your dream because of some experience you have had with it in your waking life.

Many times, the taboo power does not exist in an object, but in a relationship transaction that violates a moral code (such as incest, marital infidelity, or theft). Others times, the symbol of taboo is something shrouded, such as a STRANGER that you instinctively knew not to mess with. All of these are taboo representations.

The key to dream interpretation is to discover why your particular taboo experience was revealed through the particular object or person in question. Dreams often have a peculiar rationale in their storylines. It is a product of childhood MEMORY organization being overlaid with adult reasoning and moral subtlety. Sometimes, the moral subtlety of adulthood is tempered in dreaming by the absolute right and wrong of childhood. Consequently, taboo IMAGERY can crop up almost anywhere in dream life.

These taboo moments should be treated with importance. Many times, our most self-destructive emotional or relationship patterns are seen most clearly in dreams. Your mind may be trying to warn you, through taboo images, to avoid repeating the same mistakes over and over.

TAROT CARDS

Tarot cards have recently received renewed popularity. Often times, dreaming about a psychic reading indicates a desire for a third party to illuminate and validate some big decision(s) you are facing. A contrasting possibility is that you feel as though your decisions are not important and your life is in the hands of fate, outside your personal control. Whether or not you subscribe to psychic practices in waking life is the most important element of discerning the meaning of this dream event.

TEAM SPORTS

Team sports are prevalent in our world and seem to be increasing in popularity and diversity. Dreams of team sports include the dreamer as observer, player, or coach. Many times, it's a dream of WISH-FULFILL-MENT—just wanting to be a sports legend. However, it the coaches and other players seem very familiar to you, or are actually people from facets of your waking life, the dream has more to say.

Most times, the dream is about participation and connectedness to the common goals held by others in your life. "Being a team player" and "getting with the program" are emphasized often in work and FAM-ILY these days. Whichever of the three roles you most identify with determines your self-awareness within the team sport.

Observing from the audience may indicate that you are feeling "off the team" or outside the action. Observing as a player who does not enter the game indicates that you feel others are ambivalent about your skills, or you yourself may be so. Being a player shows your willingness to participate in the game. If you have too many roles on the team or do the work of several players, it may be that you are feeling as though people expect too much from you.

Finally, being the coach is a position of leadership, control, and decision-maker for the success of others. In this case, determining how the team did is important to appreciating the message of this dream.

TEETH

Dreams about teeth and losing teeth are common. Often the dream is troubling, although it does not contain the same fear or ANXIETY as a NIGHTMARE. In the dream, the teeth often are a concern only to the dreamer. Other characters in the dream either do not notice, or do not care, about the loose teeth.

A 19-year-old woman reports:

> *I am in the bedroom combing my hair. A guy comes in and asks me if I am in a relationship. I say no. Then, he asks me out on a date. I say yes. He is about to kiss me and I ask him to hold that thought for a second. I go to freshen up a bit. When I wipe my mouth, my teeth begin falling out! Every one I touch falls out. No bleeding, just*

empty spaces in my mouth. I go back out of the bathroom, concerned,
but the guy doesn't notice. Meanwhile, I'm a wreck.

In waking life, the woman reports feeling conflicted about ending a relationship with a man. She would like to renew it. Potential embarrassment is preventing her from doing so.

Dreams of losing teeth are often dreams of embarrassment or potentially embarrassing situations. The parallel waking experience could be summed up in the phrase "losing face" publicly.

Other possible teeth-loss dreams may come from physical sensations such as grinding your teeth or having particularly sensitive teeth.

Do your teeth get knocked out or do they fall out for no apparent reason?

TELEPHONE

The telephone often appears in dreams as a link between you and other dream characters who are physically inaccessible, but influential on the dream outcome. Many times, you will know who is on the other end of the phone before you pick it up to speak in your dream. The way you connect yourself to others with the dream phone is important. To whom is also important. The phone is often called "the next best thing to being there." Consequently, using the phone in your dream indicates that while a person is influential in you life, they are not as connected with you as perhaps they could be or you would like them to be.

TEMPLE

Temples and spiritual dwellings are common in dreams. This is because many dreams include events of cleansing, preparation, moral judgment, or divine communication. Often times, these dreams occur at times in your life when inner peace is elusive and sought after.

Often, such dreams involve STRANGERS as temple ministers or priests. These ministers will often give clues about what type of temple service is needed and what area of your life is to be effected. They may be presented as all older than you, all of one particular gender, or dressed in particular ways.

If ministers and priests are absent from the temple, that could indicate an inner journey or struggle that needs resolution, versus the outer moral choices illustrated above.

THEFT

Ask anyone who has been a victim of theft and they will undoubtedly tell you how horribly violated they felt by the experience. In early childhood, we learn that to take a toy from another is TABOO. Likewise, having a toy taken away hurts our feelings. However, sneakiness and acts of theft are common dream images. Whether you are the thief or the victim, there are several interpretations to explore.

As a thief, you could be feeling a lack of resources or an unfairness about the distribution of resources. For example, if you dream of stealing essentials—bread, food, items needed to survive the dream environment—you may see yourself as a pauper. In waking, this may play out as behavior that isolates you or leaves you feeling as though you have no choices. However, dreaming of stealing from people you know may reflect a perception that you feel their lives are better than yours, even though you do not perceive them as better people.

As the victim, fear of loss seems to be a possible theme. The suspect list in the dream will help refine this further. If you are the victimized and the stolen items are central, then material loss is creating ANXIETY. However, if the lost items are of secondary importance to the suspect, you may feel as though someone you know is violating or taking

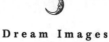

advantage of you. Still, it is important to consider the objects taken and their significance to you. What the objects symbolize for you may indicate the area or life where your BOUNDARIES are being violated and help find solutions to reestablish yourself.

THROWING THINGS
Throwing things is a dream of either removing influences from your life or seeking to reduce the clutter in your life. If you throw things directly at someone, this could also be a dream of ANGER, beating, or power against another.

THUNDER
Sound effects in dreams work much like movie soundtracks. Thunder in dreams may occur in scenes that otherwise preclude any storminess or threatening weather. When this happens, there is often psychological ANXIETY that things in the dream may not be as pleasant as they seem. This dream may occur if your relationships in the dream would have devastating consequences in waking life.

TIDAL WAVE
Dreams of impending disaster generally indicate that the dreamer is feeling out of control. In the case of the tidal wave, this out-of-control feeling is often combined with the need to make a fresh start.

A 16-year-old boy reports dreaming:

> *I am running, trying to get away from a tidal wave before it crashes over me. Finally, I realize it is hopeless. I turn around and let the full impact of the wave crash over me. Remarkably I stand up in spite of the wave's power. When I turn back to the direction I was running, everything—my house, my parents, my car—it's all gone.*

This youth presented numerous complaints at the outset of counseling, all of which revolved around home life and the absence of his father. Upon further inquiry, the youth admitted that he was a drug abuser with sexual identity problems. He desperately wanted a second chance, feeling as though he had undermined his own life.

Often to dream of a catastrophic event is to wish for a catharsis in real life.

See END OF THE WORLD

TIME, TIME RIDDLES

Time and time riddles can be a difficult element of dream interpretation. Since dreams occur in a fantasy-like mindset, there are few controls on how time is perceived. One dream may seem to happen in real time: twenty minutes of events in a given REM cycle. Another dream may occur in a series of edited scenes that happen over the course of days, weeks, years, or an unfathomable period of time. Other dreams still may seem outside of any time constraints whatsoever.

One way to discern elapsed dream time is to simply recall the scenes and then try to identify any chronological changes. Another is to think about numbered items in the dream and associate that number with time periods in your life. If your dream watch says 5:15, this could be the time, the date, or an elapsed time between two ages; in this case, perhaps five and fifteen years old.

These riddles are both frustrating and wonderful. In them are the deeper nuances of dreaming. You may readily observe a cyclical pattern to life that repeats periodically. You may recall when your maturity or self-awareness changed and how long that transition took. Numerous insights are available in these ways.

Sometimes the aspect of time within a dream may affect the

emotional milieu of the dream; a "real time" dream will probably offer a different emotional background than a "scattered time" dream.

TIME TRAVEL

Time travel is a common dream event. There is rarely a time machine involved. Rather, the dream story simply unfolds in another era of time, past or future. These dreams often represent either the romance or hopes we attribute to moments other than our present. You may find that the dream stems from your desire to identify with particular mores of a time period or to influence certain events.

If you spontaneously dream of going backwards in time, it is most likely a dream of romantic WISH-FULFILLMENT. The "good old days" seem to conjure images of heroism, nobility, morality, and social life that, while not altogether accurate, draw our admiration. Often there is a facet of your PERSONALITY that you feel you could more easily tap into as a pioneer, statesman, damsel in distress, or some other stereotypical image of history.

Most times, the time travel is confluent with your particular image of an archetypal dream character. For example, if you are dreaming a warrior/HERO ARCHETYPE, you may personify yourself in the dream as a medieval knight.

TOPAZ

Topaz is the crystal of spiritual wisdom and INTUITION. Often, it is found in dreams of PROBLEM-SOLVING concerning interpersonal relationships.

TORNADO

See END OF THE WORLD

TRAFFIC

Traffic is a fascinating dream image. If traveling is required in a dream, it is often central to resolving the dream story. Consequently, the traffic and whether it cooperates with or hinders the dreamer's achievement is important. Since most everyone encounters traffic everyday, dreams concerning traffic reflect the extent to which your environment cooperates with or hinders your goals.

These dreams may be indications that more patience, more self-assertion, or more creativity is needed to reach your goals. Of course, to dream of traffic can also mean that you were simply stuck in it all that day and you need to work out the frustration in a dream.

Did the traffic cause you to miss an important appointment?

See CARS

TRAINS

Trains are the cross-country transport of antiquity and therefore are often perceived as romantic. Dreams of this nature often reflect a hope for liaison on the part of the dreamer. The dream may unfold with the object of romance as a companion.

The train station, like the SUBWAY STATION, is the place of life choices in the dream.

TRANSFORMATION

Since most people are never completely satisfied with their physical appearance, transformation dreams come to us easily. We all see our ideal selves as in our minds. These ideal selves work into our dreams.

Other times, you may transform into ANIMAL, not human, form. These transformations can have numerous expressions. You may see yourself as needing to assert a particular PERSONALITY attribute. Other times, you may transform in order to disguise yourself. In these dreams, who you are disguising yourself from and why the particular animal is a good choice are interpretive issues.

TRAVEL

Whether it is done by conventional or extraordinary means, travel is a central feature of many dreams. When traveling in a dream, companionship, purpose, and obstacles are central interpretive questions to ask.

Companionship may include known relationships or STRANGERS. Generally, the companionship either helps or hinders progress toward the dream goal. The effect of your companions on your travel should be interpreted metaphorically as a symbol of that person's impact on your life. If you are traveling alone, with only occasional assistance, that too may be a picture of how you experience personal growth and progress through life.

The purpose of travel is an often ambiguous or unclear image in the dream. It feels like you are going with no direct understanding of destination or itinerary. Dreams of this nature often reveal a particular feeling about direction or purpose in life. If there doesn't seem to be a point or a destination in a travel dream, you should consider the possible desire to vacate your current locale for a time. If the destination is clearly defined, then determining what that destiny may mean to you is a good step to take.

Obstacles may correlate with companionship, or come along symbolically apart from companionship. In this case, consider how obstacles are overcome and what resources you use to defeat them, including other persons in the dream.

TREASURE

Searching for treasure is often about adventure and life wisdom as much as it is about a desire for MONEY. You may have very real financial needs that inspire this dream. However, the treasure may be a symbol for wisdom and experience that you seek to acquire in waking life.

To gain insight from this dream, consider the nature of the treasure being sought. Sometimes, the object of the quest is an artifact of historical or cultural significance as opposed to monetary. If you are able to conclude this search by finding the object of your quest, you are probably about to acquire new insights into your life and whatever relationships are symbolized by the treasure hunt.

However, if you spontaneously discover treasure in the midst of a dream story where it would not be expected, another scenario is possible. You may not be fully aware of your opportunities in waking life. Your SUBCONSCIOUS may be saying, "Look, dummy, right at your feet! The answer." Dreams of this nature are not too unusual and should be given close scrutiny. The elusive answer to a problem may be closer than you think.

TRIAL (COURTROOM)

Being on trial is a common dream event, although it sometimes gets acted out in uncommon ways. Our society is oriented towards PROBLEM-SOLVING through litigation. The result is that lawsuits have become the new lottery of our era.

Being tried for your actions in dreams can be a non-sense sort of dream insofar as you may be tried for something against which there are no laws. In addition, the roles of the court characters may be filled by friends, co-workers, a spouse, SIBLINGS or other FAMILY members.

In dreams of this case, you may FEAR that your life is being over-scrutinized in waking. There may be secrets that you are keeping deep within the SUBCONSCIOUS that need to be processed.

If you are in one of the legal roles in your dream it is likely that you feel a need to protect yourself. This may be protection from the influences or dishonest conduct of others, or a general feeling that people are not leveling with you. If you are defending another, it may be that you feel life is taking advantage of you at some level. Your defendant will be a clue as to how this is occurring.

Where is the trial taking place—is it in a normal courtroom, or perhaps in your office or home?

Do you get the sense that you have been wrongly accused of something? Do you feel that you will certainly be found guilty of something you know you did?

UGLINESS

In dreams, your body image can be a topic of concern personally or among the other dream characters. Only occasionally do these concerns accurately reflect actual physical attributes. More often, dreams of this nature may indicate paranoia about what others think of you. The central interpretive question is whether you conclude your own ugliness or whether others impose it on you.

If you conclude your own ugliness, is this due to a particular change, such as being pregnant? In pregnancy, you may dream that you are being considered overweight by yourself or others.

Other changes that may influence your body image include a shift in physical or moral behavior, such as smoking, drinking, using drugs, becoming sexually active, or participating in sexual experiences you once considered TABOO.

This dream is worth serious consideration as how we feel about our bodies is often a significant part of how we feel about ourselves overall as a person. If you are having RECURRING dreams of personal ugliness, then counseling for self-esteem or eating disorders may be worth considering.

UNDERWATER

The great thing about dreams is that you can live anywhere. Being underwater can be a potentially threatening experience, as with drowning. However, it can just be the place you are, hanging out with the other dream characters.

Dreams of this nature may be WISH-FULFILLMENT, especially if you have an affinity for OCEAN life at some level. It may also be a desire for ESCAPE from the more mundane experiences of land-locked living.

Perhaps the most interesting effect of underwater dreams is when the appearance of the dream environment seems as if it is underwater even when it is not. People may be moving in slow motion, you may feel particularly buoyant, or there may be aquatic life intermingled with the above-water scenery. In dreams of this type, the dreamer may be feeling a need to escape or slow down the pace of life in order to observe the circumstances more accurately.

If you have been underwater in a dream, do you recall feeling like it was a "normal" environment for you, or were you nervous in the situation?

See WATER

UNIFORMS

Dreaming of uniforms is most often a dream of self-awareness. Conformity through clothing is one of the unspoken rules of CULTURE and we often perceive parts of our wardrobes as our "uniform" for particular roles we fill in life. In dreams of uniforms, it does not matter if the uniform is officially recognized or simply identical clothing on numerous persons.

If you are in uniform, and there are others dressed the same way, consider who is with you in the dream and what camaraderie you share with them. It may be that you are recalling a satisfying tenure in military service, employment, or identity with a particular group. If you are in uniform and others are not, it may reflect a feeling that you perceive yourself as more loyal than others.

A 24-year-old man reports dreaming:

> *I am in the Navy. They have not trained me. I report to my ship with my only uniform, which is summer whites. Everyone around me is in dress blues. Nothing on the ship goes right.*

This dreamer, a college student, was contemplating an officer's commission in the navy. He was excited, but hedging his commitment. This dream reflected those concerns and warned him to examine the situation more closely.

Uniforms can also be a symbol of authority. Note the person wearing a uniform in your dream. Was it a logical situation for that person to be wearing a uniform?

URINATION

In the modesty of the human race, elimination of body waste is a task that we often prefer not to share with others. We either feel that our privacy is being invaded, or that another is forcing themselves on us. This often reflects not only the base nature of the act, but also the genital exposure that accompanies it.

A 25-year-old student reports dreaming:

I am sitting in my apartment. One of my instructors enters and urinates in my kitchen. He makes it a point to expose himself to me prior to leaving.

Not surprisingly, this student felt as though the instructor violated not just his free time, but also his person. Upon further questioning, the student revealed feelings of underlying aggression, as well. The student feared the teacher could willfully affront the student for little cause, simply by "pissing on" a term paper with an unwarranted "D" grade, for example. The message of the dream seems to include a sense that the student felt powerless to prevent the intrusion.

Urination is a symbol for territorial disputes. It is also a signal of dominance.

Who is taking part in this activity in your dream? Where is it occurring and why?

If someone other than yourself is doing the urinating, do you confront them, keep quiet, or ESCAPE?

VICTIMIZED IN A DREAM

The awareness of crime in our society is creating sensitivity about the potential victimization we all face. Dreams of being victimized are common and on the increase.

You can be victimized by almost anything in a dream: beating, RAPE, THEFT, MURDER, a monetary swindle, an abusive SIBLING, parent, spouse, partner, object . . . anything. Each means of being victimized carries with it certain explicit, as well as subtle, implications.

The primary considerations are how vulnerable a position were you in prior to the victimization occurring, and who was the aggressor.

Did a relationship that generated a sense of security suddenly turn evil?

Was it a random act of violence committed by a STRANGER?

Did you observe or have the feeling that the aggressor knew you or that you were somehow connected with them?

After these considerations are elaborated, turn inquiry to the specific crime and the implications of it.

VIOLENCE

In dreams, facets of PERSONALITY that never get displayed in waking life can become quite animated. Nowhere is this more apparent than with violent behavior. The violence may be justified or random, but it is often extremely graphic. It is so graphic, in fact, that you should understand that this is normal—albeit disturbing—and that its presence is almost always an exaggeration of another point.

Violence can be an off-shoot of heroic behavior, especially in rescuing dreams. Terrorism in the news has made all of us aware that the enemies can be in our midst. KIDNAPPING dreams, ESCAPE dreams, and protecting dreams are other versions of this type of violence.

Violence may come unexpectedly, as well (suddenly, you are just stomping some poor guy's head with no apparent provocation). Often these dreams deal with repressed ANGER towards authority figures. While wanting to become physically aggressive toward others is a common desire, it should never be acted on in waking life, and it very rarely is. However, the dream releases the anger for you. If you have RECURRING dreams of this nature, you may want to consider a mediated session with the object of your anger; or re-arrange your circumstances.

If you are the aggressor, does the violence frighten you or make you feel powerful?

If you are the witness to violence, do you feel ambivalent to it or does it somehow affect you?

VOMITING

Vomiting is a difficult and humiliating experience for many people, especially children. In dreaming, in may occur it the midst of almost any kind of dream. While it is often associated with illness in waking life, it is appears in dreaming when our lives are most out of control. Most likely, this phenomenon has to do with the relationship between vomiting and nausea, or other common ill feelings in the gut.

A woman in her early forties reports dreaming:

> *I am on a playground. I am a child, about eight years old. The turntable ride is going faster and faster. I am enjoying it. A man I don't recognize is pushing it. He stops and walks away. I vomit on my yellow dress and am very sad.*

This dream is fascinating for numerous reasons. First, the dreamer imagines herself in an earlier stage of life. This is an indication that her memories of childhood will be essential to interpreting the dream. In the dream, a man walks away and she vomits. The dress turns out to be significant because it is a dress she was given the summer her parents divorced.

In her waking life this dreamer was just finishing what she had called the "infertility merry-go-round." She and her husband had been deeply hurt and disappointed by the experience of not being able to give birth. They felt out of control of their own lives. The vomiting dream seemed to stem from ANXIETY about her future in a potentially childless household.

VULNERABILITY

Vulnerability has numerous expressions in dreaming. Many times, dreams will begin with symbols concerning the dreamer in relationship to other dream characters. The symbols usually show the dreamer as being vulnerable to, in power over, intimate with, or estranged from other dream characters.

Situations in which the dreamer is vulnerable include dreaming of being ASLEEP, being only partially clothed, being unable to communicate, or being physically limited through handicap or restraint. Dreams of vulnerability often resolve as rescue or VICTIMIZATION dreams.

Because your person (either physical or spiritual) is at risk in dreams of vulnerability, the exchanges and conclusion of this dream indicate much about your life and how you see it. You may be wanting someone to come along and make things right, or experiencing a self-destructive pattern that needs resolution. This dream can often open your waking mind to ways out of the position that has you in a subservient or defensive posture.

When feelings of vulnerability arose in your dream, where were you? Did you try to ESCAPE or did someone try to protect you?

VULTURE

This is the ultimate scavenger. If you dream about a vulture, it may be that you are feeling like a bottom feeder or that others are picking your bones clean. It is seldom a comforting dream or herald of good prospects for the future.

A vulture appearing in your dream can also be symbolic of loneliness.

Was the vulture eating or hovering over the feast of other ANIMALS? What was it eating?

WALKING

You may be trying to slow down your pace or lack the means to make speedy progress. Walking is a dichotomous symbol in that it can be both frustrating and relaxing to walk.

Walking is much more of a discovery-oriented JOURNEY than driving, FLYING, or other modes of transit. When walking, you are forced to experience your environment in much more detail since you are moving through it so slowly. To walk in a dream, especially if your perceived destination is far off, may indicate that you are missing some of the pleasure life has to offer by fixating on destinations, rather than on journeys.

In order to see the interpretive value of the walking, it must be determined why walking is the preferred mode of transit.

Are there other dream characters involved in walking, marching, or hiking? Are you trying to walk in an environment that is normally traveled by CAR?

WALLS

In psychoanalytic technique, walls are generally held to be a symbol of the male PERSONALITY, with a focus on power. This thinking seems to stem from the impressions a young child would have of dominant male power in the home (which is a "fortress" surrounded by walls and dominated by the patriarch). In dreams, many people encounter walls as a random barrier and/or a projection of power.

In your dream, do you come upon a wall in your travels, or do you find yourself immediately surrounded by walls?

Do you try to scale the wall, find its end, or simply ignore it?

WATER

Water is central to the human story. Whether it is the deep, fresh lake, the river that brings life, or the ocean that must claim her dead, water is both friend and enemy at once. When dreams contain this powerful image in any of its forms, understanding the role of the water is essential.

Water is a strong symbol in dreams because so often it is the exclamation point of the feelings in the dream. If other objects in a dream are relaxing, a bubbling brook through a meadow is more relaxing. If some symbols generate feelings of fear or ANXIETY, the tumultuous ocean creates the most anxiety. Water has symbolic, archetypal meaning in that it either provides life, or harbors mystery and danger. This is a reflection of our human experiences with water.

In early human history, the hunter-gatherers quickly learned that water was the central ingredient of life. (We die of thirst much more quickly than we starve.) More importantly, to know where the water was meant knowing where the FOOD was. However, as commerce expanded water became a necessary evil that harbored unknown dangers. Water TRAVEL was dangerous and uncertain as sea creatures, storms, and rough seas claimed numerous voyagers. Polluted water affected livestock and spread disease.

To emphasize the positive, water is often a symbol of new life, refreshment, and vigor. Water in manageable amounts or controlled settings almost always conveys this sentiment to the dreamer. Controlled water is the key.

If a dream contains a lake, is the entire shoreline visible and likely attainable?

If a river or creek is dreamed of, is it within its banks and apparently traversable by usual means? These are all examples of controlled water.

Water presented in this way is often indicative of renewal. For example, while traveling and growing weary, the dreamer suddenly happens upon a creek. Refreshment for the journey is close at hand.

Perhaps a dreamer is out on a BOAT, moving over the water gently. One should anticipate a season of respite or sabbatical in life, or perhaps create an opportunity such as this intentionally.

Uncontrolled water will often create a sense of unease for a dreamer. Raging rivers, rapids, and lakes without borders often reflect being out of control of one's circumstances. Still deep water, while sometimes refreshing, may also create unease. This is because of the murkiness or uncertainty of what lies below the surface.

One exception to the generalities listed above is water faucets. In a dream, it is important to recognize if the dreamer or another is controlling the faucet and whether this is done to effect the comfort or discomfort of the dreamer. If the dreamer is controlling the faucet ineffectively, the assumption may be made that the dreamer feels out of control or unable to master what should be apparently simple circumstances (or, what's worse, perhaps there is no water to be had). If another controls the faucet, one may conclude that the dreamer feels his circumstances, for good or ill, are dependent on the whimsy of another. This whimsy may reflect either greater discomfort or comfort, whether it is an unpredictable boss, lover, or other significant relationship.

WEATHER

Dreams can have very unique weather. It may be sunny and thundering, or pouring rain everywhere except for where you are standing. Weather images in dreams often reflect your feelings about your environment. You may view the world as contrary to your goals; thus a dream would have bad weather in it. On the contrary, pleasant dreams or dreams at a time when life is going well usually feature good weather. The weather in dreams is generally not as significant as other images unless it is somehow aberrant from normal, waking world weather.

Did the weather in your dream prevent something good from happening, such as a planned event?

WEDDING CEREMONY

Obviously, one would want to examine possible TRIGGER EVENTS, such as other weddings in waking life, before too much interpretive work goes into this dream. This dream may be simple WISH-FULFILL-MENT or personal anticipation. However, if you aren't in the midst of such activities, other scenarios may exist.

Initially, it is worth examining other commitments in your life.

Are you becoming over-committed, or on the brink of making a major commitment to an employer, romantic partner, or other relationship? This dream may be commenting on how appropriate the commitment is for you. If the wedding goes well, you may see yourself as entering a sound union. If the wedding is a catastrophe, or your role in it is unclear, you may need to reexamine your commitments.

WHITE HAIR

White-haired characters are archetypal figures of wisdom in most cases. This includes most major theorists' and cultural IMAGERY. It is one of the few dream symbols that seems universal.

A 42-year-old woman reports dreaming:

> *Three old women enter my room to tell me Methuselah (a legendary, 969-year-old man of great wisdom) is coming to see me. I am interested, but fall asleep. They wake me later and scold me, telling me I missed him. I am crushed, because I've always been fascinated with Methuselah.*

In this dream, the old women have particular knowledge about an ancient, wise figure that they offer to share. However, the dreamer does not fulfill her obligation to the knowledge that was offered to her, and so it went unreceived. She felt responsible for missing the chance to gain wisdom by giving in to laziness.

WILD ANIMALS

Wild animals may reflect an area of our lives that is out of control. Many animals have stereotypical meanings that can tell more of their presence. Think of what the wild animal means to you in waking life to understand the reason for its presence in your dream.

Wild animals that are domesticated in dreams may not be animal dreams, but rather dreams of interpersonal success or self-discipline. Many times, making peace with animals is a sign of harmony in our lives and hope for smooth interpersonal relationships.

Is a wild animal posing a threat to you in the dream or do you have it under your influence?

WINDOWS

Windows often show a world that is possible, but not being directly experienced. The windows can be tricky, because they can reveal something we cannot experience directly. This can infer frustration, protection, or illusion in the dream. If dreaming of confinement, the window may expose a very desirable person or setting that we cannot experience directly. This is a common event in life.

If the environment outside the window looks hostile, and you can get to the other side of the window to experience it, you may find you have been tricked. Windows in dreams sometimes show one thing, but the actual experience is something quite different. It may be time for you to overcome your ANXIETY and experience life directly rather than watching it go by. If the converse is true, and a pastoral window scene yields a troubled reality, you may feel as though life is deceptive in some area.

The window may be a passage from this world to others. Dreams of this nature are common among those who pursue astral projection or OUT-OF-BODY EXPERIENCES. Windows of this kind may be revealing potential realities for you to experience.

Did you open a window in your dream, walk by one without looking, or close a window?

Were the images on the other side of the window clear or murky?

WITCH/WARLOCK

Encountering persons with SUPERNATURAL POWERS, or becoming those persons ourselves, is a common dream image. In the case of occult power dreams, there may be unique elements of personal projection of will power by you upon others or by others against you. Who is the occult PERSONALITY, you or someone else?

How these powers are projected is important. If they are projected by you onto others, you may feel as though they have an unfair advantage and you want to level the playing field. Another version of this dream is that you may want others to appreciate your influence more. A third option is that you have repressed ANGER towards another. Still another possibility is that you may want someone to become romantically attracted to you. You may be projecting the power onto a STRANGER, who is likely a representation of someone else in your life or a representation of a part of yourself.

If another is projecting power on you, it is likely that you believe others are pulling the strings in your life or are plotting against you.

If you or another are trying to wield witchlike powers, is the spell successful or thwarted?

WOLF

The wolf is often a symbol of loneliness or predator behavior in dreams. If you dream of a wolf, you are probably in a situation where you lack friendship or companionship. Another scenario may be that you feel others are preying on you, or you are preying upon others for personal gain.

Does the wolf appear close up and snarling, or do you notice it far off at bay?

WRINKLED SKIN

According to African legend, death entered the world in the following way:

> *Long ago, people were able to shed their skins, like a snake. Every-one did this and lived forever, renewing their youth. One time, a woman forgot that she should do this and put her old skin back on, and death came into the world.*

Dreams of wrinkled skin may be troubling because they create images of age and death. You may feel as though you are wasting your time in waking life and your SUBCONSCIOUS is reminding you that life is short. Another version of the wrinkled skin dream is accelerated aging, where your skin seems to visibly shrink or wrinkle in minutes. This dream may be revealing how you feel about your progress towards your life goals. You aren't getting any younger, after all.

These dreams can be troubling, but should not be. Dreams of this nature often are your mind's way of saying, "Hey, it's time for something new," and encouraging you to take steps in a new direction. Turn in your old hat for a new one.

Are you resisting the maturing process at some level?

Do you feel as though others are preventing you from attaining the stature or wisdom of your age?

Are you experiencing a rebirth or removal of "old" limitations?

X-RAYS

As truly benign as it sounds, most X-ray dreams seem to reflect a desire for inner knowledge concerning the dreamer or someone with whom the dreamer has an ongoing relationship. We often think that life would be better if we knew what made others tick. X-ray dreams often reveal the desire to know more of the inner self.

Another scenario is medical. If you have not been feeling well lately, but do not seem genuinely sick, you may dream of X-rays in a desire to resolve uneasiness about your health. Many times, our minds will go searching for solutions to waking problems through dreams. In the case of health, this would mean typical medical associations.

YOGA

If yoga is a feature of your waking life, then dreams of it usually do not have substantial interpretative content—they are merely replays of normal events. However, if you are not a yoga practitioner in waking life, this dream may indicate a desire for more mind-body balance or harmony with the universe. Or, it could indicate some sort of reference to a convoluted situation in your life.

ZEBRA

Dreams of zebras often reflect a sense of changeability in your waking life. You may see yourself as having two (or more) distinct identities that compete for predominance in your behavior, morals, and other life roles. This is especially true for persons who struggle with workplaces that demand questionable ethical practices; or those who are unfaithful to others.

ZIPPER

Zippers are a convenient, yet potentially frustrating or painful, invention of the fashion world. Dreaming of zippers is often dreaming of efficiency, convenience, or maintaining a well-groomed personal appearance. However, if the zipper is stuck, it can become a dream of being thwarted, feeling incompetent, and lacking PROBLEM-SOLVING resources.

ZODIAC

The zodiac may come into dreams in numerous ways. If you are a fan of astrology in waking life, dreams of the zodiac often reflect your desire for fuller understanding of the world.

Each sign, such as Cancer, Leo, and Pisces, has stereotypical meaning to illustrate various facets of life and PERSONALITY traits. Think about the zodiac symbol and the gems, NUMBERS, and other elements associated with it.

When dreams of reading astrology occur, you are often trying to categorize events of your life according to your understanding of what will be best for you.

Do you come across signs of the zodiac on your own in the dream or are they presented to you by someone else? Who is that person? If it's a STRANGER, try to figure out who in your life they best represent.

ZOO

Zoo dreams are often similar to MUSEUM dreams. The actual content of the zoo may be true to life, or it may contain some nonsense inhabitants such as co-workers, past romantic interests, or RELATIVES. You may also be a display, rather than an observer.

If others are on display, you may feel as though these people need to be confined or that they draw too much attention to themselves. If you are on display, you may feel that your life is somehow "abnormal" and on display for others to observe and critique.

Do you feel as though others keep you "on-display" or "caged-in"? Perhaps you are uncomfortable with a particular sense of notoriety you have attained.

Still, a dream that takes place in a zoo may have to do with ecological concerns, memories of childhood, or a sense of adventure.

book 3

◆

Theories and Theorists

I believe it to be true that dreams
are the true interpreters of our inclinations,
but there is art required to sort and understand them.

—Montaigne

Dreams have confounded minds for seventy centuries, give or take a few years. The results have divided the intellectual community into two camps. The first, and somewhat less interesting camp, are the proponents of the purely physiological study of dreams. For these scientists, a dream is a purely electrical event that is a necessary and universal part of sleep; a way for the brain to release excess energy, and nothing more. Thanks to the development of the EEG, scientists can determine exactly what the brain is doing while a person is asleep, and can say exactly when and how intensely a subject is dreaming. They mark their charts with scribbly lines and say, unequivocally, "That there is a dream." Any meaning you wish to ascribe to the images that result from the random electrical activity, this camp would say, is hogwash.

This camp also makes an intriguing, although unprovable, assumption. In a science-based world, we often assume that knowing where a thing originates, what it is made of, and how to predict its occurrence is the same as understanding the value of it. The argument seems to be that since dreams are identifiable physiologically, their value can then be defined in exclusively quantitative, medical terms. That's what the physiological camp says. . . .

Then, there's everybody else.

Such neglect for the soul value of dreaming is disconcerting to the second camp of dream study, which consists of anyone who believes their dreams have meaning and relevance to their waking life (including such famous names as FREUD, JUNG, and ADLER). Undoubtedly, the medical findings of sleep research are valuable and necessary. However, purely quantitative research often ignores the possibility that dreaming is an important qualitative mode of intrapersonal communication. When we are dreaming, and because of dreams, we intuitively discern new ideas of ourselves and our circumstances in the world.

Ultimately, the interpretation of dream images belongs to the dreamer. One may dismiss their own dreams as static energy being released in the form of nonsense images, or one may consider the possible connection between the appearance of those images and waking life. Since dream images come out of and speak to the context of a person's life—their history, circumstances, and emotions—it can be no other way.

Needless to say, seventy centuries of discussion within this second camp has resulted in many different ideas about dream study from which to seek guidance. The points of view include CULTURE,

RELIGION, psychoanalysis, spirituality, occult, and even science (but not that first camp of scientists mentioned above!).

The most critical skill to develop in dream interpretation is recognizing the central images, emotions, and events in the dream, and discarding the "wrapping." This holds true to any theory you may employ for any dream. Sometimes traumatic dream events are not oracles of doom, but psychological problem-solving at a deep level. Likewise, nonsensical transactions can be SUBCONSCIOUS similes for archetypal struggles.

Once you've determined the key elements in your dream, it's time to start analyzing. Remember, in almost every dream you have, there are elements from many different schools of interpretation that can be useful. So keep an open mind, and have fun!

ARCHETYPE

An archetype is an idea or concept that has become innate to humans as a result of past human experience and which affects our perception of the world today. Basically, human evolution has been shaped by numerous forms of self-awareness. These forms sprang from the actions of real life people (example: Ulysses is an archetype of the "HERO.")

CARL JUNG popularized this approach to psychology. He theorized fourteen self-aware conditions of the person in the world. By using studies from world RELIGIONS and literature, he would then illustrate nuances regarding each unique circumstance of these archetypal conditions. The importance of these archetypes is that each one can influence behavior and self-perception of how to act. The result is that the archetype impinges on the autonomy of the self.

Many psychologists have continued to use archetypal work as a means of understanding neurosis and unlocking the potential of the psyche to continue growth. Literature for counseling of this kind includes texts from mythology, RELIGION, and parables.

ADLER, ALFRED (1870–1937)

Adler represents another school of psychological thought that branched out from FREUD'S work through the "Wednesday Night Club." Adler was fourteen years junior to Freud, born in 1870 in Vienna, Austria. He was the son of an unsuccessful merchant, and the poverty of his upbringing affected his political positioning, as well as his PERSONALITY theory. Like Freud, he was raised in a Jewish home and, also like Freud, never developed an elective affinity for the Jewish faith.

Adler was raised in Vienna and became part of Freud's circle of professional mentoring for several years. Although he never enjoyed the same collegiality as JUNG did with Freud, he was a respected contributor. However, like Jung, he had problems with Freud's commitment to regressive sexuality as a means of interpreting personality.

For Adler, involvement in early socialist movements seemed to have influenced his theory of personality and, consequently, dreams. Adler held that the development of personality was a reflection of a "will towards power." Dreams were not regressive visions of mental antiquities, but rather forward-thinking projections. The goal of dreaming was not to use the past to define the self in the present, but rather to solve problems in the intrapersonal and interpersonal worlds of the present and future.

Personality, for Adler, was the interaction of the autonomous self with the autonomous world. Sleep was an extension of the waking activity, including aspirations. Therefore, the symbols of dreaming were given not to disguise, but to express the thoughts and feelings of the personality. Dream interpretation was a tool of social adjustment rather than SUBCONSCIOUS impulse—it was, for him, a very practical exercise.

Adler had trouble maintaining notoriety after his departure from Freud. Although his work is now widely regarded, he died in relative obscurity in Scotland in 1937.

AMORALITY IN DREAMS

Often, the dreamer becomes a participant in an action that he or she finds morally repugnant. In fact, these are the dreams we most often wrestle with since they exist outside the comfort zones of our PERSONALITY. There can be many causes for this type of dream behavior.

Freud theorized that the ID is an amoral facet of the personality—it is driven only by pleasure and aggression impulses and lacks any governance over potentially bad consequences of its desires. The wishes to express ANGER, to overpower, to make threats, or to experience gratification are the only concerns of the id. Morality is left for the SUPEREGO and EGO to negotiate over the protestation of the base drives of the id. The id is practically the living definition of amorality.

Many times, especially in dreams of RESCUE, romance, ESCAPE, VIOLENCE, anger, or SEX, our dream images are very explicit. These explicit images can be quite troubling. Yet, within these dreams are the most powerful SUBCONSCIOUS expressions of what we desire from life.

AMPLIFICATION

Amplification is the theory that you can take images from your dream and expand on them—using similar images from literature, RELIGION, and CULTURE—to encourage further explanation and extract more meaning for the individual.

This highly practical technique of dream interpretation is JUNG'S. The purpose is to use various nuances to create clarity of the self.

ANCIENT DREAM INTERPRETERS

There has been interest in the meaning of dreams as long as there has been an awareness of dreaming as a human experience. The interpretation of dreams has been the business of philosophy and religion for nearly forty centuries prior to the present era. Whether spiritual or rational methods were used was often a function of where the seat of global POWER was located. For example, during the reigns of Egypt and Persia, dreams were religious material, interpreted by religious structures structures and dignitaries. In classical Greece, dreams were philosophical material, interpreted through the Pantheon (as all Greek thought was).

Persia and Egypt represent the earliest accounts of dream interpretation and narrative. The *Epic of Gilgamesh* (Mesopotamia, 3,000 B.C., the world's oldest narrative tale) and the tombs of the Egyptian pharoahs include explanations of the origin, incubation, and meaning of dreams. In these accounts, the similarities revolve around dreams as divine revelation—the gods revealed their favor or judgement through dream content. In Egypt, dreams were often perceived as opposites of actual reality—good dreams were bad omens, and vice versa. Interpretation was the business of priests who would direct sacrifices to fulfill a promising dream, or forestall the onset of bad omens revealed in dreams.

The Greeks began to influence dream interpretation around the fifth century B.C. The problem encountered by Greek thinkers such as Plato and Aristotle was the challenge presented by irrational dreams that conflicted with the rational nature of their Pantheon of gods. As such, some dreams were attributed to the gods while others were considered the nonsense expression of depraved human minds. Religion was influential inasmuch as TEMPLE priests ministering in the name of Hypnos (the god of sleep) would elicit sacrifices from dreamers to incubate favorable dreams. Morpheus would then negotiate communication from the gods through the incubated dreams of the temple.

The influence of these earliest interpreters of the meaning of the human experience continues to be important. Plato's theories show up, albeit greatly revised versions thereof, in JUNG. Egypt and Persia have continued to influence many of the present-day "new age" dream thinkers. Because dreaming has been viewed as meaningful to the human story for so long, we must consider seriously the foundations that were carefully and thoughtfully constructed by the earliest ancestors of the human FAMILY.

BOSS, MEDARD

Naturally, it should not be forgotten that no new dream theory could ever have seen the light of day had it not been preceded by the decisive, concrete observations of Freud, Adler, and Jung. Yet the dream theories of these pioneers led us astray. . . .

Thus Medard Boss, a Swiss existentialist, attempted to set a new course for contemporary dream theory. His book *I Dreamt Last Night* challenges us not to make our dreams mean something, but to make ourselves mean something because of our dreams. His basic theory is that dreaming is equally real to what is generally considered "reality."

Existentialism is a big word for a concept which is not terribly difficult. Basically, existentialism addresses the question, "Who in the world are you?" The complexity comes from the realization that plumbing the depths of human contemplation—which this question seems to ask you—is risky business.

A possible answer for this existentialism question is, "Three dollars worth of chemicals, seventeen liters of water, and a heartbeat. How much more is there?" Boss and his entourage would be inclined to answer that question with something like, "Since you are aware of yourself, there is more. Namely, the soul."

Yet this answer would be confounding to FREUD and many other dream analysts. Freud, JUNG, and others have wanted to somehow validate and quantify the science of psychology. Basically, they'd say that even the SUBCONSCIOUS, although repressed, is logical. Boss sets his bets directly against this sort of scientific positivism because he'd have little to do with such a constrained view of the self.

In the typical world of science, the observable stuff counts the most. We live in a world of objects, after all. These objects tell us things we need to know about our world. We are helped to understand ourselves by the objects around us. Thus reactions to our world (including dreams) are effects, not causes.

In Boss's world, the being of a person in the world counts most. How we feel about objects—not the objects themselves—count the most. Reality is a veiled experience that is at times convoluted by the objects that press into our awareness. Dreams, because they so directly impact our self-awareness, are real causes of how we address the world.

Think of it this way:

Sit at your desk. You see your books, pens, and envelopes. They are right there in front of you and they do not rely on you as such. They are simply there. You can touch these things and pick them up, but still, they exist apart from you.

Now consider that you are dreaming about your desk (surely it is not farfetched to dream about such a common yet important thing in your life). Now, in your dream, again you see your books, pens, and envelopes. They are right in front of you, but their presence feels different than it did when you were awake at your desk, doesn't it? You get the sensation that these things, while being somehow separate from you, are actually a part of you—a part of your mind. You can manipulate them in much greater ways than those of your waking experience;

however, this isn't about having power over these objects. It's more about communion with them. In a dream, everything is one.

This illustration best describes Boss's theory of dream importance and evaluation. Boss is not interested in searching for some possible cause of the dream, he simply wants to appreciate the dream in itself. It is a radically different way to approach the phenomenon of dreams. He would contend, "Because I dream, I can know meaning in myself."

Boss is interested in learning how to experience dreams as a mode of being human. When we dream, we often feel ourselves to be mentally awake and aware, even though we are ASLEEP. Thus the self—as being aware in the world—is as much awake in a dream as in the office, school, home, or on the highway. Relationship transactions and our awareness of them is also as real in either condition. Upon waking, we may feel particularly happy or disappointed that dreamed scenarios cannot be experienced with others as they were within ourselves, but the reality is not lessened.

Thus, existential dream interpretation moves dream interpretation away from what dreams mean about us, and into what we can mean because of our dreams. We are constantly confronted with the reality that we have been thrown into this world under circumstances that are beyond our control. However, despite the world that functions autonomously from us, we may be aware of our potential in the world.

COMPENSATION

Compensation is a function of dreaming within the economy of the mind. Your life is filled with pleasures and threats that you consciously deny yourself as well as limitations you impose on yourself in many areas. The result is that the self-aware, waking EGO struggles with how to integrate numerous unresolved desires of the personality.

Dreams can compensate for this disunity by drawing on universal ARCHETYPES of being to attempt integration of waking life desires into dreams. So as your ego and SUPEREGO withhold pleasurable pursuits from your waking world, your UNCONSCIOUS can compensate by indulging these things in the dream world.

Jung held that all dreams, at some level, were compensatory for waking ego deficiencies or interruptions.

CONDENSATION

The definition of condensation we are most familiar with is this: the moisture found on a glass of lemonade on a hot summer day. In this phenomenon, the presence of the cold glass draws water molecules out of the surrounding air and causes the glass to "sweat." Psychologically, FREUD theorized, the same thing can happen in our minds.

While dreaming, we often see a collection of symbols that do not logically fit together. However they seem to have sufficient unity to all show up in the same dream. The reason for this is condensation. Basically, an image becomes symbolic due to emotions or associations surrounding that object in waking life.

Freud records a dream of a woman. In the dream there is a pair of may-beetles. The time of year was May, but the woman had also been married in May. Consequently, Freud discerned that the beetles were a condensation image of this woman's marriage.

CONTEMPORARY DREAM INTERPRETERS

The history of dream interpretation has swung on a broad pendulum of thought. The initial work was religious, occasionally couched in the philosophy of classical thought. This domination extended through the nineteenth century, when the human sciences emerged. Most recently, a new spirituality and self-awareness—part transcendent, part psychology, and part existential philosophy—has emerged. This advent, most notable in this country in the post-1960s era, offers some of the most interesting insight into the human potential discovered through dreaming.

Carlos Castaneda, a student of Native American and Mexican shamanism, has written extensively on dreams as a potential, or even co-equally true, reality. His work, *The Art of Dreaming,* includes extensive dialogue on the dreaming process. He says that dream content is an astral level of reality that serves to locate energy-producing points (or personal empowerment) for this common reality of the waking world.

Gayle Delaney, a Ph.D. from Princeton University, is more "clinical" in terms of traditional Western thought, but recognizes a mind potential in dreaming that she believes can have an expansive effect on our waking lives. Her work, *Living Your Dreams,* is a guide to dream creation, incubation, and interpretation. Not surprisingly, her work reminds one of spiritual meditation and a nearly "prayer-like" experience of preparation, followed by a psychological interview and evaluation of dream content.

David Fontana, a lecturer in Wales and Portugal, emphasizes teaching oneself to dream as a means of gaining larger access to the mind. Clinically, humans have been evaluated as using only 10–20% of brain capacity. Perhaps his book, *The Secret Language of Dreams,* can lead a person to access larger perceptions and interpretations of reality.

These new trends in dream interpretation share the common conviction that dreaming may impact positively on waking conditions. Other titles, such as *Sensual Dreaming* and *Mutual Dreaming,* indicate that linking our waking and dreaming lives will clarify and strengthen relationship potential. These relationships may include self-awareness, work, friendship, and romantic interests. There are many other contemporary writers and students of this sort of new-age dream interpretation.

DISPLACEMENT

Displacement is the phenomenon whereby the SUBCONSCIOUS introduces a dream character to take the place of an actual person from a relationship in the dreamer's waking life. In dreams, relationships are often displaced this way to prevent trauma. If you have a serious problem to resolve with someone in your life, your dream world may present this person as someone else and then allow you to act out your aggression on this representative character. This way, if you are sick and tired of your boss's intrusions into your desk, for example, your boss will turn up in your dream as another character who you end up bludgeoning with a staple gun. No harm, no foul—thanks to displacement.

One example that FREUD often referred to was the presence of famous people, especially politically powerful ones, to represent parents in a dream. However, almost any displacement scenario is imaginable. These displacements often temper the blind amorality of the EGO towards objects of sexual desire or anger. They may also transpose our WISH-FULFILLMENT projections from inappropriate to more appropriate objects.

ECONOMIC PERSONALITY THEORY

A theory, first articulated by FREUD, that PERSONALITY attributes followed economic theory. It has nothing to do with MONEY, per se, but rather is similar to the nature of economic transactions.

Basically, personality is the product of tensions expressed and repressed within the self. The job of the EGO is to manage these tensions in such a way as to maximize productivity and minimize conflict. When operating in a healthy environment, this economy minimizes neuroses. The economy is affected by supply and demand of various ANGER and pleasure impulses as guided by the ego. So, if a person can manage to manage their impulses well, they will have less neuroses and will be stay "out of the (emotional) red," so to speak.

FREE ASSOCIATION

In order to understand the relationships between dream symbols and waking life, a technique called *free association* can be useful. Often, this is caricatured by the psychiatrist who says to the patient, "I'm going to say a word, and I want you to tell me the first thing that pops into your head." This is actually a fairly useful psychological technique.

The intent is for someone to draw relationships between the internal images and themes of the mind and the external world of relationships and objects in which the dreamer lives. This is where the creativity is so important. Sometimes you need to plow around the field of MEMORY a good long while to find the SUBCONSCIOUS associations with the waking events and memories.

This theory of interpretation applies to dreams because our subconscious will say something out loud while the dream is happening. This is the image we wake up with that makes us feel like the dream meant something. But then we have to begin the free association process to find links between what was said out loud and the meanings and memories associated with that statement. In these associations, we become more aware of relationships between waking and sleeping life.

FREUD, SIGMUND (1856–1939)
His Life

Sigmund Freud is arguably the founder of psychotherapy. Much of what we commonly know about psychotherapy, dreams, and personal insight came from the initiative of Sigmund Freud. He invented and brought understanding to personal psychoanalytic theory. While not all of his work received wide attention during his life—and some continues to be disparaged or caricatured to this day—the value of his efforts can scarcely be underestimated.

Freud's life began May 6, 1856 in what is now the Czech Republic. He was the son of a "sentimental" MOTHER and a wool merchant FATHER. Numerous accounts of his early life are important to understanding the choices he made and how those choices ultimately affected his thoughts and life choices.

Little Sigmund was the eldest of the Freud children. As such, he enjoyed his mother's exclusive attention until his brother, Julius, was born. Julius died suddenly at the age of eight months. Since Sigmund recalls feelings of jealousy concerning the attention received by his newborn brother, he felt as though he had somehow caused the boy's death. This thinking would take root and become a central theory of Freud's dream interpretation: WISH-FULFILLMENT.

Another event which Freud recounted as formative was an event of seeing his mother naked. His response was one of sexual arousal. This experience would find later expression in his theory of Oedipal desire. Briefly summarized, Freud felt that a significant portion of PERSONALITY was developed by romantic attraction to the opposite gender parent and by how those feelings were repressed or resolved.

The most troubled of Freud's childhood experiences was the act of URINATING in his parents' bedroom. After this event, his father concluded, "that boy will never amount to anything." Later in life, Sigmund would report dreams of feeling successful as COMPENSATION for this event and the fall-out from it.

Freud's final formative event, which he discussed frequently in adulthood, stemmed from the anti-Semitism he experienced as a child. On one occasion, he recalled, his father was particularly shamed by the taunts he received. These experiences created substantial struggles for Freud in faith and RELIGION.

Freud began his education at the University of Vienna as a medical student in 1873. Upon completion of his studies, his early work as a professional was in the field of Meyneris Amentia (hallucinatory psychosis). This work allowed Freud to see how hysteria and constructs of the mind could dramatically affect human behavior.

About ten years later, Freud began working with Dr. Josef Breuer. A patient that Freud observed was a woman prone to outbursts of hysteria. A "talking cure" seemed to help lower the woman's ANXIETY level and control the episodes. The patient would describe thoughts, feelings, fantasies, and memories that caused the hysteria episodes. Through the talking, the patient processed her feelings calmly, and finally bypassed the hysterical episodes. Freud quickly understood the value of this "talking cure." And so, psychotherapy was born.

Through the mid-1880s and into the 1890s Freud began to work intently with the ideas that wish-fulfillment, Oedipal transactions, and the influence of the infantile life on adulthood were the pillars of personality development. All along, his thinking about the nature of humans had been influenced by Darwin (specifically, Darwin's theories of evolution and survival of the fittest). This influence also came into play in his dream research. His theory was that the biological origins of dreams was as follows:

What was seen became dreams.

What was heard became fantasies.

What was sexual became neurosis.

Dreams, Freud held, were the place where our earliest mental images, as well as pre-historic evolutionary impulses, were catalogued. Consequently, dreams were a gateway to insight concerning the mental antiquities not only of individual life, but of human existence.

Freud said of dreams, "Dreaming is an example of the regression to the dreamer's earliest condition, a revival of childhood, of the instinctual impulses which dominated it, and of the methods of expression which were available. . . . Dreams have preserved more mental antiquities than we could have imagined."

His first book on the topic, *The Interpretation of Dreams*, was completed in 1899, but dated as 1900 by his publisher. Although it is widely held to be his best work, and is read by many as a foundation to dream work, it received a tepid reception at best. In its first two years of publication, only 451 copies were sold.

Aside from this book, Freud made two other great contributions to dream work. These offerings came through the "Psychological Wednesday Circle" that Freud started in Vienna. Every Wednesday evening, Freud would host a group of four to twenty practitioners in his home for dinner and a paper. Frequent paper contributors were Carl JUNG and Alfred ADLER. Both of these men—able-minded, but relatively unknown psychologists—were soon invited by Freud to participate in the Wednesday Circle. Although each would later abandon Freud's theories, their fame can be traced, in part, to their relationships with and critiques of Freud.

Aside from *The Interpretation of Dreams*, Freud published several other works. The most controversial was *Three Essays on the Theory of Sexuality*, released in 1905. This work resulted in Freud being ostracized from the medical community for the balance of his career. Other significant works include *Totem and Taboo* (1913), *Beyond the Pleasure Principle* (1920), and *The Future of an Illusion* (1927).

Freud had been an avid cigar smoker, consuming as many as twenty a day at times. He eventually developed mouth cancer. The cancer became so advanced that he lost almost his entire hard palette. To eat and speak, he wore a prosthesis to separate his mouth and nasal cavity. This device slurred his speech considerably, which is why Freud is often character- ized as speaking unintelligibly or with grunts. On September 22, 1939, Freud went to see his physician and euthanized himself with pain killers.

His Legacy

If Sigmund Freud were to rerelease his magnum opus of psychother- apy, *The Interpretation of Dreams*, the new title may very well be *Sex, Lies, and Videotape*. Each of these themes comprises a piece of Freud's approach to dream interpretation. While Freud was sometimes diffi- cult to comprehend, his work on dreams is the body of knowledge that we now accept as being the most heavily traveled avenue into the lan- guage of dreams. Even those who have diverged from his path to other inquiries have willingly paid homage to his work.

Sex. The first step to understanding Freud is understanding how he thinks we are all put together. His best guess is that we're all comprised of a three-part harmony. These parts are the ID, EGO, and SUPEREGO. The first of these present in us is Id. This is our "in-born" personality. Over time, ego and superego develop.

This id seeks to satisfy your most basic desires, without any reluc- tance or shame. It is governed by the pleasure principle. In other words, id says, "What will make me feel better right now is what I want most." Watching a small child in action can validate this theory. Kids are moti- vated by being at peace through food, contact with momma, and comfort in their surroundings. Reality from day one forward is inter- preted by this pleasure-principle approach to problem solving.

As far as the sex part goes, well, that's the id in action. Since sex is one of the most intense human pleasures, Freud theorizes that it is central to human drive in most any given situation. Freud does not limit sex to the genital experience, but rather has an all-encompassing perspective of sex as anything that brings pleasure. All experiences and emotional transactions are weighed based on their ability to move us closer to or further from fulfillment of our pleasure needs.

Consider the man who, after marriage, acquires a knack for doing dishes and running the vacuum. This is a Freudian illustration of the id influencing behavior on the ego. To get pleasure, the man wants the woman to be pleased. Pleasing the woman includes doing chores. The more chores he does, the more pleasure he receives. Over time, doing the chores may even become a pleasure in themselves for the opportunities that stem from them.

Since we cannot develop solely as sex-driven persons, Freud theorized that something else has to develop along the way to govern or suppress the id. (Did anyone tell the men this rule?) This is the part of the PERSONALITY he labeled ego. This facet regulates the id by identifying appropriate and inappropriate transactions—"transaction" meaning either interpersonal (with others) or intrapersonal (in your own mind) emotional events. The ego's job is to take what the id taught it and appropriate it for maximum effectiveness.

The ego needs help to keep that wild id in check, though. So there is a superego to help it. This superego is the place where our inhibitions and sense of social propriety form. These include things that are polite ("You just don't do that in polite company"), as well as TABOO ("You just don't do that ever!").

The id and the superego are constantly in conflict. The ego is the mediator. While id says "More with everyone!," superego is saying, "Be careful, restraint is valor." The ego's negotiation of this conflict becomes the CONSCIOUS self. The id and the superego form poles of the SUBCONSCIOUS self, while the ego is at the center. People with strong egos are often considered to be "very centered."

Lies. Freud would say that the EGO and SUPEREGO are the least true selves. They suppress the truest self, the ID. The technique for doing this is a two pronged attack on the id. First, a claim that the id is flat out wrong. Superego makes it a point to say "No!" often and loudly. The second attack is more subtle. The ego says that the id may not be flat out wrong, but it is wrong because of XYZ factors that, if we could change or dismiss, would make it right.

It seems that Freud viewed personality as one big power struggle. Within that struggle, dirty tricks were perfectly acceptable. Whatever one facet of the personality needed to develop to balance the other two was all right. After all, all's fair in love, (sex), and war. These become our neuroses.

The healthiest people are able to integrate the id, ego, and superego perfectly—making it so that each of the three could play with others and share their toys happily. The least healthy people are not able to integrate the three with any sense of balance. Not one of the three (id, ego, superego) could play well together or share.

This is where the "lies" become important. The one facet of personality needing the most compensation would often try to manipulate the other two in the dream state to work out in the SUBCONSCIOUS what could not be accomplished while awake. Thus, the meaning of dreams was central to the Freudian psychoanalytic method.

Videotape. Freud more or less considered the brain as a sponge metaphor. He believed that earliest childhood experiences were recorded and held in MEMORY for interpreting later events in life. To Freud, a dream was equal to an infantile scene that was modified as to become transferred onto an adult experience.

If childhood were utopia, this would be no problem. Very few dreams would be unsettling and most would have happy endings. However, the "videotape" has everything on it, including some of our most bizarre desires and anxieties as children. These included Freud's famous theories of Oedipus and Electra (romantic attraction to the opposite-gendered parent), castration anxiety, anal retentive disorders, oral fixations, and a host of other pre-adolescent trauma. These traumas create the conflicts between what we ought to do and what we want to do.

Listen to Freud in his own words: "Dreaming is an example of regression to the dreamer's earliest condition. It is a revival of childhood and the instinctual impulses which dominated it and of the methods of expression that were available. . . . Dreams have preserved more mental antiquities than we could have imagined." Freud sees the dream as the recalling of our earliest and most actual selves in our appetites and desire for self-fulfillment. Thus, it is no surprise when you consider Freud's major principles of his dream interpretation.

His Major Theories

Free Association. For Freud, the dream is something like a rebus—a picture-word puzzle. To understand it, his method encourages the use of free association between dream images and waking circumstances. In this way, he hopes to capture subtle meanings or conflicts from the CONSCIOUS world that have been projected into the SUBCONSCIOUS.

An Asian graduate student in her mid-twenties reports the following dream:

When I was in [Asia], I dreamed of flying to America in a heli-
copter with a wealthy American who was much older. He had his
own helicopter and would fly me off to different places. He was the
most romantic type of guy and this romance was such as in those
romance novels that all girls read.

This is the kind of dream Freud loves. It involves an overt sexual
overtone and a female patient. It also includes an important Freudian
phenomenon called displacement.

When first related to me, I felt this woman may not be too close
with her father. The fact that her romance was with a man "much
older" led me to think that she was trying to represent something that
was missing from her CONSCIOUS life. Indeed, when I asked her about
her father, her response was kind of painful. "We get along better
when we're not together, or right when he gets home from a trip." Her
rationale for the pained relationship was that they are "too similar."

The overt sexuality of the romance is Freud's grist for the mill.
Freely associating with the client, Freud would probably explore ideal-
izations of father-daughter relationships. If the dream were happening
near puberty, the romance would be a representation of affection not
otherwise obtained earlier in life. Diagnosed, it would likely be characterized as an unresolved Electra complex.

Free association is crucial to Freudian dream interpretation. What in
waking reminds you of anything you encountered in the dream event?
In this case, the much older man and America would be those items.
The patient's father is an international import and export businessman.

This free association technique can be useful. Many times, images
appear in dreams that are outright bizarre and disjointed. Yet if we keep
rolling them around in our minds, probing for things that somehow they
have in common, psychological themes may begin to emerge. The key is

to try and find every MEMORY that has a relationship of any kind to the dream image you are trying to interpret. While the relationships may seem strained, or even obtuse, Freud's analysis can make use of them.

Displacement, Condensation, and Representation.

Three dream tools central to Freud's interpretation are displacement, condensation, and representation. Each of these is a tool the self uses, even in the SUBCONSCIOUS, to prevent the conflicts in the psyche from getting out of hand. In dreams, these tools are used to create psychological images that have subconscious meaning, even if they lack apparent meaning in the CONSCIOUS.

Displacement means putting thoughts and feelings about one person or situation onto another. For example, the ID wanting to kill the FATHER to be the MOTHER's lover is inappropriate. Besides, the child's ego knows it would be overwhelmed by the father's power. (Yes, Freud thought this is something we all want to do.) However, you can kill numerous authority figures in dreaming without actually killing your father. That would be too traumatic.

Condensation is the combining of several characters or events into a single dream experience. Having one or more UNCONSCIOUS stimuli in the same dream can make interpretation difficult. However, through free association, relationships can be identified that unlock the mystery of the condensed dream event.

Representation is similar to Jung's ARCHETYPES. Although he may not have ever admitted to it in so many words, representation was a germinal idea for Jung's own dream work. Freud had a great appreciation for the universal images of the world and our experience of them. He would often connect water and birth, using images of Osiris, Moses, Adonis, and Bacchus to defend his position.

Wish-Fulfillment. Wish-fulfillment is another important facet of Freud's understanding of dreams. Many times, there are things we want out of life that the SUPEREGO talks us out of getting. The ID may at times try to obtain for itself in sleep what the EGO and superego deny it in waking. This is wish-fulfillment dreaming. Wish-fulfillment may often be present in dreams. Many people go through life feeling as though their potential has not been appreciated or that their ambitions are unfairly impeded. These wishes may, at times, be an outgrowth of the childhood traumas that are becoming our adult neuroses.

Sexual Content. Freud's weakness, in many scholars' opinion, is his commitment to sexual content. Every knife, dagger, snake, column, spear, and hot dog is a phallus for him. It makes little difference what the dreamer's world actually is. Freud is helpful, though, in many ways. However, he ultimately leaves little to be desired due to his firm commitment to image meanings apart from the dreamer's understanding of the content.

GOODISON, JANE

In the late twentieth century, gender and the psychoanalytic process have come under scrutiny. One of the most interesting theorists is an English woman, Jane Goodison. Her published dream work deals exclusively with the matter of women's dreams. While this may not sound earth shattering, look at the other names in this section; Sigmund, Carl, Alfred, Medard. They are all male. Consequently, they can only speak to one dimension of personhood in the dream event.

Goodison represents an existential approach where the unique condition of the self as a woman is a primary consideration of the existential self. In so doing, Goodison seeks to elevate the unique attributes of womanhood as central to the dream event. For all of us, male and female, our bodies are the primary mode of our being. Each of us is a certain kind of person with a certain kind of body that has obligations and inherent potentiality. Dreams can be very illuminating to how we experience that potential, how we are pained by it, and what requisite obligations of care we feel toward our bodies.

Insight is creating an awareness of potentiality and insight as a self acting in the world. Since our bodies are a vessel of our potentiality, the awareness of them is most completely expressed by those who share them.

If the CONSCIOUS is described as the self-aware person in the world, the SUBCONSCIOUS could be described as the not-yet-aware or becoming-aware person in the world. It is from this platform that Goodison makes a well developed plea for unique appreciation of the dreams of women. If a man, who lives in a body unique to his worldview, cannot be fully self-aware, how can a man be aware of the subconscious processes of a self-identity he does not share.

For women, dreams of fertility, menstruation, lactation, and motherhood are experienced much differently than for men. Moreover, the relative value of these experiences as a facet of a woman's awareness can only be fully appreciated in a feminine context.

To the extent that gender reflects a unique mode of existence, Goodison follows Boss's thought.

What Goodison does offer is a genre of female symbolism that comes from being a female as an end in itself. In contrast to FREUD and JUNG, who interpret dream symbols as a process of the PERSONALITY, Goodison allows the symbol to simply be. It is refreshing. Through her dream groups, a number of symbols have developed, some of which challenge the traditional way of looking at Western icons. She tries to create equivalent female icons to compensate for fifty-five centuries of primarily patriarchal literature. In doing so, additional POWER ARCHETYPES are discovered to tell the female story.

Goodison departs from Freud to the extent that Freud's symbols are often tied to his maleness. Women's dreams often reflect different image meanings based on similar theories of personality development. Goodison also applies archetypal interpretation, but again it is uniquely formed around her primary commitment to womanhood.

This work by Goodison develops a very interesting contrast to Freud. Freud's theory of sexuality as the causal influence of dream content was limited by his understanding of male identity and the central characteristic of maleness, the penis. However, he was limited because he viewed the rest of psychoanalytic theory through his own eyes. Goodison reorders sexual awareness around the features she is primarily associated with, namely the woman's body.

Consider this woman's dream:

> *At a medical examination, the doctor listens to my abdomen and hears a heartbeat. A sonogram confirms this fact. I am uncertain how exactly to feel about this. The scene changes and my child is now larger, but still attached to me. Her breasts suddenly fill and lactation occurs not from me, but her.*

Freud and Jung would each have a lot to say about this dream, mostly in the areas of wish-fulfillment and psychological archetypes. Many of their conclusions may even be true. However, this dream, dreamt by a woman and filled with woman's unique self-aware potential, will have insights that men cannot comprehend apart from women's narrative. Insight is awareness that comes comes from within and reaches within to expand the potential of self-awareness.

Some persons from more conservative perspectives will have trouble accompanying her on this journey. The language of the female as a central figure of self awareness is often discordant and difficult to recognize following such an extended heritage of maleness.

Unfortunately, little biographic information about Goodison is available. She is a British counselor and community politician.

HINDU

The Hindu interpretation of dreams can easily lapse into a metaphysical fog. Creativity, reality, and self-awareness exist in a multi-dimensional reality for Hindus that is difficult to condense with succinct clarity. Potential and insight are not limited to a single dimension and consequently are difficult to define. Those who were not born Hindu but who have gone on to study the RELIGION have spent lifetimes trying to understand the complex system.

Doctrine regarding dream interpretation has an ancient foundation in the Indian concept of *maya*. This concept is concerned with the idea of converting an idea, imagination, or vision into dimensional reality.

In the hymns to Visvakaran recorded in the Rig Veda (sacred Hindu scripture), the creator god, Rudra, is imagined as an artisan with whom all possibilities for reality reside. God is the artist who paints the pictures we mistake for the world. The consequence of this is that possibilities are randomly distributed through our awareness.

In sleep, our minds are more available to be conjoined with the gods. As a result of this, dreams are actually a greater reality than our waking world. Rudra's mind joins with ours, thus revealing the actual state of our being.

Many people use Hindu interpretations of dreams that include both co-creativity with the gods and karma (basically, the theory that what goes around comes around) to illuminate this reality and its meaning. RECURRING dreams of relationship deficits and uncertainty are often part and parcel of incomplete karma. There is a need to resolve lessons in karma in order to allow the soul to progress to its next level of growth.

INCUBATION

How often have you gotten a song stuck in your head? It's the last thing you hear as you walk out the door and it sticks with you the rest of the day. It can be frustrating if it's a bad song, or it can keep you upbeat all day long if it is a good one. Basically, we can stick things in our heads to generate (i.e. incubate) dream matter, too.

Dreaming is like any other mental discipline—with practice you can draw it into a more meaningful role in your life. This includes both dream content and dream recall. However, it isn't an automatic result of desire—it also requires design and hard work.

Because of a lack of recall, some people feel that their dreams may not mean anything while others believe that they just don't dream. While it is true that not every single dream is packed full of insight, it is also true that everybody dreams. To recall dreams, it is helpful to cooperate with the natural rhythm of the brain. We can scientifically observe that sleep runs in ninety-minute patterns. Moreover, people who are awakened during a REM cycle are three times more likely to recall at least some dream images. Coordinating your bedtime and waking time to this ninety-minute pattern can be very helpful (see FOUR STAGES OF SLEEP).

Dream incubation has physical, emotional, and spiritual dimensions. Good health and fitness can have a huge impact on dream vividness and recall. Certain herbal supplements that address metabolism, energy, and nervous system health can also influence dreams. Also, eating too close to bedtime can impact dreams.

Emotionally, dream incubation means intentionally plotting the thoughts, attitudes, and relationships you want to develop in the UN-CONSCIOUS state. Allowing these thoughts to permeate your awareness as you go to sleep can often help translate them into the dream state. This is especially true of interpersonal relationship problems that have no apparent solution; it also is helpful with intrapersonal dilemmas.

Spiritually, communing with the source of your being can be essential to dream outcomes as well. Meditating on special writings and songs can be a good way to develop a connection with your higher being as you dream. Others may need to burn incense or complete a sacred preparation ritual before dreaming.

The goal of these preparations is to have a harmonious and open relationship with reality at the highest level of your perception before going to sleep. Intentional dream incubation is about being open to acquiring the largest possible view of your potentiality for better or worse.

INDIVIDUATION

According to Jungian theories of PERSONALITY, individuation is the primary task of personality. Basically, it is the process of becoming a unique and whole person, identified with, yet separate from, archetypal forms of being. The trick is that many times our self-awareness gets "stuck" in a particular mode of self. In other words, rather than integrating all the ARCHETYPES into a cohesive self, a particular archetype wields undo influence and prevents integration of the entire self.

In dream interpretation, it is useful to see how you portray yourself in relationship to these archetypes and your individual identity. Do you often feel trapped, feeling as though you have no choice but to act as you do? This is a problem of individuation, Jung would be prone to say.

The key is to move beyond the suggestive force of the collective UNCONSCIOUS, liberating yourself from the mask-like collective psyche.

INFLUENCE OF INFANTILE LIFE ON ADULTHOOD

At the center of FREUD'S theory of PERSONALITY stood the idea that childhood events cast the perspective of adult behavior. This theory arose out of the fact that many childhood experiences, for better or worse, were formed by the child's powerlessness in relationship to the world around them.

"The cause of hysteria," Freud stated, "is a passive sexual experience before puberty, that is, a traumatic seduction." Freud, after all, held that the ID was present even in the minds of small children. Consequently, experiences of sexual awareness, difference from the opposite gender parent, seeing naked bodies, and other similar events are considered passive sexual trauma. In turn, these events would impact how a person sees themselves in the world. For Freud, this was critical to dream interpretation. If every dream contains expressions of the id, then it follows that the way these expressions were resolved or repressed in early childhood affect how the dreamer sees himself or herself as living in the world today.

INTERPRETING DREAMS

As you can see, there are many different schools of dream interpretation, many particular tools to use in the interpretation process, a variety of reasons to attempt such dream work, and a million reasons why any of these things is right or wrong.

However, it can be stated with confidence here that the most important thing you can do to effect positive dream analysis is to have a plan.

See APPENDIX A—KEEPING A DREAM JOURNAL.

ISLAMIC DREAM WORK

The body of literature concerning Islamic dream interpretation is perhaps the most extensive of any of the ancient Near Eastern RELIGIONS. While most modern dream literature is restricted to psychoanalytic materials, Islam continues an impressive proliferation of literature on the subject.

Islam was started with a dream. Mohammed was given divine instructions to "read." When he reported that he could not, the angel Gabriel appeared to him, and so revelation came to him. To this day, the dream continues to be the path par excellence to wisdom, spiritual insight, and interpreting reality.

However, various sects of Islam now view dreams with varying enthusiasm. Shiites and Sufis have regarded prophecy as continuous today, rather than accepting that it closed at the end of canonical writing. In their Islamic faith, the dream is a sacred instrument of God's communication. Allah may foretell his wishes and plans through the dream event.

Sects that believe prophecy from Allah ended with the end of canonical writing, view prophecy dreams with slightly more suspicion. However, the high place of dream interpretation in Islamic faith experience has remained. Published accounts exist concerning conversion of faith solely due to dream content within the corpus of Islamic literature.

JUDEO-CHRISTIAN INTERPRETATIONS

Judeo-Christian dream interpretation requires a breakdown into early and late literature. Although Judaism started with a fairly high commitment to dreams as revelation, with the influence of Aristotelian thought and later prophecy, the place of dreams has waned. Christianity has tacitly endorsed this trend. Although no overt literature has refuted the meaning of dreams, the dream does not receive nearly the warm response it does in ISLAMIC, New Age, or Eastern RELIGIONS. Rationalism seems to have taken its toll on the value of dreams in more recent years for Judeo-Christians.

The Hebrew scriptures are replete with dream accounts through the Torah and Kethibim corpus. The biblical books of Genesis, Ecclesiastes, Esther, and Job all recount dream activities as central to God revelation and interpretation of his people's circumstances. In the prophetic, or Nebeiim, scripture the dream accounts continue, but begin to wane with the later prophets.

In Christian scripture, dream accounts are scarce. The only references are one in the gospels and one in the second Corinthian letter of St. Paul. The APOCALYPSE of John may have some dream content, but it is often left to interpreters to discern the symbolic meaning.

The purpose of dreams and interpretation of them in Judeo-Christian literature seems to be revelation. The corruption and insensitivity of the EGO/CONSCIOUS self inhibits the ability to receive divine illumination. During sleep, God has unmediated access to the ego for communication and PROPHETIC content. Consequently the dream is a tool for accomplishing God's revelation and purpose.

Interpreting dreams of religious significance in this context seems to revolve around an understanding of God's purposes and priorities for human lives. If a person feels convinced that divine communication is the content of a dream, verification comes through applying scriptures to the dream events for further insight.

JUNG, CARL (1875–1961)

Carl Gustav Jung entered the world on July 26, 1875. The son of a Lutheran minister, his thought and theories of personal psychology form a complex and deeply spiritual understanding of the human condition. Jung was gifted with a particularly acute sense of self-awareness that would become both his greatest adversary and a foundational pillar of his theory of PERSONALITY.

Jung's autobiography, *Memories, Dreams and Reflections*, relates an interesting anecdote concerning his earliest dream awareness. In it, he recalls a dream he had at age four. The account of this dream includes a detailed narrative of encountering a wall, inner chamber, and throne room. Interpreting his own dream as a phallic ARCHETYPE, he considered the experience his initiation to the realm of dreams.

"It's just a dream" are four words you would never want to utter in front of Jung. You could, but then he would intellectually dissect you like a biology class frog. When he was done, you would fully appreciate that no matter what you understand the dreaming life to be, his influence is far reaching. Trying to boil down Jung is like trying to boil down a rock, it's already so dense there isn't that much to strain out.

To understand Jung's thought, one must explore his childhood and formative years. Throughout his life, Jung seemed to be on a search for human authenticity, both his own personal self and the human FAMILY'S. Jung seems to experience much of his own life and his early relationships with a sense that the true self is somehow shrouded from awareness by the neurosis that we call our "self."

Through his teenage years, Jung recounts a double life of sorts. His personality, Jung thought, had two distinctive facets. The first was his mundane life in the world. This personality was concerned with academic disciplines and the "guy stuff" of a nineteenth century Swiss schoolboy. The second facet was the inner, spiritual Carl. This facet of Jung, as he describes it, had an almost transcendental quality. He felt himself "looking down with God on creation."

During this time, church became a place of torturous insincerity for

Jung. During the theological catechism administered by his father, young Carl grew bored. Out of that boredom came the realization that his father had no experience with God, only general knowledge of Him. This was horrifying to Jung, who felt God to be something immediately experienced rather than a benign awareness. This ANXI-ETY may have been influential on his later thinking concerning the problems of the personality as primarily spiritual in nature.

Throughout his later educational period, Jung had a particular affinity for the classical Greeks, especially Plato. This exposure also became central to his thought concerning the nature of the personality. Jung completed his education in 1900 and entered medical practice through the Psychiatric University Clinic of Burgholzi. There, his reputation as an able-minded psychiatrist grew. Eventually, he was invited to Vienna to participate in the Wednesday Evening Circle led by Dr. Sigmund FREUD.

Jung and Freud shared great camaraderie from 1907 to 1912. Freud, being twenty years his senior, fancied Jung something of an eldest son. He lavished great attention on the young scholar, including presentation of gifts and a ritual ADOPTION of sorts.

Jung was a regular participant in the Wednesday Circle until at least 1908. However, the relationship would not last. Freud was deeply committed to the sexual theory as essential dogma. This was untenable to Jung, who felt the need for further inquiry. Eventually, Jung struck out on his own intellectual path. In 1912, Jung published his *Transformations and Symbols of the Libido*, knowing that its release would be the beginning of the end of his relationship with Freud.

In this work, Jung drew contrary conclusions to his mentor Freud on the issue of incest, among other things. For Jung, incest was a symbolic spiritual struggle of the personality as it was expressed through dreams. Freud, however, saw incest as a much more literal sexual power struggle within the family. This literalism was too much for Jung, who felt personality was more complex than manifestation of the singular expression of sexuality.

He rejected much of Freud's theory of the individual as a mostly sexual being. And, although he would never be considered orthodox, Jung believed in a presence of divinity in the universe that was contrary to Freud's thesis as articulated in *The Future of an Illusion (1927)*. The religious commitments that Freud was so eager for humanity to outgrow represented a level of truth to Jung that could not be separated from individual personality theory.

Jung's thought was much more focused on what he perceived to be universal human experiences that were occurring among individuals in his therapy practice. His thesis was that, "Ultimately, every individual life is the same as the eternal life of the species." This meant that our individual thoughts and ideas, including the dream life, are determined by a common self-awareness that arises and continues throughout the human race. This common self-awareness was, after a fashion, his image of God.

This thinking was heavily influenced by the Darwinism of his era. The evolved species had an evolved CONSCIOUSNESS in common. Humans, as a self-aware species, had developed a sense of collective soul. This collective soul, or universal conscience, was the ground of personal being in the world. Jung theorized that the goal of personality development was the individuation of a person from this common ground of being into a unique soul. This was done using the commonality to move toward a self who was uniquely defined.

Plato, about 800 B.C., had an idea that apart from this world of perception, there were perfect forms or ideas. For all the cubes to exist in the world, there had to be a perfect form of a "cube" that existed on some ungraspable level. Jung took this idea and applied it to people's personality traits, and consequently, to dreams. The forms of Plato were Jung's collective soul of humanity.

Jung called these perfect forms of people archetypes. The idea of archetypes is hardly original to Jung, but his use of them in psychology was revolutionary. They were Platonic forms of who we are, active in our self-awareness. These archetypes had the capacity within the Self (a person aware of their quest for meaning) to initiate, control, and mediate behavior.

The source of neurosis is the overexertion of archetypal influences and the neglect of other facets of personality. Archetypal autonomy may exert power that drives the persona to madness, unable to fathom the self apart from a singular, unique perspective in and upon the world.

An innocuous example is the proverb, "Why does a young girl's heart turn to love in the springtime?" Jung would say, "Simple, because that's what young girls do." They can't not do it because it is the archetype initiating, controlling, and mediating the young girl. The Darwinism comes into play when you try to refute the argument. Jung then can reply that the species has been behaving this way for thousands of generations without coaching. Why? It's in the genes.

However, if the young girl is unable to comprehend or integrate a self that moves beyond springtime infatuation, neurosis will occur. Rather than progressing toward motherhood, responsibility, wisdom, and preparation for death, her personality will be stuck in the mode of seeking out infatuation.

Dreams were purposeful to Jung because the archetypes contained in them offered a mirror in which the dreamer could look for feedback concerning the condition of the self. Dreams were caused by the world, but were purposeful in explaining the self in the world as well.

Jung's life-cycle archetypes are:

Being Mothered	*nurtured or cared for*
Exploring the Environment	*discovering who you are as a separate person*
Playing with Peers	*socialization*
Adolescence	*transition*
Rights of Passage or Initiation	*becoming adult*
Establishing a Place for the Self in Social Hierarchy	*accepting responsibility*
Courting	*mating ritual 101*
Marriage	*mating ritual 201*
Parenting	*preserving the race*
Hunting, Gathering, and Fighting	*climbing the ladder of success*
Participation in the Sacred	*coming to terms with what is of ultimate value*
Social Responsibility of a Mature Person	*the village sage*
Preparation for Death	*completion*

Jung felt that all people had to go through all these tasks in order to be a unified or complete Self. The work of the dreaming mind was to see the self in the process of completing of these tasks. When particular tasks are not resolved, the self uses the dreaming life to identify conflicts, work through difficulties, or affirm the need to incorporate the anxiety of transition between tasks into the mind.

Many dreams, according to Jung, were illustrations of our lives going through these processes. We may feel celebration, fear, or ambivalence about the task. Our dreams would reveal this and either heighten or relieve the feelings. In certain transitions, we would be unsure whether or not we had the resources to complete the transition. In dreaming, we could see solutions that were not readily apparent. Social tensions around mating and career choices could be the source of uncertainty in waking. Through the dream state, these issues are revealed. Our relationships with characters in the dream are fodder for the resolution of our waking incompleteness.

Dreams, for Jung, reveal archetypal awareness in an emotional transaction called COMPENSATION. This term is used by Jung to describe why people do things in dreams they would never intentionally do in waking life. Our archetypal selves compensate for the deficiencies of our waking selves. Jung states, "Since everything living strives for wholeness, the inevitable one-sidedness of our conscious life is continually being corrected and compensated by the universal human being in us, whose goal is the ultimate integration of conscious and UNCONSCIOUS; or better, the assimilation of the ego to a wider personality."

What this statement means is that we are blind to much of ourselves. We strive to live our lives as something we think we should be, not as who we are. Dreams, Jung would contend, are instruments of the universal conscious, intended to open us more fully to who we really are as an individual within that universal structure.

Let's apply Jung's theories to the interpretation of a dream. A 22-year-old woman reports dreaming:

> *I'm descending down a steep stairwell. At the bottom, I encounter a*
> *door leading into a small room. An old woman gives me a glass*

with unknown liquid. "Drink it," she says. I do. The taste is awful. I close my eyes tightly to force it down. After a few moments, I open my eyes. The old woman has disappeared. I walk through another door into a large, crowded room. Everyone in the room is a man. I find it uncomfortable, then flattering. Before I can meet anyone, I walk past a mirror and see that I too am now an old woman. I run out ashamed.

Jung would say that the twenty-two-year-old patient is anxious about the passage into adulthood. The steep staircase leading to a CAVE-like area is a symbol for coming to a place of initiation. She wants a mentor. She fears that this passage may be a very bitter experience. The old woman is an archetypal source of wisdom. She forces the dreamer to confront and accept the unpleasant right of passage. The young woman wants to go through the rite so she can become a woman and begin courting. However, she also has fears that she may not be able to mate effectively and so will pass into old maid status before finding a suitable mate.

Dreams often reflect several tensions at play in the psyche at once, looking for integration. These can be seen in the following questions:

Who am I now?

Who do I see myself becoming?

Who do others see me becoming, and how do I feel about it?

Am I afraid of who I am becoming and how others feel about it?

Often times in life, we act a certain way or feel a certain way about ourselves based on where we are in Jungian passages of life. If you'd like to contend this point, first ask yourself the following questions:

Do I think about myself the same way now as I did when I was ten years younger than now?

If my marital or parental status were different, would my priorities be the same as they are now?

How do others' expectations and perceptions of me affect my actions?

In contrast, when do I act for another's fulfillment rather than my own desires?

If you respond honestly to these inquiries, it doesn't take long to see that Jung was on to something with his archetypal theory.

Another great example of a Jung story is that of Luke Skywalker in the *Star Wars* films. In the last film, *Return of the Jedi*, Luke goes through his hero quest to become a Self. He does this by going alone on his quest. He finds a mentor, the aged Yoda. Yoda leads him through a training that concludes with an initiation. Do you remember the crucial scene? Luke is alone in a cave, fighting a black cloaked figure that represents evil, but when unmasked, is himself. Then Yoda prepares to die, having completed his work.

Interpreting your dreams from the Jungian perspective entails being focused on the your state of mind during the dream and the tasks completed in the dream.

Were the actions reminiscent of any of the thirteen major archetypes of life?

Were you stuck, unable to to make a transition from one kind of person to another?

Are you looking back on your life, unable to find a symbol of an archetype?

Your Self wants to complete a puzzle with a missing piece. Were you longing to be something you used to be, but are not any longer?

Did you skip from one segment of life to another, perhaps missing something you have looked forward to with fondness?

What was your relationship to the people in your dream, and who were your helpers and detractors in resolving the dream situations?

His later works, including *Man and His Symbols* and *Vision Seminars* can guide you towards greater insight into the power of archetypal language.

Ultimately, dreams solve a problem for Jung. The problem is that we want to be whole, but our conscious lives have a too limited a perspective. Listen to his own words: "The dream is a little hidden door in the innermost and most secret recesses of the soul opening into that cosmic night which was psyche before it was ego. Ego separates and discriminates, knows only particulars. In dreams, we put on the likeness of that more universal, truer, more eternal self dwelling in the darkness of night."

The poetry of this statement enhances the power of its meaning. We are in the process, most of the time, of narrowing the field of our mind from the great potential to the mundane. Consequently, we often talk ourselves out of trying to become the person it would be best for us to be. Yet the universal conscious refuses to relent; it uses the dream avenue to access the most authentic inner self and achieve insight.

Undoubtedly, Jung's contributions to dreamwork were and are substantial. However, his unique self-awareness makes interpretation bedeviling at times. Not all people are "wired" to live their lives being comprehensively aware of their interior and exterior life to the same extent Jung was. Nonetheless, archetypal psychology continues to be very influential, primarily due to his contributions.

LATENT CONTENT
Latent content refers to what is not said or done; often what is left out is more important than what is communicated. These repressed non-expressions of the waking self are often excellent feed for the dreamwork mill. Latent content often appears as the shadow of our

CONSCIOUS feelings about ourselves, our relationships with others, and the meaning of our lives. This repression often comes out through acts of the UNCONSCIOUS , such as dreams.

The difficulty is that latent expressions are often below the reach of the conscious EGO. Even in recalling dreams, we fixate mostly on the symbols that have the most obvious significance to us. However, even though we do not recognize these latent contents directly, if at all, that does not compromise their value.

METAPHOR CONTENT

Hope is a blanket that's always too short. . . .

This dark piece of prose reflects the power of metaphor. In dreams, an event, visual image, or emotional transaction is often a symbol of something else meaningful. The fullness of meaning is not derived from the object or event per se, but rather what that thing refers to. Therapeutically, FREE ASSOCIATION is the technique used to discover this meaning. In free association, various streams of MEMORY are pursued around the dominant image or object until meanings are found that unite the dream event with a waking event through the use of story or metaphor.

This technique has its advantages and drawbacks. To its benefit, seemingly illogical events can be unified by free associating various memories and metaphors. However, if you presuppose a dogmatic position on human PERSONALITY (as FREUD did with regard to sexuality) the conclusions are limited by the assumptions initially drawn.

MILLER, GUSTAVUS HINDMAN

Wrote *10,000 Dreams Interpreted or What's in a Dream* in the nineteenth century. This is a classic book of dream interpretation, albeit incredibly prescriptive and mostly outdated. Miller takes scads of everyday items and exotic objects and tells you exactly what each one's dream meaning is. For example, did you know that to dream of a crawfish denotes that "Deceit is sure to assail you in your affairs of the heart, if you are young, after dreaming of this backward-going thing"?

Once meant to be a serious scientific study of dream images, this book is now little more than a curiosity piece. However, it is still in stores today, enjoying its twenty-fourth printing!

OEDIPUS/ELECTRA COMPLEX

In Greek mythology, a young hero is separated from his family. After growing up, going away to war, and returning victoriously, he is unknowingly wed to his mother. Consequently, the gods judge him for incest. The play dramatizing these events is Sophocles's *Oedipus Rex*. FREUD used this archetypal story to explain the passive sexual trauma of romantic attraction toward a parent. (Oedipus being boy to mother; Electra being girl to father.)

The Oedipus/Electra complex offers a huge reservoir of dream information in Freudian analytic theory. Many times dreams of helplessness, incest, DEATH of FAMILY members, and romantic liaisons with strangers are expressions of this psychological tension in Freudian psychoanalysis.

Freud's theoretical weakness, as always, is overplaying the hand. While there are certainly many observations of this phenomenon in waking life, it is hard to fathom implications as far-reaching as Freud often suggests. Many times, little boys especially go through a phase of wanting to marry mommy without consciously grasping the implications of what that means. However, attempting to cast the shadow of that experience through all of life's interpersonal relationships seems a far stretch.

What can be asserted is that the event is somewhat common. Moreover, it does create an unsolvable tension at some levels due to the inability to actualize the desire. Consequently, many dreams of representation in relationships can include some expression of this event.

REACTION FORMATION

If you have ever been excessively nice to a person you secretly despise in a social setting, you have experienced reaction formation. In dreams, this is expressed by harming people you love or by rescuing people you despise. The motivation for creating these reaction formations lies within your feelings about the persons.

SECONDARY ELABORATION

This is the trick we play on ourselves and others when recounting our dreams. While dreaming, particular images are presented with various degrees of importance and meaning. However, in waking, we recall the dream according to the desires, prejudices, and expectations of our waking life. The filtration by the EGO of the dream narrative is the secondary elaboration.

Many times, when recounting dream stories, you may be tempted to add editorial comments. These may include drawing an ego-gratifying connection between yourself and dream CELEBRITIES, making intuitive comments about why things were presented as they were, and so on. One way to try to see your dreams more clearly and avoid secondary elaboration is to avoid commenting on the intuitive content of the dream. When recounting the dream, try to simply recall the symbols and images in the order they occurred with no additional insight or comment.

After you have recalled the symbols, then begin associating the symbols with your intuitive understanding of them. This may be done through writing down the images; this will discipline the impulse to add meaning as you verbalize.

SPIRITUALIST WORLDVIEWS ON DREAMS

Spiritualist worldviews often emphasize the search for revelation from the spirits of the world about the condition of the world. Seeking out these omens can include both ritualistic searches (i.e. Native American use of peyote in religious events) or spontaneous revelation, such as in dreams.

The dream is regarded as an explanation of the self in relationship to the waking world. The omens produced may then be realized, if positive—or avoided, if negative. This negotiation occurs through the direction of the medicine man or shaman and includes ritual sacrifice or protective behavior to bring about the desired result. Many contemporary dream interpreters base their theories on the dream work of Native American and Aboriginal peoples.

TAOISM

Taoism, or the teaching of the Tao ("the way"), has a contribution to make to dream interpretation. A primer on Taoism is appropriate before the insights for dreamwork can be appreciated.

Taoism, as articulated by Lao-tsu in the sixth century B.C., has as its goal the appreciation of natural laws: the simple life. All things, heavy or light, wet or dry, fast or slow, have a particular nature within them. When abstract or arbitrary rules are placed upon them, struggle becomes inevitable. The world is not inherently good or evil, but a teacher of lessons. Upon learning, one will have access to the Way. The Way has unlimited power, as it is the presence behind all things in the universe. No life can exist apart from it.

Tao thought is illustrated in the following parable:

> *There was a man who disliked footprints and shadows. On seeing*
> *his, he became frustrated and started to run away. Of course, his*
> *shadow kept up with him easily while his footprints followed close*
> *behind. Eventually, he became exhausted and collapsed dead. If he*
> *would have stopped, no footprints would have occurred. If he would*
> *have rested under the shade, his shadow would have disappeared.*

What does all of this have to do with dream interpretation? Dreams may reflect a truer and plainer self than could otherwise be known. Many times, especially through compensatory dreams and ARCHE-TYPES, we are confronted with aspects of ourselves that we choose to ignore or even suppress in waking life. Moreover, seeing ourselves in dreams is one of the only times to observe ourselves apart from our struggles to become someone.

WISH-FULFILLMENT

This was FREUD'S central instrument of dream interpretation. What the ID wanted, but was unable to achieve due to the restraints of the EGO and SUPEREGO, was often received through the wish-fulfillment of the SUBCONSCIOUS in dreaming. Wish-fulfillment can have both positive expression, those thing you desire to have happen; and negative expression, an expressed non-desire of what you hope will not happen.

appendix A

Keeping a Dream Journal

A dream journal is a great tool to use if you are serious about learning what your dreams are trying to tell you. You can buy an extravagant journal at a specialty shop that includes nice illustrations of stars and moons, or just a simple notebook from a drugstore. Some people find that the specialty books give them more inspiration while recording dreams. Either way, the most important thing to consider when keeping a dream journal, of course, is how you use it.

By recording your dreams, you will accomplish two things:

1. You will learn to understand the images in your dreams as they affect your waking life.

2. You will have a stronger sense of your dream patterns, and so you will have a better chance of incubating dream ideas.

There is no standard procedure for keeping a dream journal. It is a very personal book, and so you should set it up in a way that feels most comfortable to you and which will inspire you to use it on a regular basis. If you can use it everyday, that would be great—it means that you are not having any trouble remembering all your dreams, and you will be gaining much insight from your dream world. However, you may not recall every dream, or you may just want to record the dreams that motivate you to do so. Whatever works for you is the best system to employ.

Here are some basic tips and model entries which you may find useful in setting up your own dream journal:

1. Keep your journal next to your bed. Since dreams are so elusive to the waking mind, it is best to record them soon after they come to you. Keeping your journal handy not only makes it easier to jot things down on the spur of the moment, even while you may still be in a dreamy state, but it also helps your mind prepare to dream when you see it laying next to you as you doze off into sleep. You may also want to keep candles, crystals, or other fond objects near your journal. Some people just like to throw it on the floor—again, whatever works for you!

2. Record your dream soon after you have it. Immediately upon waking, even if it is 4 A.M. record your dream in story form. Just write down exactly what happened in a quick paragraph or two—longer if you need to or if you can remember more details. By doing this, you will have captured the essence of the dream; this will make it easier to decipher at a later time.

Example:

> *I was in France at the Eiffel Tower and an old French woman was talking to me but I had a hard time understanding her. She offered me something, a package, but I had to keep saying "No thanks." I walked away from her and found myself in front of my childhood*

home in New Jersey. The house had just blown down and my
whole family was standing around. No one noticed me or listened to
me when I talked to them. . . .

The key to this aspect of journaling is similar to the theory of free association. The goal is simply to record the most important aspects of the dream before they dissolve back into your SUBCONSCIOUS. In this particular example, there were more objects involved in the dream, more characters, and plenty of emotion. But for this step in the journaling process, the best thing to do is just to jot down the skeletal story of what happened in the dream.

Usually, whatever you choose to record in the minute or two that it takes to complete this step are the most important or most compelling features of the dream.

3. Later—say, in the morning after you fully wake up, or in the evening when you have some free time—take a few minutes to write down, in list form, they key elements from the dream.

Example (continued from above):

> *The Eiffel Tower*
> *Old French woman*
> *Gift from the French woman*
> *My childhood house in ruins*
> *My family*

At this point, if you remember more details, write them down, too:

> *The woman was wearing shabby clothes.*
> *The weather seemed bad at the Eiffel Tower.*
> *None of the other houses in my neighborhood were blown down.*

4. The next step, which you can complete at the same time as Step 3 or at a later time (perhaps before going to sleep the next night), is the interpretive step of dreamwork. You have the basis to discover the meaning or meanings of the dream, but it may take some in-depth thought and consideration. Refer back to several of the theories in Book 3 for a starting point to interpretation—there are many different theories, and it is up to you to discover which ones work best for you. It often works best to employ a few of them.

Here is an example (based on the above dream) of successful dreamwork:

> *I was in France but it felt uncomfortable to be there. The old woman was offering something to me, but I felt as if she really didn't want me to take it. When I left her I found myself back at my childhood home, and my family seemed to be ignoring me. I think this all has to do with the fact that I was the first bird to fly the coop in my family and that I have been living two thousand miles away from them in New Orleans the last year-and-a-half.*

The fact that I am away from home is represented by an exotic place (The Eiffel Tower), the fact that I am rejecting a native woman's offer represents the possibility that I am not comfortable there (New Orleans), and the fact that when I leave the old woman it is to return to my roots represents that I miss living near my family (blown-down home).

That just about covers a single, complete entry in a dream journal. Sometimes dreams are more emotionally driven than object- and character-driven. In those cases, it is best to not worry so much about covering all the objects that appeared in the dream and what they were doing, but rather to elaborate on how you felt during the dream and possible explanations of why you felt that way.

It is always a good idea, then, to go back through your journal after several weeks or months and re-read some or all of the entries you have recorded. If you notice any patterns, you may want to rely on your dreams and what they are telling you, to affect positive change in your life!

appendix B

◆

Common Dream Types

The "Polar Bear Theory" says that not every polar bear needs to be studied before polar bears can be understood. In fact, after studying the mating habits of one hundred or so bears, the mating habits of all bears become fairly predictable. While polar bears may act out uniquely in many instances, the general principles of polar bear behavior remain true.

To a limited extent, this is true about dream interpretation as well. In the context of human experience, there are as many dream scenarios as there are individuals. Since dream composition is dictated by individual experiences and individual reactions to them, there is virtually no limit to the dream accounts available.

However, there are patterns observable in dream content. These patterns seem to be organized around two themes. The first theme involves external factors that we all share such as marriage, death, birth, archetypal events, etc. The second theme is derived from internal issues. These could be characterized as PERSONALITY-driven dreams based on your own relationship conflicts, personal uncertainties, or archetypal neuroses.

The first (external) group of events are difficult to comprehend because of their inevitability. As an individual, you can shape your opinions about, but not deflect, the reality of certain experiences. All people can anticipate a life of becoming a sexual, adult being. All people can anticipate death, their own and others. Interpersonal transactions of POWER affect all people. We dream to help comprehend the implications of these events. Although the scenarios vary widely, there are specific types of dreams that convey the meaning of these experiences.

The second (internal) group of events is best explained using the psychotherapy of FREUD and others. In these cases, theories of how people react to their lives are important to discerning the meaning of dreams. Freud, for example, was deeply committed to the sexual theory of personality as essential dogma. Thus, his dream theory reflects deep and far-reaching implications of sexual expression.

By offering several types of dreams for your deliberation here, it is hoped you will be able to find inspiration to understand better your own TRIGGER EVENTS and dream content. In the examples that follow, you will find dreams about jobs, marriage, relationships, and significant transitions of life. In each of these dream scenarios, the central elements of interpretation have been elaborated and defined.

Be careful to look at your own dream from several perspectives when trying to choose a comparison that fits best. Your dream may read like a classic Freudian dream, yet be more directly interpreted as an archetypal self-awareness dream. For all the good-natured teasing directed at Freud and psychotherapy, the truth of the matter is dream interpretation is rarely completely wrong. Most often, it is a matter of finding the method that is most right for your situation.

ARCHETYPAL SELF-AWARENESS DREAMS

When our self-awareness is in a stage of transition (i.e. moving from identification with one ARCHETYPE to identifying with another), our dreams can be traumatic and troubling.

A 20-year-old woman reports a RECURRING dream she had in pre-adolescence:

> *I am at a mall with my family (mom, dad and two younger siblings). Suddenly, pirates overrun the mall. Everyone escapes but mom. I am alone with my brothers outside the mall. My dad goes back in to rescue mom and we are reunited eventually.*

By using a Freudian therapy approach, much meaning would be placed on the dream, especially with regard to the HEROIC FATHER and removed MOTHER. However, what does the dream mean to the dreamer?

She reports that she was deeply concerned about two aspects of the dream, her mother's safety and the responsibility for younger siblings while dad orchestrated a rescue. The indication of being anxious about the shift from child to "in charge" says much about how she viewed herself in the dream. She was becoming a young woman.

Being concerned for her mother's safety was important because she was entering a time when she felt an acute need for a woman mentor figure in her life (besides the literal fact that she was concerned for her mother). As a girl beginning the passage into womanhood, it would be devastating to face those challenges in a home with three other males and no female. She was separating from her mother as a child, while reaffirming her relationship to her mother as a different kind of person, more of a colleague in the sisterhood of all women.

Interpreted, the dream shows ambivalence about rites of passage and not wanting to go through them alone. Indeed waking life reflects this same tendency. The dreamer has struggled to clearly identify herself in college or progress through that passage into adulthood. She also struggles to assert independence in other areas, showing a propensity for highly dependent relationships.

COMPENSATORY DREAMS

Compensation dreams allow us to experience in the dream world what we would like to experience in the waking world but repress (from the waking world) for our own good.

JUNG himself reports as good a compensatory dream as any:

> I see Dr. FREUD. However, I realize he is not in his usual form.
> Upon closer examination, he is a ghost dressed in the uniform of a
> defunct Austrian customs inspector.

Jung saw this dream as compensation for his waking admiration of Freud. As a doctor, Jung was aware that critical examination of Freud's theories was essential regardless of his admiration for the man.

Compensatory Dreams as Resolution of Emotional Energy.

Many people experience dreams that replay life situations. These replays often include a resolution that would be more pleasing than the resolution found in waking life.

One 40-year-old male, a married truck driver with children, describes his dream as follows:

> I am interacting with people I know in an unfamiliar, yet comfort-
> able setting. There is a neighbor whom I had not seen in more than
> twenty years; there are my parents, my siblings, and some old

friends. I wonder if we are working out karmic debts of some kind through astral projection? I get the sense that everyone is telling each other that they're doing fine; and there is nothing more to the dream.

This idea of "karmic debts" could be described as a version of compensation related to Jung's dream theory. Since Jung saw most psychological problems as spiritual in nature, the compensation in no way impacts on the dreamer's spiritual evaluation of the dream.

Interpreting dreams in this way is often an excellent use of dream theory. Many times, we replay scenarios of waking life, to look for better resolutions of the problems we face. To the extent that dreams provide a laboratory for that experience, they are useful to us.

FREUDIAN DREAM WORK

Just when you think FREUD is useless, a presentation occurs that confirms at least some of his IMAGERY and symbolism.

A middle-aged husband who had been attending marriage counseling with his wife reports dreaming:

I am digging a pond in our backyard to go fishing. I sit down next to the pond and realize my hand has come to rest on a snake. Terrified, I throw it as far as I can. It slithers off. I catch a couple of small fish. They are similar, but each is unique. I feel emotional pain for having caught them. They look at me knowingly. I awaken.

Taking each symbol in its most literal Freudian meaning, this dream breaks down as follows: Digging the pond is an image of identification with womb experience or female genitalia. Finding a snake is a phallic symbol. The fear and throwing away the snake indicates some level of revulsion over phallic power. The small fish represent semen, or the product thereof.

The man in this dream realizes a great investment in his wife and family. However, his own sexual identity and struggles are often his own worst enemy. Often, they crop up in unexpected thoughts and feelings. He would like to expel these concerns from his life. Moreover, he realizes that his children bear the largest brunt of any emotional injury caused by his struggles.

Freud's symbols are not terribly removed from this dreamer's condition in life. It is important to realize that this dream functions more as a representation of the present than an aspiration towards the future. Dreams may do either, or both, in the same dream.

GRIEVING DREAMS

These dreams are prone to occur immediately prior to or following the death of a family member. Sometimes they can occur well after someone close has died.

A 41-year-old woman reports dreaming:

> *I am sitting on my parents' bed watching my mother brush her hair. She is taking her time doing so. I turn to see that my father has entered the room and is leaning against the door frame. He is encouraging her to get ready to go. His anxiousness seems to increase with time. Mom doesn't seem ready to go with him. Finally, she says she is ready and goes. She and Dad leave, I wake up.*

The woman who reports this dream has lost both parents. Her father preceded her mother, but both died within eighteen months. This dream occurred after the mother had passed away.

While the woman had grieved for her parents outwardly, letting go is often a more difficult experience. The dreamer felt a distinct sense that she had completed this grieving task until the occurrence of this dream. Upon having it, she allowed her grief to move further into her soul for a full release of emotion.

When a parent dies, especially the last parent, there is a sense that the soul loses an archetypal covering, or a sense of protection. There was a buffer between us and full exposure to mortality, uncertainty, and identity: the living parent. Letting go is difficult.

Yet to let go is crucial to the grief process. The dream strengthened the process of letting go by allowing the grieved one to entrust mom to the parent who had passed previously. It is a beautiful picture of love calling to love, and love releasing love to love. It is truly the gift of a dream.

JOB DREAMS

Dreaming of your job is, unfortunately, quite common. We spend so much time at work that there are always going to be issues that go unresolved in waking life. Some job dreams can be simple, real-time experiences of being at work. The message behind such dreams is usually that you have been working too hard. Other job dreams can have more to say, symbolically speaking.

A 31-year-old man reports dreaming:

> *I am walking down the street with a coworker who I consider a good friend. We walk up to a black sedan that reminds me of a Mafia car. I recognized two occupants as being from our organization. Suddenly, my coworker draws a gun and shoots the two others from our organization repeatedly at point blank range.*

Everyone in this dream is related by the workplace. Consequently, even though no event in the dream relates to work per se, the dream can be classified as a work dream. This dream is important because of how waking relationships are represented.

The two occupants of the car were the dreamer's two greatest detractors is waking life. Their administrative habits seemed particularly insidious to the dreamer because they would not communicate direction, only critique. The dreamer often felt entrapped by their unpredictability. Upon having the dream, the dreamer acquired insight into the fact that they may seek to "rub him out" of the company.

However, the coworker friend was also a supervisor. The dreamer experiences the supervisor as emotionally supportive, but lacking genuine resolution skills. He held him to be something of a puppet supervisor, capable of great emotional outburst, but little true leadership.

In waking the client reported a combination of satisfaction and distress from the dream and the insights he drew from it. The supervisor would be regarded as genuinely supportive, but unable to clearly articulate his expectations and appreciation of the employee to senior leaders in the company. Consequently, the dreamer saw his opportunity with the organization as limited.

MORAL PROBLEM-SOLVING IN DREAMS

Often a dream will give you insight into a decision you are entertaining, or something you have done, which you may consider to be wrong. Actually, you probably know that it is wrong, and your dream is simply reminding you of this and affirming what you already know.

A 37-year-old woman reports the following:

> *I am walking through fraternity row in a college town. Someone is dropping candy on me. I put up an umbrella. Suddenly the candy is thrown with enough force to pierce the fabric and strike me. I grow angry and look up at the source of the candy to express my frustration. Suddenly, it is raining candy with great velocity. It hurts.*

I never see the source of the candy, but duck for cover into a room with three men in it. It is cold and candlelit with graffiti featuring various bridge scenes on the walls. I get under a blanket. A young man is huddling there with me. He goes all the way under the blanket. I am looking at the bridge scenes. They are all very pleasing, but none seem to lead anywhere. One of the men looking at the bridges with me seems very familiar, the other is a stranger. Suddenly, I am aware of the one with whom I had been sharing the blanket. He is making sexual overtures under the covers, unknown to our other two companions. Although he is very attractive, I am unable to feel good about him or the attention he offers me. I wake up.

This dream is fascinating because it offers so much in terms of moralizing and interpersonal tension. Several of the symbols seem to have classical CONDENSATION or DISPLACEMENT attributes that initially bothered the dreamer until she saw more clearly what was being SUBCONSCIOUSLY processed in the dream. The insight gained from the dream contributed much to the dreamer's insight about commitments and choices she was making.

The opening scene is one of scattered desires. Candy, being randomly dropped, reflects a sense of looking about. The umbrella seems to be a source of protection, but also sets a phallic tone for what transpires next with the three men in the room.

The room does not seem to be a Freudian womb space, but rather a Jungian CAVE of initiation or cleansing for moral purposes. The cave itself is remarkable for the art work in it. Bridges, journey symbols leading nowhere, are the most prominent feature of the dwelling. The occupants of the cave number three. This could be a sexual or religious number. Since most moralizing comes from RELIGION, it may a condensation image for both.

The sexual overture is fascinating because of its overt, near-exhibitionist context. The cave is occupied when it occurs. This would be appalling in waking life—to have such overt genital contact with a STRANGER in the presence of others. Even more so because one of the other men in the room was so familiar.

When pressed for details on the familiarity, it was the eyes of the stranger that the woman made a connection with. Eyes being "the window of the soul" reminded the dreamer that the stranger was actually her husband, her soulmate. Consequently, the dream insight was that looking other places for sexual gratification was a no-win, and at some level, repulsive, scenario to entertain.

RECURRING ORACLE DREAM

Some people believe that time and space are so interconnected that it is possible to catch a glimpse of the future. With dreams, one's SUBCONSCIOUS may be so astute as to foresee something which the CONSCIOUS mind would not see coming.

A married, 36-year-old female reports dreaming:

> *I am in a house where I lived six years ago. I am looking out over the patio at a pond. The house and patio are true to life. In waking life, many ANIMALS would come to feed in the backyard. In the dream, there are many animals circling the house, feeding at the watering hole, but they are all African. I feel as though the scene is gradually rotating in a circular motion. It is very peaceful, dusk is falling in the dream.*
>
> *Many people are present, including some of my extended family, but the animals and people aren't bothering one another. However, as the animals circle, they draw closer to the house and the people*

*become more concerned. It is getting darker The door is locked I feel
great fear, and am winded, as if I have just run a great distance.*

*The scene changes to the next evening. The animals have moved
back to a more comfortable distance, but this time they watch the
house very intently. Usually, the cycles repeat themselves once more.*

After having this dream, someone the dreamer knows dies. It has
occurred four times in the past six years.

Upon reflection, several symbols of death are present in the dream,
including:

- **Sunset** — *the waning of our life cycle*
- **Wild Animals** — *a natural, but somewhat overpowering adversary*
- **Fear** — *our usual disposition toward death*
- **Locked Door/ Inescapability** — *everyone dies*
- **Awareness of Threat** — *normal response to realization of mortality*

This dream seems to serve as a psychic warning to the dreamer that
death is impending and inescapable. The dreamer reports skill in
LUCID dreaming that would normally empower the outcome of the
dream to change. However, lucid dreaming is to no avail in this particular RECURRING dream.

In waking life, every occasion of this dream has been followed by
news of the death of an acquaintance or relative. At times, the word of
the death has been delayed until several weeks after the dream. The
result is ANXIETY on the part of the dreamer every time the dream
occurs. This is consistent with FREUD's theory that recurring dreams

are an attempt to overcome feelings of powerlessness in the face of uncontrolled circumstances. However, this dream is difficult because death is a universal, uncontrolled experience.

Counsel for this person includes trying to be aware of the health struggles facing those around her, as well as the frailty of life in general. This dream is a precious gift, despite its foreboding content. Anticipation can relieve fear in many cases and replace panic with dignity and noble acceptance of inevitable circumstances. Often times, we are caught by surprise by the ultimate outcome of life, and feel unprepared. Sharing this dream widely among friends and family could generate paranoia and skepticism and is not recommended. However, realizing the presence of this dream in the inner sanctum of the soul could allow the dreamer to both fully appreciate the pain of death while fully comprehending and celebrating the dignity of life.

Recurring trauma dream

When a truly bad thing happens to us in life, it is almost completely incomprehensible. Wrongful deaths, tragic loss of your home to a freak accident, and disfigurement all qualify. Unfortunately, the dream state can rarely help you work through these things.

A teenage girl reports dreaming:

> *I am running through the woods. I hear a young woman crying in pain. She is being beaten. Sometimes I just see her wanting me to help, other times, she is me. Sometimes I am running toward her and feel myself being chased.*

This dream stems from the tragic murder of a relative at the hands of a serial killer. The death occurred at a time in the dreamer's life when she was old enough to understand death, but too young to comprehend tragedy or randomness in life. This particular RECURRING dream seems to illustrated FREUD's theory on the topic. He felt that recurring dreams were a means of trying to assert EGO strength at a time in life when circumstances were beyond comprehension. Unfortunately, tragedy and random violence are always beyond comprehension. Grief counseling would be the best prescription for resolution of this dream event.

TABOO RELATIONSHIP DREAM

There are lines that separate right from wrong in our waking lives, and all well-adjusted people know where they are drawn. However, actively crossing those lines or just pondering the act are two different things.

A teenage girl reports dreaming:

> *I am at church, enjoying the typical mass. Suddenly, I hear one of*
> *the ministers has committed suicide. I am saddened, but not as much*
> *as I think I should be.*

This dream is a good model of a dreamer avoiding a conflict issue. The girl is a regular churchgoer and has even found a place of importance in church as a leader of the youth group. Since she is characterized as homely and overweight—two difficult attributes to possess as a teenager—she struggles socially. Church is a successful and accepting place for her. It is no surprise that she enjoys church.

Yet, in her dream, she causes the death of a minister. She caused it because, in dreams, the images are our constructs of how we experience others.

The central truth of this girl's life in relation to the dream is that she has a crush on the minister who killed himself. What could be more TABOO for a church-going child than to be confronted with the desire for a romantic interlude with an adult minister? The dream was a way to resolve the conflicts of the psyche surrounding her relationship with this minister. What could create more relief than having the minister take matters into his own hands to absolve her of responsibility for having to solve the problem?

This type of dream plays itself out in many of our lives. In waking, we often find ourselves playing the "what if" game of life. Often we know exactly "what if" and the consequences that would follow, which usually are potentially devastating. However, if the object of our "what if" desire scenario is inescapable, such as a coworker or another frequently met person, we have to solve the problem outside our waking lives.

appendix C

Dream Quotes

I t is a medical fact that all people dream when they sleep. It is a human fact that all people dream when they are awake, also—they have goals, aspirations, and hopes which we often refer to as "dreams." Here is a collection of some great words that express thoughts and hopes common to us all. Enjoy!

There seems to be something in dream images
that reminds us of language . . .
we have the feeling they might mean something.

Samuel Taylor Coleridge

English poet

---◆---

He who has learned aright about the signs
that come in sleep will find that they have
an important influence over all things.

Hippocrates
Greek physician

---◆---

The past is all one texture,
whether feigned or suffered,
whether acted out in three dimensions
or only witnessed
in that small theatre of the brain
which stays brightly lit
all night long.

Robert Louis Stevenson
Scottish writer

---◆---

In all of us, even in good men, there is a lawless,
wild beast that peers out in sleep.

Plato
Greek philosopher

---◆---

O God, I could be bounded in a nutshell and count myself king of infinite space were it not that I have bad dreams.

Hamlet William Shakespeare
English dramatist

*In a distempered dream,
things and forms in themselves common and
harmless inflict a terror of anguish.*

Samuel Taylor Coleridge
English poet

*The waking have one world in common,
but the sleeping turn aside
each into a world of their own.*

Heracleitos of Ephesus

*A dream is a wish your heart makes while
you're fast asleep.*

Cinderella

---◆---

I had a dream . . . crazy dream . . . anything
I wanted to know, anyplace I needed to go.

Robert Plant, Led Zeppelin
Rock musician

---◆---

When you wish upon a star,
your dreams come true.

Jiminy Cricket

---◆---

I had a dream, but it is past the wit of men
to say what dream it was.

A Mid-Summer Night's Dream
William Shakespeare
English dramatist

---◆---

I have a dream of a day when men
will be judged by the content of their character,
not the color of their skin.

Martin Luther King Jr.
American statesman and activist

---◆---

In dreams, we put on the likeness of that more universal, truer, more eternal self dwelling in the darkness of night.

Carl Jung
Swiss psychologist

Life is but an empty dream.

Henry Wadsworth Longfellow
American poet

I wonder that the great master . . . when he called sleep the 'death of each day's life,' did not call dreams the insanity of each day's sanity.

Charles Dickens
English writer

Your old men shall dream dreams, your young men shall see visions.

Joel 2:28

For hope is but the dream of those who wake.

> Matthew Prior
> English poet

I slept and dreamed that life was beauty . . .
was thy dream then a shadowy lie?

> Ellen Sturgis Hooper
> American poet

The dream is a little hidden door
in the innermost and most secret recesses of the soul,
opening into that cosmic night. . . .

> Carl Jung
> Swiss psychologist

But in dream He suddenly bestrides me. . . .
'All is well' I groan and fumble for a light
Brow bathed in sweat, heart pounding.

> Robert Graves
> English poet

I've always had access to other worlds.
We all do because we dream.

Leonora Carrington
Surrealist painter

The madman is a waking dreamer.

Immanuel Kant
German philosopher

Are not the sane and the insane equal at night
as the sane lies dreaming?

Charles Dickens
English writer

All night I dreamed I was surrounded
by the bodies of those who had been murdered . . .
now I know it was the souls of the trees
crying out to me.

Hasidic proverb

Dreaming is a nightly dip, a skinny dip,
into the pool of images and feelings.

James Hillman
American writer

Why does the eye see a thing more clearly in
dreams than the imagination when awake?

Leonardo da Vinci
Italian artist

If you can remember dreams of flying and soaring like
a bird, or dancing, or singing more perfectly than you
ever thought possible, you know that no second-hand
account of such events could ever give you the thrill
you felt in the dream.

Gayle Delaney
American psychologist

Dreaming permits each and every one of us to be
quietly and safely insane every night of our lives.

William Dement
American psychiatrist

The pleasure of the true dreamer does not lie in the substance of the dream, but in this: that there things happen without any interference from his side, and altogether outside his control.

Isak Dinesen
Danish writer

*So, if I dream I have you, I have you,
For, all our joys are but fantastical.*

John Donne
English poet

All that is true is hidden deep in the body of the world and cannot be taken by force. It must be dreamed and attended and received with awe and affection.

Rikki Ducornet
American writer

*We become what we dream. . . .
We achieve in reality, in substance,
only the pictures of the imagination.*

Lawrence Durrell
French-born English writer

---

*Existence would be intolerable
if we were never to dream.*

Anatole France
French writer

Only the dreamer can change the dream.

John Logan
Scottish clergyman and poet

---

*One of the most adventurous things
left us is to go to bed.
For no one can lay a hand on our dreams.*

E. V. Lucas
English novelist and poet

---

*If the dream is a translation of waking life,
waking life is also a translation of the dream.*

René Magritte
Belgian artist

Dream Quotes

Those who compared our life to a dream were right. . . .
We sleeping wake, and waking sleep.

Michel Eyquem de Montaigne
French essayist

All that we see or seem
is but a dream within a dream.

Edgar Allan Poe
American writer

I should have lost many a good hit,
had I not set down at once things that occurred
to me in my dreams.

Sir Walter Scott
Scottish writer

We are such stuff as dreams are made on, and
our little life is rounded with a sleep.

William Shakespeare
English dramatist

*A dream which is not understood
is like a letter which is not opened.*

The Talmud

*In dreams we see ourselves naked and acting out
real characters, even more clearly than we see others awake.*

Henry David Thoreau
American writer

*Take, if you must, this little bag of dreams,
unloose the cord, and they will wrap you round.*

William Butler Yeats
Irish poet

*I've dreamt in my life dreams that have stayed with me
ever after, and changed my ideas;
they've gone through and through me,
like wine through water,
and altered the colour of my mind.*

Emily Brontë
English writer

Myths are public dreams, dreams are private myths.

Joseph Campbell
American mythologist and writer

---

*Nothing so much convinces me
of the boundlessness of the human mind
as its operations in dreaming.*

William Benton Clulow
English clergyman

---

*Dreams say what they mean, but they don't say
it in daytime language.*

Gail Godwin
American writer

---

*There have been times in my life when
I have fallen asleep in tears; but in my dreams
the most charming forms have come to console
and to cheer me, and I have risen the next
morning fresh and joyful.*

Johann Wolfgang von Goethe
German poet

---

*People come and go in life, but they never leave
your dreams. Once they're in your subconscious,
they are immortal.*

Patricia Hampl
American poet

---

*We sometimes congratulate ourselves at the moment
of waking from a troubled dream:
it may be so the moment after death.*

Nathaniel Hawthorne
American writer

---

*We often forget our dreams so speedily:
If we cannot catch them as they are passing out the door,
we never set eyes on them again.*

William Hazlitt
English writer

---

*All human beings are also dream beings.
Dreaming ties all mankind together.*

Jack Kerouac
Canadian-born American writer

Bibliography

Alvarez, A. *Night*. New York:
WW Norton & Company, 1995.

Boss, Medard. *I Dreamt Last Night*.
Translated by S. Conway. New York: Gardner Press, 1977.

Castaneda, Carlos. *The Art of Dreaming*.
New York: Harper Perennial, 1993.

Delaney, Gayle. *Living Your Dreams*.
San Francisco: Harper, 1997.

Domhoff, G. William. *Finding Meaning in Dreams: A Quantitative Approach*. New York: Plenum Press, 1996.

Evans, Christopher. *Landscapes of the Night*.
New York: Viking Press, 1983.

Fontana, David. *The Secret Language of Dreams*.
San Francisco: Chronicle Books, 1994.

Foulkes, David W. *The Psychology of Sleep*.
New York: Scribners, 1966.

Freud, Sigmund. *The Interpretation of Dreams*. 1900.

Globus, Gordon. *Dream Life, Wake Life*.
Albany: State University of New York Press, 1984.

Goodison, Jane. *The Dreams of Women*.
New York: WW Norton, 1995.

Jung, Carl. *Dreams*.
Translated by RFC Hall. Princeton University Press, 1974.

Jung, Carl. *Symbols in a Man's Life*.

Jung, Carl. *Visions*.

Langs, Dr. Robert. *Decoding Your Dreams*.
New York: Holt Publishers, 1988.

Magallon, Linda Lane. *Mutual Dreaming*.
New York: Simon and Schuster, 1997.

O'Flaherty, Wendy D. Dreams, *Illusions and Other Realities*.
Chicago: University of Chicago Press, 1984.

O'Neill, Carl W. Dreams, *Culture and the Individual*.
San Francisco: Chandler and Sharp Publishers, Inc. 1976.

Parsons, Elise Clews. *Pueblo Indian Religion (Volume 1)*.
Lincoln: University of Nebraska Press, 1996.

Porter, Laurence M. *The Interpretation of Dreams: Freud's Theories Revisited*.
Boston: Twayne Publishers, Inc. 1987.

Scott, Charles E., *On Dreaming, an Encounter with Medard Boss*.
Chico, CA: Scholars Press, 1977.

Wehr, Gerhardt. *Portrait of Jung, an Illustrated Biography*.
New York: Herder and Herder, 1971.

Index of Entries

Index of Entries

The Dream Directory